The Year of the Queer

The Year of the Queer

Thoughts, Blogs, Letters and Sermons / 2013-2014

Rev. Jeff Hood

WIPF & STOCK · Eugene, Oregon

THE YEAR OF THE QUEER
Thoughts, Blogs, Letters and Sermons, 2013–2014

Copyright © 2016 Jeff Hood. All rights reserved. Except for brief quotations in critical publications or reviews, no part of this book may be reproduced in any manner without prior written permission from the publisher. Write: Permissions, Wipf and Stock Publishers, 199 W. 8th Ave., Suite 3, Eugene, OR 97401.

Wipf & Stock
An Imprint of Wipf and Stock Publishers
199 W. 8th Ave., Suite 3
Eugene, OR 97401

www.wipfandstock.com

PAPERBACK ISBN: 978-1-5326-1262-6
HARDCOVER ISBN: 978-1-5326-1264-0

Manufactured in the U.S.A.   NOVEMBER 29, 2016

To Jim Mitulski, Prophet of Queer Love
To Will Campbell, Queer Baptist Preacher
To Quinley Mandela Dillard Hood, With Deep Prayers You Will Be Just Like Them

Throughout the tumult and triumph of the times contained in this book, I have felt the presence of God. In writing during the last year and a half, I have sought to decipher and share what has met my ears and experience. I've grown in knowledge and conviction that God that is queer or different beyond anything we can ever imagine. To follow such a God, I believe we have to be queer or different in order to make a difference. With every stroke of the pen, I discovered more of my own queerness. I have written all of these words, so that you might be inspired to find more of yours.

Amen.

Contents:

1. March 31, 2013: "Resurrecting Jesus"
2. April 7, 2013: "Resurrecting Love"
3. April 14, 2013: "Resurrecting Hope"
4. April 21, 2013: "Resurrecting Justice"
5. April 28, 2013: "Getting Over Our Fear of Jesus"
6. May 5, 2013: "Overcoming Our Fear of Love"
7. May 11, 2013: Hate Translates / San Pedro de Atitlan, Guatemala
8. May 13, 2013: Perspectives / Guatemala City, Guatemala
9. May 14, 2013: "Borders" / Quetzaltenango, Guatemala
10. May 15, 2013: Environmental Consciousness and Gender Equality / Chicostenango, Guatemala
11. May 16, 2013: The Fiction of Neutrality / Panajachel, Guatemala
12. May 17, 2013: "A Tale of Two Pastors"
13. May 21, 2013: *A Poem for Moore, Oklahoma*
14. May 23, 2013: "The Root of War is Fear."
15. May 26, 2013: "Getting Over Our Fear"
16. June 1, 2013: Resurrected Pieces of the Queer Christ
17. June 2, 2013: "The Queer is Here"
18. June 9, 2013: "The Courage to Move"
19. June 9, 2013: A Sermonic Eulogy for Ray Emory Hood
20. June 13, 2013: The Danger of Identity
21. June 16, 2013: "A Diaconal Ordination"
22. June 16, 2013: "The Water into Wine"
23. June 23, 2013: "TELL THE TRUTH!"
24. June 26, 2013: The Religious Case for Queer Marriage
25. June 26, 2013: "Speech at The Denton Day of Decision Rally"
26. June 27, 2013: Remarks on SCOTUS Decision in Denton Record Chronicle
27. June 30, 2013: "Daring to Love Beyond the Closet"
28. July 2, 2013: Learning to Fight for Life and the Rights of Women
29. July 3, 2013: CAN WE BELIEVE IN LOVE OR LOVE OR LOVE
30. July 3, 2013: GOD
31. July 3, 2013: PEOPLE
32. July 4, 2013: LIFE
33. July 4. 2013: TODAY
34. July 4, 2013: you and me
35. July 4, 2013: history
36. July 5, 2013: THE HOSE
37. July 5, 2013: THE SNAKE
38. July 6, 2013: FRIENDS
39. July 6, 2013: hospitals
40. July 7, 2013: "Loving Justice Enough to Shut Up and Let Others Get the Credit for Achieving It"

41. July 8, 2013: completion and reflection
42. July 9, 2013: THE JUDAS REMIX
43. July 10, 2013: The TriP
44. July 11, 2013: travel
45. July 14, 2013: "The Woman, Transgender Person, & George Zimmerman at the Well"
46. July 14, 2013: in and through you
47. July 15, 2013: "Prayer at Justice for Trayvon Martin Rally"
48. July 16, 2013: AMEN
49. July 21, 2013: "Remarks Upon the Retirement of Chief Jeff Hood : My Dad"
50. July 21, 2013: "God is Sweet. Love is Sweet. Now, go and be the sweetness…"
51. July 24, 2013: The Activist
52. July 25, 2013: exhaustion
53. July 26, 2013: Is this what you call love?
54. July 28, 2013: A Plea for Universal Healthcare
55. August 4, 2013: What does belief look like? Just run.
56. August 7, 2013: the hidden danger of privilege
57. August 9, 2013: beau ties
58. August 12, 2013: borders
59. August 13, 2013: queer jesus
60. August 14, 2013: "Feeding"
61. August 15, 2013: "Queer Love or God Finds Us in Queer Spaces"
62. August 18, 2013: "I'm Here! Presence in the Storm, Parade, and in Life"
63. August 20, 2013: abscence
64. August 25, 2013: martin's dream and us
65. August 25, 2013: Jesus in Drag
66. August 29, 2013: I Will Not Eat! A Pastor Responds to Potential Strikes on Syria
67. August 30, 2013: hungry
68. August 31, 2013: Remarks at The March for the Beloved Community
69. September 1, 2013: Remarks Upon Ending My Fast For Peace in Syria
70. September 1, 2013: Turn off the Swerve and Embrace Your Destiny
71. September 4, 2013: generosity
72. September 8, 2013: "Standing Against Patriarchy, War & the Self Takes Courage"
73. September 10, 2013: messages
74. September 14, 2013: eight-year-old commits suicide
75. September 15, 2013: I Am The Light of The World
76. September 22, 2013: The Blind Man
77. September 27, 2013: Remarks from the Inaugural Denton Meeting of Pastors for Texas Children

78. September 29, 2013: Jesus was a man under attack
79. October 2, 2013: The Danger of Language
80. October 6, 2013: A Church Under Attack!
81. October 7, 2013: faggot
82. October 13, 2013: National Coming Out Day
83. October 15, 2013: Liturgy From The Wedding of Two Brides
84. October 17, 2013: Peace
85. October 20, 2013: Betrayal, Love & Feet
86. October 27, 2013: Things Grow Queerer or from Mable Peabody's to My House to Beyond
87. November 2, 2013: death penalty penalty death
88. November 2, 2013: tears
89. November 3, 2013: Energy=God?
90. November 5, 2013: Pastors for Texas Children and the Fight for Neighborhood Schools
91. November 10, 2013: The Risky Queer Path of Love
92. November 12, 2013: The Prayer
93. November 18, 2013: The Crucifixion of Jesus, Transgender Day of Remembrance & Crimes of Hate
94. November 19, 2013: Stop the Damned Drilling!
95. November 25, 2013: The Courage to Feel a Resurrection
96. November 27, 2013: if god be in / a queer rhyme for our time
97. November 30, 2013: Jesus has AIDS / World AIDS Day.
98. December 1, 2013: The Calling Past...to Birth
99. December 5, 2013: The Birth of a Child & The Changing of a Name : A Living Tribute to Nelson Mandela
100. December 6, 2013: i waited and we found / a story of us
101. December 8, 2013: The Baby of Belief
102. December 15, 2013: Birth and the Queer
103. December 15, 2013: An Invitation to Birth
104. December 16, 2013: Phil Robertson and the United Methodist Church
105. December 19, 2013: demons
106. December 21, 2013: Response to Being Given the 2013 Fort Worth PFLAG Equality Award
107. December 22, 2013: Bethlehem & The Way
108. December 24, 2013: Embrace the Incarnation: A Christmas Message
109. December 30, 2013: Beyond The Language of G-O-D
110. December 31, 2013: eschatology
111. January 5, 2014: The Baptism of Quinley Mandela Dillard Hood
112. January 5, 2014: The Year of Living Dangerously: The Dangerous God
113. January 5, 2014: Gloria Evangelina Anzaldúa, Jesus & the Space Between
114. January 9, 2014: Empathy is An Act of Imagination

115. January 11, 2014: 1 Corinthians 13:13
116. January 13, 2014: I am, Ground of Being and the Courage to Be: A Dangerous Proposition
117. January 13, 2014: Stay Awake With Me
118. January 16, 2014: Jesus the Atheist : Beyond the God of Theism : A Response to "A Year Without God" former pastor Ryan J. Bell
119. January 18, 2014: A Prayer from the Dr. Martin Luther King, Jr. Parade in Dallas, Texas
120. January 19, 2014: The Year of Living Dangerously: Loving Your Enemy or Jumping in the Gelatin Dessert
121. January 19, 2014: Gone to Mixing
122. January 22, 2014: Love Your Neighbor: The Case of Edgar Arias Tamayo
123. January 25, 2014: North Texas Fellowship of Reconciliation: A Beginning Benediction
124. January 27, 2014: The Year of Living Dangerously: ...on the Bible
125. January 28, 2014: The Terminal
126. January 29, 2014: The Beginning: North Texas Fellowship of Reconciliation
127. February 2, 2014: Phillip Seymour Hoffman, Us and the Denial of Death
128. February 3, 2014: somewhere to lay my head
129. February 3, 2014: being and healing: responding to the call
130. February 3, 2014: the ice pellets on the head of God: reimagining church
131. February 4, 2014: air: who in needs it anyway? / a short tale from the city with the worst air quality in Texas...Denton
132. February 5, 2014: Suzanne Basso. Take a second and repeat that name. Suzanne Basso.
133. February 6, 2014: Remarks to Fort Worth Pastors for Texas Children
134. February 6, 2014: Islam, Rihanna & the Surprise of Belief
135. February 9, 2014: The Paralytic Church, Queerphobia & Frank Schaefer
136. February 9, 2014: The Wise Men...Reinterpreted or The Lack of Wisdom in the Wise Men
137. February 11, 2014: The Journey to Abolition: Remarks to the Dallas Texas Coalition to Abolish the Death Penalty Prayer Breakfast
138. February 12, 2014: We Can End This: Remarks to the Fort Worth Texas Coalition to Abolish the Death Penalty Prayer Breakfast
139. February 15, 2014: Turning Shitheads into Prayer Partners
140. February 16, 2014: The Withered Hand, The Undivided Heart and The Undistracted Church
141. February 17, 2014: Leading with the Withered Hand

142. **February 19, 2014:** The Reason I Will Walk Prayerfully from Dallas to Fort Worth: Dallas County DA Craig Watkins, Tarrant County DA Joe Shannon, Jr. & the State of Texas' Death Penalty
143. **February 20, 2014:** A Letter to Dallas DA Watkins
144. **February 21, 2014:** The Start: A Faithful Pilgrimage to Abolish the Death Penalty
145. **February 21, 2014:** The End: A Faithful Pilgrimage to Abolish the Death Penalty
146. **February 23, 2014:** love.
147. **February 24, 2014:** Get in the Way / Bring them Close / Tell the Stories that Obstruct
148. **February 24, 2014:** Coconspirators in Uganda's Recent Homophobic Bill: Mainline Christians
149. **February 25, 2014:** Love Dangerously Dallas
150. **February 26, 2014:** The Judgment: Christians and the Ruling in Texas
151. **February 26, 2014:** Delivered Tonight: A Question for Dallas County District Attorney Craig Watkins
152. **February 28, 2014:** The Week : Close to Death
153. **March 2, 2014:** My First Job in Ministry, Forgiveness & the Imperfect Pursuit of Perfection
154. **March 2, 2014:** The Guys with the Guns on the Denton Square
155. **March 3, 2014:** Cathedral of Hope Devotional for March 28
156. **March 3, 2014:** A Sermon Entitled "Jesus for President" or The Reason I Will Never Endorse a Political Candidate
157. **March 4, 2014:** apoem: the why of ashe wednesday
158. **March 5, 2014:** The Push of the Ashes: A Manifesto of Defiance for Clergy Colleagues
159. **March 7, 2014:** The Danger of Missions in a World Desperate for Salvation
160. **March 10, 2014:** A Girl Named Peter and the Path to God
161. **March 11, 2014:** A Love Letter to Mark Driscoll
162. **March 13, 2014:** apoems from a plane to dallas-fort worth
163. **March 15, 2014:** The Trouble with Bishop Spong and Embracing the Mystery of Faith
164. **March 16, 2014:** Prayers for a Child of God
165. **March 19, 2014:** Double Homicide Tonight: Racism Reigns in Texas
166. **March 20, 2014:** Jesus the God of Rage: Tossing the Moneychangers Out of Our Government, Our Churches and Our Self
167. **March 21, 2014:** Why We Can't Wait: A Sunday Letter from a Baptist Pastor to my Methodist Colleagues Here in North Texas
168. **March 26, 2014:** Power in the Blood: Oscar Romero, Bullshit Churches Teach and the Seed of Liberty
169. **March 27, 2014:** Would We Execute Moses?: The Case of Anthony Doyle

170. March 30, 2014: doubt the poem
171. March 31, 2014: The End of Gay Marriage
172. April 2, 2014: The Danger of Being Called Pastor
173. April 5, 2014: The Danger of Calls to The Wilderness: A Lenten Response to Rachel Held Evans and Other Progressive Evangelicals
174. April 8, 2014: Actions Talk and Bullshit Walks: The Story of A Real Christian: Major Kathy Cox of the Salvation Army: Witness to 60+ Executions in Texas
175. April 9, 2014: Hand Washing: The Case of Ramiro Hernandez-Llanas
176. April 9, 2014: Finding Inspiration on Immigration in Strange Places // When Jeb Bush Sounded Like Jesus
177. April 14, 2014: Traveling into the Darkness
178. April 14, 2014: The Enemies Cometh and in them Lay Our Salvation
179. April 16, 2014: The Passion of Jesus Comes Early: Standing on the Via Dolorsa at the Execution of Jose Luis Villegas Jr.
180. April 18, 2014: Jesus Didn't Die for Your Sins. Jesus Died to Show You the Way...the Way to the Cross.
181. April 22, 2014: Jesus Sells Drugs: An Easter Message
182. April 25, 2014: Bent: Why I Decided to Act.
183. April 25, 2014: A Child of God and the Violent Hate that Killed Her
184. April 26, 2014: Glen Stassen 1936-2014 / A Tribute from a Southern Baptist
185. April 27, 2014: Donald Sterling, Churches and Race
186. April 28, 2014: Stand Up! : Remarks at Pastors for Texas Children-Dallas
187. April 29, 2014: Botched Executions: A Visit, Jesus in Oklahoma and Us
188. May 3, 2014: Courage Not Comfort: A Word to the Rich Young Rulers of Our Churches
189. May 6, 2014: Lives Less Valued: Why Black Girls Matter
190. May 10, 2014: The Ethics of Our Table: Jesus and Meat
191. May 11, 2014: apoem: beloved & the next day
192. May 12, 2014: The Cross and The Needle: Deep in the Heart of Texas
193. May 16, 2014: Progressive Christians Often Seem to Not Give Two Shits About the Persecution, Imprisonment and Martyrdom of Fellow Christians and I Think I Know Why: A Retrospective
194. May 19, 2014: To the Muslim Student at Southwestern Baptist Theological Seminary: A Satire
195. May 21, 2014: A Few Thoughts on the Occasion of the Second Birthday of My Sons Jeff and Phillip
196. May 23, 2014: Jesus is Calling...Please Pick Up: An Open Letter to Brother Bill Haslam, Governor of Tennessee
197. May 25, 2014: The United States Flag at the Front of the Church is Blasphemous
198. May 29, 2014: The Danger of Dr. Maya Angelou

199.	May 30, 2014: Cathedral of Hope Devotion
200.	May 31, 2014: Jesus' Rampage or a Quick Lesson on Jesus and Guns
201.	June 12, 2014: On the Eve of Pilgrimage: Contemplating Walking 200 miles from Livingston to Austin in Opposition to Execution
202.	June 12-19, 2014: The Complete Pilgrimage Journal: A Short Story of a Long 200 mile Journey
203.	June 25, 2014: My Struggle with Stonewall
204.	June 27, 2014: The Tragedy of Mark Mayfield and The Call of Love
205.	June 28, 2014: The Danger of Debating with Jesus: Hobby Lobby and the Incarnated Christ at LaGuardia
206.	July 2, 2014: Don't You Dare Turn Your Head: The Self-Immolation of The Rev. Charles Moore
207.	July 7, 2014: Jose Antonio Vargas at Cathedral of Hope
208.	July 13, 2014: Across the Borders and Into the Flames: Rev. Charles Moore, Dr. Robert Jeffress, Bishop Yvette Flunder and Us
209.	July 14, 2014: The Pilgrimage: Reflections on 200 miles
210.	July 15, 2014: God is Our Passive Enemy: Reacting Fairly and Honestly to a Day Like Today
211.	July 19, 2014: Eric Garner, the Silence of White Churches and Sins of Omission
212.	July 21, 2014: The Borderless God in a Time of Borders
213.	July 24, 2014: The Last Testament of Joseph Wood: The Prophet of a Botched Execution
214.	July 27, 2014: God is in Hell
215.	July 29, 2014: Twins Again! : A Tale of Unexpected Love for the Hoods
216.	July 29, 2014: Let the Children Come to Me: Arriving for an Immigration Action in Washington D.C.
217.	July 31, 2014: There Are Children to Love
218.	July 31, 2014: An Open Letter to the Cathedral of Hope
219.	August 1, 2014: The Danger of the Immigration Debate is Forgetting God's Love for the World
220.	August 9, 2014: The Cost Scandal of Theological Education
221.	August 11, 2014: The Night I Almost Took My Life
222.	August 13, 2014: Emily: An Ode to Three Years
223.	August 13, 2014: The Souls of White Folks
224.	August 17, 2014: Prayer for Racial Reconciliation and Justice at Cathedral of Hope
225.	August 19, 2014: The Call to Ferguson
226.	August 21, 2014: The Death in Ferguson
227.	August 22, 2014: The Violence of Demanding Peaceful Protest: The Missteps of Clergy in Ferguson
228.	September 7, 2014: "Becoming Queer and Growing Queerer"
229.	September 8, 2014: Claiming Justice and Killing Jesus: The Execution of Willie Trottie

230. September 13, 2014: the weather
231. September 16, 2014: Remembering Queerly: Words from A Conversation on Queer Theology and Activism at Galileo Church
232. September 16, 2014: A Lesbian is Murdered and Nobody Cares...
233. September 18, 2014: LOVE: Wrestling with the Wrestlings of Paul and the Root of Our Self
234. September 18, 2014: Book Review: I AM TROY DAVIS
235. September 19, 2014: I AM the Light of the World: Connecting Queerly with the Gospel of John at Living Faith Covenant Church
236. September 20, 2014: Would Jesus March at Dallas Pride?
237. September 21, 2014: Prayers from Pride Sunday at Cathedral of Hope
238. September 22, 2014: A Gender Revelation: The Forming Hood Twins
239. September 24, 2014: following jesus
240. September 29, 2014: The Inaccessible Pulpit: Rev. Justin Hancock and the Struggle for the Rights of Disabled Persons
241. October 5, 2014: jesus is where?

1.

March 31, 2013

"Resurrecting Jesus"

We begin with the word queer. What does this controversial word mean?

The definition of the word queer at a very basic level is something that is not normative. Ours and other societies throughout human history have sought to normalize human beings. We want everyone to be easy to figure out. We want everyone to fit labels and categories.

Our lesbian, gay, bisexual, and transgender friends know well the many pressures of normativity. Why can't you just date guys like the rest of the girls? Why can't you just become accustomed to the identity that God gave you? Why can't you just date girls like the rest of the guys? These are just a few of the many pressures of normativity, labels, and categories. I and this community choose to be queer. We choose to shun normativity, labels, and categories so that all might be able to embrace the uniqueness with which they are made by God, the queerness of which they are made. The word queer is a radically inclusive term that encourages people to recognize the queerness in themselves so that they might learn to accept the queerness in the other. We stand with all who have been labeled queer because we recognize the queer within ourselves.

How should the word queer function in a church setting? If we are going to call ourselves a queer church, then what will that mean for our community?

Using the word queer as we do, the Church at Mable Peabody's is going to be a house of love and hope for all people. We will turn no one away. This is a queer construct in a society that wants to consistently create categories of acceptance and rejection. We accept everyone. We are going to be a queer church and this means that we are going to be a radical prophetic voice of change for our community. We are going to be the change that we want to see in ourselves and in our community. We are going to be queer and the queering that we want to see in our world.

So, why be a church?

We are a church because we feel like there is something to the idea that people work better in community as opposed to individually. We are a church made up of followers of Jesus because we feel like there is something queerer in the life of Christ than in all of the other humans who have ever lived.

Queering Jesus

In Chapter 25 of the Gospel of Matthew, Jesus declares that what you have done to the least of these, the marginalized, the oppressed, you have done to me. Rather than shunning or oppressing the margins, our God takes residence on the margins. The queer community constantly experiences oppression, therefore Jesus is Queer.

I use the term Queer Jesus as a clean break from the oppression and homophobia that is constantly associated with the traditional Jesus.

You see the life of the Queer Jesus does not look all that different from the experiences that we have all had as queer folk. The Queer Jesus was rejected by family, oppressed by traditional religion, misunderstood, and ultimately persecuted by those the Queer Jesus loved. The Queer Jesus experienced all of the pain and marginalization then and continues, through inhabiting our community, to experience marginalization and oppression. The Queer Jesus was harassed and killed in a violent hate crime perpetrated by religious folks for refusing to conform. Throughout the life of the Queer Jesus, there was an expectation to be normal and not be queer. Constantly in the Gospel accounts, the Queer Jesus deals with the fear of being Queer.

On the days and nights leading up to the death of the Queer Jesus there were many wounds inflicted. On the night the Queer Jesus was killed, folks started betraying the Queer Jesus. Trusted family and friends abruptly turned their backs. How many of you have known times when the folks you love don't show up at the showdown? Later, as the Queer Jesus prays for the courage to be queer and face what is about to come. The Queer Jesus asks the disciples to stay awake so that the Queer Jesus won't have to experience all of this alone. How many of you have needed people to stay awake with you so you won't be alone and looked out to find everybody asleep?

There is no question that the Queer Jesus was terrified of what was coming. A very painful time was approaching that would require the Queer Jesus to open up and there was a need to push through the fear. How many of us have struggled with the pain of opening up and being who we are called to be?

Later, the Queer Jesus is betrayed with a kiss. How many of us know the pain of something that feels good, but ultimately kills us? When the Queer Jesus goes before the Roman Governor Pilate, the government denies the Queer Jesus due process and civil rights. How many of us know about a denial of due process and civil rights? Just last week, the Supreme Court heard arguments with regard to marriage equality. Which side do you think that Jesus is on…the side wanting to deny rights or secure rights? After being beaten and gaybashed over and over the Queer Jesus is crucified. Above the head of the Queer Jesus was a sign that read queer. The Queer Jesus was outed and nailed up on a cross for all the world to see. In spite of the hate and oppression, the Queer Jesus shouts, "Forgive them for they know not what they do." These words change all who hear them. People can't believe the love and compassion of the Queer Jesus in spite of the pain. Sacrificial love is a queer construct, it simply is not normative. Sacrificial love flies in the face normativity and loves anyway. The Queer Jesus dies so that queerness, love might reign.

The death of the Queer Jesus is a hate crime of the highest order. The proponents of bigotry and hate thought they had one. Queerness was defeated. The proponents thought they killed love and hope, but normativity and death never win with the Queer Jesus.

There were some really shitty things that happened on Friday. There was a tremendous amount of pain and fear on Friday. But we are not a Friday kind of church.

Early on that fateful Sunday morning, some of the women who were closest to the Queer Jesus went to check the tomb. They intended to spread some oils and spices to make the stink go away. How often when we are used up and feel dead do people try to put some spices and oils on us to make us smell better? Mary Magdalene led the group and saw the stone removed. She cried out, "They have taken my Jesus and I don't know where they have laid my Jesus."

I look around our town and see a tremendous amount of celebration at churches this morning for Easter, but I didn't see a whole lot of pastors at the marriage rally. They have taken my Jesus and I don't know where they have laid my Jesus. Churches don't seem to care much about queer folk. They have taken my Jesus and I don't know where they have laid my Jesus.

Friends, the traditional church has stolen Jesus and for that matter has killed Jesus by weighing the construct down with an unbelievable history of oppression and hate. We are seeking to resurrect the true Jesus. The Queer Jesus who heals and loves through queerness.

Like the Queer Jesus, we use our wounds to help and not to hurt others.

When the Queer Jesus meets Thomas after the resurrection. Thomas asks, "How do I know it is you?" The Queer Jesus steps forward and shares the unique wounds inflicted during the hate crime, nail prints. Our wounds are often one of the more queer things about us. They help us to discover who we are and how we can help others. When you give your wounds away you are saying they have no power over you and you are using them to help others get out from under the grip of their wounds. Displaying your wounds shows sacrificial love. We all, like the Queer Jesus, must push through our fear in order to heal by our wounds. The scripture says that by the Queer Jesus' wounds we are healed. We, like the Queer Jesus, can heal with our wounds.

When we come out with our wounds and refuse to be afraid of fear then we can transform this community, this nation, and this world. The question is one of courage. Will we push through and share our wounds, our queerness, our vulnerability with others? If you do have such courage, then you, like the Queer Jesus, will transform yourself and the world.

Jesus is queer and I pray that we will all have the courage to let everyone see that we are too.

Amen.

2.

April 7, 2013

"Resurrecting Love"

What is love?

People have been asking this question for a long time. How do you define love? I think the best answer that I have ever heard is: "I know it when I feel it." I think it is far easier to tell someone what love is not, rather than what love is. Nevertheless, let us first survey common definitions of love found in traditional models of church.

Often time for our more traditional brothers and sisters, love is centered on correction and rebuke to get you to conform to a normative model. There is a desire to conform the individual to the community and therefore make the individual like everyone else. Doctrine and dogmatics become more important than the whole of the individual. There is a consistent belief that there is a need to strangle eccentrics and suffocate uniqueness. The individual has consistently been one of the most consistent casualties of traditional religion. The individual spirit is consistently trampled and stomped upon in the name of love.

I think this type of religion is bullshit. What has it done to help us?

There is a need to let die the traditional religion, the traditional Jesus. Their idea of love is an imposter. The truth is that Jesus is Queer.

I believe we will only find the meaning of love when we are willing to discover the Queer Jesus who is the author of love and the queerness that each one of us carries.

The Queer Jesus is an entity that believes that the glory of God is a human being made fully alive through love.

You can't be fully alive when you are told your sexuality is sinful. You can't be fully alive when you are told your identity is a mental illness. You can't be full alive when you are under a constant microscope of oppressive rules. I have been told that the rules are there to make you a better person. Does this sound like horseshit anyone else beside me?

I say that if you believe in a God that oppresses people, takes away people's sexuality, perverts people's identity, pushes people to the brink of insanity trying to keep up with the rules, and winds up mostly on the side of don't rather than do *then* your God is a fucking asshole.

Can I tell you about a God that loves every piece of who you are because she made all those pieces?

Can I tell you about a God that wants you to succeed and thrive just as you are?

Enter the Queer Jesus. In John 15:13 we are told, "Greater love has no one than this…that they lay down their life for their friend." The Queer Jesus demonstrated that love on the cross. In that moment, we find that love is sacrificial, willing to be wounded, and forgives the persecutor. This is real love. How are you demonstrating such love?

In John 20, Jesus meets up with Thomas after the resurrection. Thomas inquires of Jesus, "How do I know it is you?" Jesus replies, "Put your fingers where the nails were." You see we love by sharing our wounds.

To love you have to know where your wounds are. You have to know where to tell people to put their hands. To love you have to sacrifice the time for those around you. The Queer Jesus came just for Thomas. We must never forget to go to that one person who needs us. To love we have to keep our mind on the end game. What do you want to accomplish in this life? Do you want to be known for love or for hate? If you want to be known for love, then do it. Love is an action.

I hope that our church will follow the example of the Queer Jesus and Thomas. I pray that we will love sacrificially, exhibit a willingness to be wounded, and a desire to forgive those who persecute us. I further pray that we will become familiar with our own wounds, give of ourselves to others, and keep our lives centered on love.

Later, Thomas went on to found the church in modern day India. Christianity in India is quite vibrant, mystical, and loving.

What will we accomplish in this space?

I don't give a shit about all that traditional stuff.

I want real tangible substantive wounded queer love.

I will no longer cede love to the oppressive assholes that have never felt true love.

Love is Queer. God is Queer.

May we use this space, Queer people following a Queer Jesus, to teach this community how to love.

God make it so.

Amen.

3.

April 14, 2013

"Resurrecting Hope"

What does hope look like?

Can you smell it? Can you hear it? Can you taste it? Can you hold it? Can you see it?

I held a bottle of pills in my hand one time. I unscrewed the cap. I put the pills in my mouth. I was a student at the Southern Baptist Theological Seminary. I lived in an apartment on campus. I lived in a place where we were supposed to be taught about a God that is love. The only God that I found hated everything I loved in the world. I unscrewed the cap. Something made me stop.

I experienced something or somebody declaring, "I love you."

Hope to keep me from ending my life came in a queer fashion, love.

I was still clinically depressed. Then the ministers started arriving. They were closeted Southern Baptist seminarians that revealed their secrets and wounds.

I found hope to continue and keep pushing through those secrets and wounds.

I met the hope of the Queer Jesus in a space of darkness, through secrets, wounds, and love.

I am here today because of that encounter. I am passionate about the Queer Jesus because the Queer Jesus offers hope to the world.

Are we willing to be the vessels of hope? Had it not been for my closeted ministers at the Southern Baptist Theological Seminary, I would have never made it. Will we be the vessels who give life to others? Will we follow the Queer Jesus and be wounded healers our self?

What does it look like to tell your story? What does it look like to share hope? What does it look like to be a savior for others?

Jesus in Matthew 25 states:

"I was hungry and you gave me something to eat, I was thirsty and you gave me something to drink, I was a stranger and you invited me in, I needed clothes and you clothed me, I was sick and you looked after me, I was in prison and you came to visit me... Whatever you did to the least of these, you did it unto me..."

Hope looks like this:
Food for the hungry
Shelter for the homeless
A visit for the lonely
Justice for the just denied
Siding with the voiceless
Clemency for the imprisoned
On and on and on...

Where do you stand with regard to the least?

We are a community that has known oppression. There is no question about that. The Queer Community is marginalized and oppressed everyday...but we must not only fight for our self...for the oppression of one is the oppression of all.

Since you are the least, Jesus is present in this space. Since Jesus is liberating us, we have a responsibility to liberate others. We are hope.

We must be a church that is outwardly focused and fighting to help others. If we cannot do this, then we shouldn't call ourselves a church.

The Queer Jesus will be with us in our efforts.

Amen.

4.

April 21, 2013

"Resurrecting Justice"

This has been a difficult week.

In Boston, Krystle Campbell, Lingzi Lu, Sean Collier, and eight-year-old Martin Richard were all killed in a heinous crime spree.

In West, Texas, 14 people were killed. Most of them first responders and firefighters, just like my dad.

We mourn and hurt for those killed. We long for justice to take the place of the injustice of lives cut short. Who are we to be in such times? What are we to do? What about them?

Two men in Boston are victims, Tamerlan Tsarnaev and Dzhokar Tsarnaev. These guys killed multiple people and injured hundreds more. They have shattered the stability of tons of people. How are we to view them? These men are victims of a fundamentalism that taught them the way to spread their ideas was to kill. They are victims of the sway of evil and intolerance. They are also perpetrators of a heinous crime.

In West, Texas, West Fertilizer Company reportedly stored an otherworldly amount of ammonium nitrate. I will put it to you this way, I read in the news that the maximum amount of ammonium nitrate, without a consultation with the Department of Homeland Security, is 400lbs. The news media is reporting that West Fertilizer Company had 270 tons on hand. For those who are not good at math, that is close to 1,350 times more than what they were supposed to have. These folks got greedy and now people are dead. How do we view West Fertilizer Company? West Fertilizer Company is a victim of its own greed. Unfortunately, the company thought the way to make a dollar was to endanger the lives of everyone around them. This company is the perpetrator of a heinous crime.

This congregation knows a thing or two about injustice and oppression. We have people in this room who are victims of hate crimes. We have people in this room who have endured oppression based on their sexuality, marital status, race, identity, and on and on. If you want to know about injustice, start talking to each other.

So what are we to do about injustice? How do we resurrect justice?

It all begins with love.

In fact, all queer things begin with love. Love is the glue that holds us together. Love is the only thing able to make us whole. Love is love.

One of the queerest things about Jesus was whom Jesus decided to love. Sound familiar?

In John 8, the religious folk of the time, the traditionalists, brought a woman that was caught in adultery to Jesus. These traditionalists are not all that different from those meeting in the traditional Baptist, Methodist, Bible, Episcopal, Lutheran, and other Christian congregations all over town this morning. I know that many of you have been the woman caught in adultery in these and other spaces of worship. Well the traditionalists of Jesus' time were following the law. The law stated that this woman was to be killed. She was caught in the very act of adultery. The evidence was there. She was guilty. Now what did that old queer we love do, Jesus lunged to be down in the dirt with her. Loving someone and acting out a just ethic of love often means getting dirty. Jesus looked up at those traditionalists and silently declared, 'If you are going to kill her then you are going to have to kill me.' Then, he loudly and audibly declared, "Whoever is without sin can go ahead and cast the first stone." For the Queer, love is the first order of business. Love is always siding with the marginalized and oppressed.

The woman was being mistreated and Jesus pursues justice by placing the body of Jesus between the oppressee and the oppressor.

This situation is also an act of love toward the oppressors. This is another queer aspect of the life of Christ. Jesus loves the oppressor as well as the oppressed. By defending the woman, Jesus is telling the oppressors what justice looks like. Jesus is asking the oppressors to allow their capacity for love to replace their capacity for hate.

There are other times where we are simply called to love the oppressor even when we can't correct them.

Jesus was beaten, crowned with thorns, whipped, spit upon, made fun of, humiliated, marched through the streets bloody and bruised, and simply treated like shit. Jesus was the victim of a hate crime. In the midst of the crime, upon the cross, Jesus looked down and asked for forgiveness for all of the people who did these things. "Forgive them for they know not what they do…"

How queer is that?

Being the queer that we are called to be begins with love. We must love the oppressed and love the oppressor. It is not enough to simply to love the victims we must love the perpetrator. The justice that is from God cannot exist until we are prepared to love both sides.

I want to share my translation of some verses with you:

Matthew 5:44: "Love those you want to hate, those you call your enemy. Pray for those who have hated, oppressed, or gaybashed you."

Matthew 18:22: "What does pure and undefiled forgiveness look like? Forgiving seventy times the seven times you think you are supposed to. Forgive until you can't forgive anymore and then forgive again."

Mark 12:30-31: "Love God with all that you are, including your heart, mind, body, soul, and all your strength. Love everyone you come in contact with like you would your self."

Luke 6:29: "If someone knocks the shit out of you on one cheek, then turn your head and let them knock the shit out of you again."

You can't love and hate at the same time. It is impossible. What side do you want to stand on?

You can't love your neighbor when you can't stand the sight of them. What does it look like to bring those we hate to the table of love?

You can't hold a gun and love your neighbor. Violence is the antithetical action of love. What does it look like to put down our weapons?

If humanity is to survive, we must learn to love. If we as a church are going to lead our community, we must learn to love. It all begins with love.

I forgive Tamerlan Tsarnaev.
I forgive Dzhokar Tsarnaev.
I forgive West Fertilizer Co.
I forgive the Denton City Council and all other governmental bodies for not fighting harder for the rights of queer folk.

Justice is found in the restoration of forgiveness.

If we don't forgive these aforementioned people then we will have to carry too much through life and be ill prepared for the next struggle. You can't reach your hand out to help people when your arms are full of hate. I want to love my enemies so that I don't have to carry the heavy burden of hate around. Forgiveness makes us free.

Resurrecting justice is learning how to love the oppressed and forgive the oppressor, to drop off the hate and embrace the love, and to realize that forgiveness is the only path that will bring about wholeness.

We cannot resurrect justice until we free ourselves for the struggle.

Who do you need to forgive?

Who needs your love?

Amen.

5.

April 28, 2013

"Getting Over Our Fear of Jesus"

I spent most of my early life terrified of Jesus. Our church taught about hell much more than it taught about grace and mercy. We seemed to learn much more about the Book of Revelation and getting left behind by God than we learned about the Gospels and the message of Jesus. To make a long story short, I don't want to have much to do with the traditional Jesus of my youth. I am still afraid of that Jesus. After a few of these stories, you will understand why.

The stories are endless.

I can remember our church consistently pressuring people to walk down the aisle and give their lives to Christ. I did. The sermon asked, "Where do you stand in relation to Jesus?" I knew I wanted to be on Team Jesus so I ran down the aisle. The problem was that after I went down the aisle, our church consistently told stories about people who went down the aisle and didn't really mean it. I was constantly afraid that I wasn't a real Christian. I prayed and prayed and prayed. I asked Jesus into my heart thousands of times. I never had any certainty, only fear.

In middle school, our church got into studying the Book of Revelation. All everyone could talk about was getting left behind after the rapture of God's people and having to endure the end of the world if you were not a Christian. We would go to this haunted trail called "The Tribulation Trail." The goal of this event was to scare the shit out of you and make you become a Christian. For me, it worked. I was terrified for years that I wasn't really a Christian and would get left behind to be destroyed at the end of the world. I couldn't be alone because I thought the end of the world was happening and everyone I loved had gone to heaven and left me here. I would get my little brother to sleep with me all the time. I asked for help and people replied that I probably wasn't really a Christian. This made things worse. For years, I lived in fear and constantly asked Jesus to come into my heart.

I spent most of my early years trying to believe the answers I was given and being terrified by their consequences.

Later, in college, I found a theology that fit my desire for answers and my vices quite nicely. The system is called Calvinism or Reformed Theology. The theology posits that God has chosen people for heaven and hell before they are ever born. This theology also speaks to wealth and privilege. If you have wealth and privilege then you were chosen by God to have it. This sounded pretty good. There were many answers, but not a tremendous amount of questions. The fear arose here when I realized the heinous consequences of the theology. I also figured out that the Dutch

Reformed Church in South Africa used this theology to justify the perpetuation of apartheid. It wasn't long before I realized that I was a part of a heinous system.

I spent most of my college years trying to believe the answers I was given and being terrified by their consequences.

When I was in seminary and still very conservative, I got a call that one of my closest mentors was dying. I spent the last few weeks of his life learning from him. At the end, he called me into his room and spoke, "I am gay and always have been. Go back to seminary and fight for those who have no voice." I spent the next few years seeking God and becoming more and more progressive, until finally God called me to be an advocate and activist for Queer folk. My mentor opened his heart and started the change.

Do you believe in miracles? You are looking at one.

In Matthew 14, there is a big teaching taking place. Queer Jesus is teaching thousands of people the meaning of life and love. Ultimately, the disciples ask Jesus to send the crowds away so they can go and buy some food. Often in this life instead of helping people, we send them away and tell them to buy their own way. Queer Jesus told the disciples that they don't need to go away, we can give them something to eat. Queer Jesus believed in the queer and was teaching the disciples to believe in the queer. We only have five loaves of bread and two fish. Queer Jesus blessed the loaves and fish and started passing it out. The people were hungry. Everybody ate, about five thousand, and then some off of five loaves of bread and two fish. How? The miraculous took place. The people were hungry and Queer Jesus opened the diving heart and fed them.

Do you believe in miracles? The people are hungry.

Had my mentor not opened his heart, I wouldn't have experienced the miraculous.

Do you believe in miracles? The people are hungry.

Answers will not get you over your fear of Jesus. I only overcame my fear when my mentor gave me his heart. I believe, because he believed.

Will we believe? Will we believe that love is bigger than hate? Will we believe that we can feed the world off of our little breads and fishes? Will we believe that we too are vessels connected to God capable of the miraculous?

They need you heart not your answers.

If you want to be like the traditional spaces then keep giving answers and the fear will continue for everyone.

But, if you want to be queer, just like Queer Jesus, then queer the world by giving your heart away.

Love is the solution to fear…embrace the love of Queer Jesus and be the change you want to see.

When we open our hearts and give them away, we leave fear behind.

Amen.

6.

May 5, 2013

"Overcoming Our Fear of Love"

What is love? Everything.

What is God? Everything.

1 John 4: 8 argues, "If you don't know love you don't know God for God is love."

We are created in the image of love, the very image of God, the very image of everything. So, why can't we love other people? Why can't we see the God in them? Why are we so closed off? Perhaps, it has to do with the fact that we can't find a way to love ourselves. Perhaps, the way that we view our self and the world has too many qualifications and boundaries.

Often when we travel somewhere we look for a map. The map tells us that there are certain paths to get to a certain place. The map tells us that there are certain boundaries on the map. Unfortunately, we are the ones who drew the map. When you begin to think freely as God has created us to, then life begins to look differently. We begin to realize that there are many paths to get to where we want to go. Love always goes off the trail. When you begin to think freely as God has created us to, then life starts to look differently. We begin to realize that the boundaries shouldn't have been created in the first place. Love has no set path or boundaries. Love is love.

I can't help but think about the immigration debate when we talk about boundaries. There is grave danger in thinking that just because you live on the other side of a line you are better than someone. Does love abide by arbitrary lines drawn by men to protect privilege?

What about human sexuality? Do you think that the God of the universe gives a shit about whether two men or two women love each other?

We are taught to love each other. When Peter slices off Malchus' ear as Judas came to get Christ for the crucifixion, Jesus declared, "Those who live by the sword will die by the sword." Let me translate that for you, those who live by guns will die by guns. It is hard to love anyone when there is a gun between you. I think you have an answer of where I stand in the gun debate. How many more tragedies will have to happen before we start producing love and not guns?

When we look across the world, we see bombs being built and dropped. Just a few days ago, Israel bombed Syria. The U.S. government has the capabilities to shoot a missile from a drone and never have to look at who was killed. War has become easy. Peace has become harder. Will this community be known for war or violence?

How do we start to love and move past our addictions to fear?

The journey begins with surrender. No matter when the time comes, we will all either live free or die afraid. I choose to surrender my fears and to live free in love. Love begins with surrender.

The journey then moves to our wounds. We must become cognizant of what wounds we have and what boundaries we have set if we are going to realize to what distance we must travel to love. Love is a process that begins with recognizing the limitations we have set.

The journey then progresses to our heart. Are we willing to rip our heart out so that others might have live? Do we seek to have the ever-bleeding heart of Jesus? Can we give our heart away? Love begins with discovering our heart behind our walls and being willing to give it away.

The journey is just getting started when we must make a choice of whether or not to die. Death is a scary thing, yet we are a people who believe in resurrection. Will we have the faith to die and know that God will raise us up and all around us in love? Love begins with the death of control and the birth of love.

Lastly, we must be willing to live. You cannot give love away until you are willing to live into love, until love becomes a very core part of who you are. Are you ready for a revolution of love?

Trust God.

When love takes over things start to look different, take John 3:16 for instance, "For love so loved the world that love gave love's only begotten love that whosoever believes in love shall not perish but have everlasting life."

1 John 4:16 - "Whoever lives in love lives in God."

Amen.

7.

May 11, 2013

Hate Translates

San Pedro de Atitlan, Guatemala

When I stepped off the boat in San Pedro de Atitlan, I was greeted by a giant poster proclaiming, "Jesus is the way, the truth, and the life. No one comes to the Father but through him." Now, I have been a Christian long enough to know that posters reciting John14:6 usually are not placed by people inviting dialogue about the ins and outs of spirituality. There is no question that San Pedro is a conservative place, about sixty percent of the residents are evangelicals and forty percent are Roman Catholic. At night one can hear the whistles of the policia de etica or ethics police chasing the drug using and sex-craving gringos all over the tourist district. Sometimes I think the men who run the policia de etica get close enough to take a nice long gander before they blow their whistle, literally or figuratively. Regardless, there is a clash of cultures in this place, one western and one distinctly conservative Mayan.

The Mayan people have endured much in this region. Since the Spanish conquered present day Guatemala, there has consistently been conflict bubbling beneath the surface between persons of Mayan descent and persons of Spanish descent. The conflicts have exploded into all out war on numerous occasions. There has never been a fair fight. The Mayans have always been outgunned. Often their only chance at deflecting total defeat is to endure. One such occasion of endurance occurred during the Guatemalan Civil War of the 1970s, 1980s, and 1990s.

Yesterday, 86-year-old Rios Monte, the former President of Guatemala from 1982 to 1983, was convicted of the genocide of 1,700 people of Mayan descent and sentenced to 80 years in prison. During the civil war, the military consistently exterminated people of Mayan descent. There were death squads and hit lists. The only way to break the fight of the Mayan people was extermination.

There were pastors and priests all over the Mayan regions who said no to the often indifference of their hierarchies, who were often connected to the government carrying out the exterminations. One such priest was Father Stanley Rauther of Oklahoma. Father Rauther was responsible for the parish in Santiago de Atitlan, which is very close to San Pedro, for many years. In 1981, after enduring numerous threats for his work and protection of the Mayan people, members of the military broke into the parish residence and exterminated Father Rauther as well. Tens of thousands of people mourned the loss of their beloved "Ap'las" or father in the native Mayan dialect. Though his body is buried in Oklahoma, his heart is buried in the parish church in Santiago de Atitlan. Yesterday, I prayed with his heart and the bullet that killed him, which is lodged in the floor of the parish.

This is my third time visiting San Pedro de Atitlan. I have stayed with the same family every visit. They are beautiful people. The grandmother is in her late eighties, the parents are both in their sixties, and their are four children, three of which have children of their own, all living in the same house or close by. I have had many conversations with them about their brothers and cousins who were lost during the Civil War. When I ask why they died, they respond for being Mayan and loving freedom. These are a people who are painfully aware of the consequences of hate. Last night I was with the entire family and the conversation got interesting. We talked for a brief moment about the conviction of Rios Monte and then the conversation shifted to questions about the church I pastor, The Church at Mable Peabody's. When I told them that about ninety percent of our church is lesbian, gay, bisexual, or transgender, you would have thought I told them that Jesus comes down in drag from heaven and preaches a sermon to us every Sunday. It was that foreign to them. I asked them to think about the oppression that they have experienced and are experiencing for being Mayan. I told them that in the United States and around the world the situation is similar for persons who are lesbian, gay, bisexual, or transgender. After much conversation, they began to get it. The family has always known that I have a heart for the marginalized and oppressed no matter the location. Finally, after more explanation, the mother said, "Jesus is always with the marginalized. Jesus is with the homosexuals. They are us and we are them." Hate translates.

Amen.

8.

May 13, 2013

Guatemala City, Guatemala

Perspectives

"16 of my friends and classmates disappeared."
"My brother had his testicles cut out with razorblades and bled to death."
"My cousin had all of his fingernails pulled out before he was shot in the head."
"Our bishop was beat to death with one rock."
"The soldiers consistently remarked, 'The best way to stop the insurgency was to kill the insurgent in the womb.'"

Comments like these filled my day. The interactions were unbelievably intense. Tears welled up in my eyes. The weight of these realities left me exhausted with many thoughts.

How are we to react to a world gone mad? Where in these hellacious realities is Jesus?

I think the best answer is incarnated directly in the hellacious realities. Jesus disappeared. The testicles of Jesus were cut off with razorblades. The fingernails of Jesus were pulled out before the shot to the head. Jesus was beat to death with a rock. The womb of Jesus was cut open and her child was pulled out. If we are to believe in a God that has taken on human form, joined us in our struggle, and incarnated into the least of these, then there is no question that all of these statements are true.

The nature of the incarnation continued to surface.

I encountered two ministers. One knew that he was a minister. The other had no idea, but I found him to be a minister of deep secular conviction.

I encountered the secular minister first. He was the consummate professional, briefcase and all. During the Guatemalan Civil War, he was a clandestine communicator between various guerilla organizations and students at universities. Many of his friends were killed and he was forced to go into hiding on numerous occasions. The minister presented a short history of Guatemala then moved to the present day conviction of Rios Monte. The level of passion in the room skyrocketed. The minister declared the perpetrators of the genocide evil and demanded justice. He spoke lovingly of his friends and family who died. "Rios Monte should be tortured and killed," he declared. In his world, there was good and there was evil. Justice could not come without vengeance. The only way that he could remember his friends was to hold those who killed them responsible. There was no mistaking his conviction.

I encountered the other minister second. He was disheveled and rambunctious. During the Guatemalan Civil War, he was threatened and forced to leave Guatemala on multiple occasions. The gentleman told his story. Throughout the 1950s and 1960s, his dad was in and out of jail on six different occasions for subversive activities. In 1978, his brother was tortured and killed. When the conviction of Rios Monte came up, passion in the room skyrocketed once more. He spoke lovingly of his friends and family who were killed and persecuted. Then, much to the surprise of everyone in the room, he thrust his whole body forward and boldly declared, "The 86-year-old Rios Monte is a victim in need of our attention. He was a victim of the oligarchy of Guatemala, greed, corruption, and the foreign policy of the Reagan Administration. Why can't we just forgive him and move on? You scream of justice, but forget that justice is in the hands of God. Will we be the voice of Jesus asking for forgiveness for those who have persecuted us? Or will we be the ones sick with vengeance and hate? Forgiveness is the only way to free us all." There was no mistaking his conviction.

I know which minister was the incarnation for me.

Amen.

9.

May 14, 2013

Quetzaltenango, Guatemala / "Borders"

I met a forest of trees this morning. The pines exploded toward the sky like rockets. The ground was covered in a dense rug of clovers. There were no borders in this sanctuary, just an invitation for communion. I spoke the words of Jesus to the trees in this place, "I was a stranger and you welcomed me in."

As I stood in silence in this space, a Mayan spiritual guide joined me. "The Mayans ask for all people to join the God, who represents all people," he beckoned. For the spiritual guide, there were no borders to the forest and there were no borders to God.

Borders are an important topic of conversation right now. Conversation of who is in and who is out seems to be all the rage.

The truth is that the United States has left out most of the developing world already. The Central American Free Trade Agreement (CAFTA) has successfully pillaged the countries of Central America, making the rich richer and the poor poorer. We want to close the borders, but it is our economic policies that have destroyed the lives of those trying to get in. In turn, they must risk theirs in order to support their families. We consistently create borders to true communion.

The forest is a good metaphor. There were no boundaries of communion in the forest. It was beautiful. In our forest, will those we encounter be able to use the words of Jesus, "I was a stranger and you welcomed me in?"

There are people right now standing at our borders, the literal and metaphorical ones. They are standing at the borders we have created nationally, locally, and as individuals. Folks of various races, genders, orientations, identities, races, nationalities, religions, and statuses, all knocking and asking for true communion. Will we open the table?

How long will we sit around and try to figure out ways to partially open the door of communion? The truth is that we are either welcome the stranger or we don't. There is no place called between. For the people at our borders, between is the place where they die in the desert starving for hope.

May we be the radicals who make the choice to believe in love and communion above all constructs of borders.

Amen.

10.

May 15, 2013

Chicostenango, Guatemala

Environmental Consciousness and Gender Equality

The mountains seemed to grow fiercer with every turn of the wheel. Then we stopped and stepped out to a place that seemed frozen in time. A forest as lush as any I have ever seemed. I asked our Mayan guides why this mountain was so lush and the other mountains were so barren. The reply came back sharply, "The people of this region fight for their trees."

The Mayan Mennonite pastor told us of a peaceful protest against deforestation that took place in October of 2012. The people marched and were confronted by government troops. After a brief standoff, the troops opened fire and killed seven people on the Pan-American Highway. Many of the dead were local church people who believed that part of loving Jesus was fighting for their environment.

I was reconvicted that the only way that I can give life is by sacrificing my own.

In this incredibly traditional region, most of the local environmental leaders are women. These are women who refused to be bound by traditional gender roles while the men sold off their spaces of worship and culture. Through their collective sacrifice, life is being created and preserved. The women are taking the people to places of environmental stewardship that the men refused to go.

When women lead, we get to go to places we previously refused to believe possible.

The Mayan village on the side of the mountain was poor. The dwellings were made out of mud and looked like they could be kicked over. In the past, due to lack of available jobs, men were forced to go to the cities to find work. The women were left behind with little money and kids to feed. Some of the progressive churches in the country combined resources to help with the resulting oppression and malnourishment. They decided to build something that would help the environment and sustain families throughout the year, greenhouses.

The churches knew that supposed equality without economic freedom was oppression by another name.

The greenhouses have revolutionized the villages. The women are able to plant their own environmentally friendly organic crops and sustain themselves. They do not have to rely on anyone else. Traditional gender roles have gone out the window. Now, the men and women take turns doing the cooking and the cleaning. When I had lunch in the village, there were men cooking and serving just the same as the women. The sight was strikingly different than many of the other Mayan villages I have visited, where gender roles are very traditional. By promoting sustainable interaction with the environment, progressive churches are freeing men and women.

True environmental consciousness and gender equality in this space were not just topics of scholarly conversation.

Amen.

11.

May 16, 2013

Panajachel, Guatemala

The Fiction of Neutrality

On the mountainside in a small rural Guatemalan village, the morning was dark and cold. Everyone was on high alert. The army had entered the town overnight under the cover of darkness. The soldiers demanded that men go to their places of worship for meetings with government officials. The small Methodist church in town sat on the side of the mountain slumped downward. Close to forty men filled the inside of the small space. The men were told if they left the building they would be shot on the spot. No one moved. This was not the first time they were called to the church. After a couple of hours, the sound of a large helicopter gunship filled the air. With a sharp thud, a bomb hit the church. Everyone inside was dead in seconds. The year was 1983.

The church was targeted, because it was deemed a threat to the oppressive society.

Today, I met the man who was the pastor of that church on that dreadful day. He had been exiled to another city and was not present for the fiery deaths of his parishioners. When asked what his response was, he said, "I had to remain neutral and couldn't say too much, my life was on the line."

There have been few times in my life were my expectations were this shocked to meet such a weak reply.

I am a pacifist. I don't believe in violence, whether offensive or defensive. I don't believe that shooting people teaches people not to shoot other people. I don't believe that spanking children teaches them not to hit people. I don't believe that this pastor should have taken up arms against his government, but I do believe that Jesus asks the church to lay down our lives. This means refusing to be silent in the face of injustice, no matter the consequences. To remain silent is to be complicit.

As I write…

Queer folk are being targeted for violence and execution. The church responds with neutrality.

Immigrants are living in the shadows and dying in the desert. The church responds with neutrality.

Minorities are being imprisoned and executed at alarming rates. The church responds with neutrality.

Our global economic policies and financial institutions are destroying and extinguishing the lives of billions. The church responds with neutrality.

On and on and on...

When people are dying, neutrality is a word that grows uglier and more offensive by the hour. I hear church people say all the time that their checks, houses, retirements, and comfortable lives are on the line with regards to issues of injustice and they must remain neutral.

No wonder people are not bombing our churches...we are not a threat to the status quo. We have swallowed the belief wholeheartedly that our comfort is more important than the lives of others. Checks mean more than people. Buildings mean more than people. Status means more than people. People are dying and we cling to a fictitious neutrality.

I have a suspicion that many of the church people I know will be hanging their heads in the future, having been silent in the midst of the grave injustices of our world, just like the pastor I met earlier today.

I pray it not so.

Amen.

12.

May 17, 2013

"A Tale of Two Pastors"

The sun was rising over the volcanoes and glistening on the water as we sped across the lake. The boat was made of straight fiberglass and really rocked your bum with every wave, but I didn't care. I was deep in thought, pondering all the people who gave their lives in the villages along the sandy shores during the Guatemalan Civil War. We arrived at the village and walked up the cobblestone streets until we arrived at the church.

One of the young ladies who worked for the church came out to take us on a guided tour of the facilities. We went to a coffee plantation, a sewing facility, a school, a sustainability project, clinic, and numerous other places. There was no question that the church was doing great work. The most striking component of the tour, however, was the continuous portraits, pictures, statues, and representations of a Father Steve in every location.

We were told that Father Steve left his home in Wisconsin to serve as a priest in this small village. Through his ingenuity, the church was able to create projects that helped the community grow and thrive. I was very moved by the stories of Father Steve until someone in our group asked a fateful question, "Where did Father Steve stand with regard to the Guatemalan Civil War?"

The reply troubles me as I type.

The guide laughed and said, "He played both sides and always gave whoever asked him the supplies they wanted."

The location of these comments weren't too far from the massacre sites were the Guatemalan military slaughtered tens of thousands of Mayan people and dumped them into mass graves. There is little question as to whether or not genocide took place in Guatemala.

Did Father Steve support the genocide by giving supplies to the Guatemalan military?

When we went back to the church, the guide proudly showed us a medal that Father Steve was granted from the Republic Of Guatemala. Since the peace accords, the presidents of this nation have consistently been former government military personnel from the Guatemalan Civil War. The medal seemed to be dripping with the blood of the Mayans to me.

Father Steve had a responsibility to take a stand against injustice, not to help both sides.

On the other side of the lake, another priest from Oklahoma was killed by government troops while seeking to protect the thousands of Mayan people of his church from being slaughtered in 1982.

Nobody ever came after Father Steve for anything but supplies.

Who would you want as your pastor?

Go and do likewise.

Amen.

13.

May 21, 2013

A Poem for Moore, Oklahoma

Where the fuck is God when all these people die?

Where the fuck is God when mothers and fathers cry?

Where the fuck is God when only the cameras are there to address the pain?

Where the fuck is God when nothing is ever going to be the same?

I don't know.

I don't have a clue.

I just have to pray and believe that God was there with them and died and arose too.

Amen.

14.

May 23, 2013

"The Root of War is Fear."

I taught a lesson this morning based on an essay by Thomas Merton entitled, "The Root of War is Fear." In this essay, Merton argues that fear is created by insecurity and insecurity provokes response. We can choose to respond to insecurity in a violent or nonviolent fashion. When we respond violently we are doing so because we think that it will make us secure. The problem is that when we respond violently to secure security we don't take the time to consider that the source of our insecurity and anxiety comes from within. We create the fiction that enacting violence against others will be the solution. Ultimately, violence is never the solution, Merton concludes, as there will always be new fear in our own souls and new reasons to harm for a false security.

The path towards peace begins with dealing with the fear in our own hearts.

Do we choose to live in love or live in fear?

I choose love.

Amen.

15.

May 26, 2013

"Getting Over Our Fear"

Fear is a dastardly construction. It creates boundaries, gives directions, and yells commands. Fear loudly tells us where we can and cannot go and what we can and cannot be. We have created this space to fight against the fear that bites at us out there.

Like the disciples many years ago, we have all pilled together into this ship we call a church. We are huddled together and rowing. We know not the length of time it will take to get to the other side. We just know where we are trying to go. We know not the troubles that might await. We just know that we are going to push through together.

It takes much love and trust to get into the ship. Some of you didn't know each other two months ago. All you knew was that there was this crazy church talking about an all inclusive and loving Queer Jesus getting started. You stepped past your suspicions and fears of church in general and came...now here we are.

I am proud of being in this ship with you. We have sailed a long way. We started in my house with four or five people. We moved locations. We have grown tremendously. But at every step, there has been fear to push past and overcome for all of us.

I wanted to inform you that our family has been the victim of various veiled seemingly threatening words and innuendos over the past few months. When we received a veiled word that someone had a very special birthday present for our boys, I decided to send Emily and the boys to New Mexico, while I was gone to Guatemala this past week. There have also been fishy actions that have seemed to present veiled threats to this community. While none of these veiled words have risen to the level of a provable or actual threat, we do know that there are people out there who do not like what this community is doing.

Those who are frustrated with us now will undoubtedly grow even more so when we start our study next week. I have constructed a volume entitled "The Queer," which is an interpretation of the Gospel of John set in modern day Denton. You can probably imagine who the queer is. We are going to study this book alongside a more traditional version of the Gospel of John each Sunday until we finish the entire book. We choose to study the Bible in this way because others for two thousand years have chosen to interpret the Bible in a way that has left out queer folk of all kinds and sorts. We are the restoration of a God that loves and cherishes all people no matter their orientation or identity.

So we choose to stay and fight with our hearts. To fight for the member of our community that was beaten unconscious and spit upon. To fight for the member of our community that had a crucifix shoved up his ass. To fight for all the queer folk in Denton, Texas and around the world who are afraid to be who they are for fear of losing their jobs, family, and friends. We are the resistance...to fear, inequality, and oppression. We are the movement of love that so many other churches in this area have failed to be. We are the very incarnation of Jesus the Christ, an increasingly queer construct in a world governed by fear.

We have chosen to get out of the boat and walk on water. We have chosen to move past the boundaries of logic and fear. We have chosen to walk on water toward that miraculous light. If we turn away our gaze, we will start to sink. But if we keep our eyes focused on the light that is love, we will reach the shore of our destiny, a place were love is not just an idealization but rather an actualization.

And so we fight with our hearts and dare to stand our ground at this moment, in this time, and in this place, so that all might be turned away from fear and toward love. We are The Church at Mable Peabody's and we intend to fight for any and all whose ambition is love.

Amen.

16.

June 1, 2013

Resurrected Pieces of the Queer Christ

A few months back, I led a time of sharing and healing for victims of spiritual violence. I asked people who were comfortable to share their experiences with the group. One particularly heinous story came from an older gentleman, Paul, who described being violently probed in his anus with a crucifix by members of his Catholic high school youth group. The intention of their attack was to let him see how painful being gay was.

The folks gathered asked me how anyone can morally claim to act in the name of Jesus when such atrocities and violence are consistently committed against queer folk in the name of Jesus. My gut reply surprised everyone present, and even me, **"We have to kill Jesus."**

My mind was channeling the Death of God movement. In 1961, Gabriel Vahanian concluded in his book *The Death of God* that for the modern mind, "God is dead." I would propose that queer folk have reached such a point with regards to Jesus in both their minds and souls.

Throughout history, the church has promoted and perpetuated a wholesale campaign of genocide against queer folk. How can we trust a homophobic racist classist sexist privileged Jesus with our bodies and faith again? The truth is that we can't.

The queer folk that I encounter want nothing to do with the traditional Jesus. They are desperate for something far more real, incarnational, and relational. It is not enough to change our traditions around so that we can say that we have resurrected Jesus for the queer community. There can be no resurrection without death.

The traditional Jesus must die.

Death is often a painful process. We are forced to rethink and reknow. Things have to be given up.

In Matthew 25, Jesus states very clearly that what you have done to the least of these, the marginalized, the oppressed, you have done to me. Jesus not only kills traditional notions of religion as primarily being about egotistical narcissistic ceremony and sacrament, Jesus places Jesus at the very center of the community outside the gates that the religious establishment has left out and oppressed.

We must give up and put to death our notions of a traditional Jesus so that a resurrection might occur.

I am no longer comfortable walking into a church and acting as if nothing has happened or is happening. We know that queer folk have been and continue to be locked out, denied communion, and brutalized in these spaces. These sins run the spectrum of institutional Christianity. We are all guilty. For the community that I serve, the traditional Jesus is dead.

Our resurrection has come in the form of the Queer Jesus.
We relied on scripture, reason, and experience to kill the traditional Jesus and discover the resurrection of the Queer Jesus, the God who is truly Emmanuel or God with us. For our people, this is a concept that they can relate to. The Queer Jesus is not the same Jesus that was used to brutalize and demean them. We are talking about love.

The Queer Jesus is leading a movement of restoration.
Scripture plays an important part in restoring a Queer Jesus that is devoid of the historical baggage of the traditional Jesus and traditional Christian institutions. We are told that Jesus is a constant companion of those that our institutions have left out. We are the ones who got left out.

After the death of the traditional Jesus and the initial resurrection or introduction, this is who we have found the Queer Jesus to be.
The Queer Jesus is not normative and rejects normativity as something created by humans to reject and stifle the unique queerness of every individual (our queerness being a result of our being made in the image of God). Our traditions have become far too normative to hold the Queer Jesus and thus we exist outside of the stifling heavy institutions. The Queer Jesus is deeply tied to the idea that we can only love our neighbor as our self only when we learn to love our self. We are learning to throw away the traditional language of affirmation and embrace the language of celebration of the Queer Jesus.

Those rejected by traditional churches are perhaps most holy amongst us, because they are following the path of the Queer Jesus, who was rejected by the traditional religious spaces.

The Queer Jesus is a rescue mission.
A rescue mission to save a humanity that has made God into a sterile normative image rather than a celebration of the image of God that every human being carries. The Queer Jesus is the essence of love and acceptance for all people. Due to the incarnation, there is no barrier between the individual and God. The Queer Jesus is a celebration of a marginalized Christ and a rejection of the privileged Christ.

The Queer Jesus celebrates all people for who they are at their core, queer.

Amen.

17.

June 2, 2013

"The Queer is Here"

This is not just the beginning of a study for our church.
This is a journey to the very heart of who we believe God to be.

Queer folk have consistently been read, translated and interpreted out of the Bible since the beginning. This was not the message of Jesus. The message of Jesus is one of radical love for all people. Such a message is queer or not normative. How do we open the scriptures to speak as such?

We open our hearts and minds to hope beyond our traditional boundaries of fear.

This book, *The Queer*, is an attempt to open the Gospel of John to a modern queer audience. It is a path to discover Jesus anew. Though it will not be out in print version for a few weeks, I wanted us to go ahead and begin this journey down the path of incarnation with the first chapter of this interpretation of the Gospel of John.

The Queer is Jesus.

"In the beginning was the Queer, and the Queer was with God, and the Queer was God." John 1

God is not normative! God's love extends far beyond the boundaries of what we would consider normative. When we think about God as a queer construct, we begin to realize that the uniqueness of every living being is a result of their having been created in the very image of God. God is queer and so is everyone made in God's image. Jesus was and is the complete earthly embodiment of queerness. When Jesus is described as the Queer, I am describing an entity that has fully recognized the queer within in order to become the queer that the world needs or the God within to become the God that the world needs.

The Queer is God.

"Light shines in darkness…"

Your queerness or difference is your light. Discovering who you have been made to be in the image of God lights the way for others to discover who they have been made to be in the image of God. Be the reflection of light that you have been called to be. God loves you. Be who you are. Share that love. Share that light.

The Queer is light.

"God sent a man to Texas named John…"

John was the forbearer of the light. Sometimes in our lives there are forbearers who cannot go all the way with us, perhaps they can only give us directions. We need to listen to those who offer directions so that we might reach that destination of light that we have longed for and become the queer that God has created us to be.

The Queer is destination.

"The Queer became flesh and dwelt here among us in Texas."

This is a God that continues consistently to become a human being. This is the nature of the incarnation of the Queer. When you hurt God hurts. When you are pain God is in pain. When you are oppressed God is oppressed. This is the God who is right here with you in Texas. You are queer and God is queer.

The Queer is here.

"The Queer was rejected by family and those who claim to know God the best."

We just spent an entire evening sharing and hearing numerous stories of rejection. The Queer knows what it means to be rejected by family and loved ones. This is the God who came out and was kicked out. The Queer knows what it means to be rejected by religious establishments. This is the God that was killed by them. In the same way that you were and are oppressed by your families and religious folk, so too was the Queer.

The Queer is a survivor.

"The leaders of the Church of the Bible sent numerous elders and deacons from Denton to ask John, 'Who the hell are you? What the hell are you? What is your identification?'"

When are we going to have the courage to live beyond the boundaries of labels and identifications? We live in a society that is constantly asking for such things? What are you? How do you identify? The problem with such thinking is that we become slaves to labels and identities that do not allow us to be individuals. You are a queer child of God, be who God has created you to be. You do not have to fit. You just have to be.

The Queer is queer.
and
The Queer is here.

Amen.

18.

June 9, 2013

"The Courage to Move"

I apologize for my absence this morning. I have grown to know absence quite well this weekend. I lost my dear grandfather and friend, Ray Emory Hood. I hurt. I am tired. Later this afternoon, I will preach his funeral. It promises to be one of the more important sermons I have ever delivered. I covet your prayers.

Death however is not the reason you have gathered this morning. Life is. So let's discuss life.

We find life today walking along East University Drive. This is the great Queer of all queers, Jesus the Christ. John demands that his caravan of cars stop immediately.

Sometimes in life we travel so fast that we don't take the time to look out the window and see what is passing us by. Perhaps, we miss life. Perhaps, we miss love. Perhaps, we miss God.

John didn't want to miss it. John was looking. John refused to keep going. John stopped.

Then John spoke,

"Here is the Queer of God that takes away the sin of the world! This is the Queer we have been waiting for. This is the revelation I have been preaching. I saw the Spirit of God descend and remain on the Queer."

Imagine that…the Queer is the one who takes away the sin of the world when most of our churches are saying that the Queer is the one bringing sin into the world. Is it possible that the church is missing the savior it seeks to promote? Is it possible that the salvation of the church and all humanity is sitting right here in this room? Perhaps, that which is Queer amongst us or that which is God amongst us is moving at this very moment to restore humanity to a place of love. Is it possible that we are the ones bringing the Queer that will restore the world?

When we speak of the Queer Jesus outside of this beautiful bar, is it possible that we might actually hear from those who hear, "This is the Queer I have always been waiting for"?

Revelation comes when we discover our self, our love, and our hope in God. The Queer exists to help us discover God amongst us. Will we be willing to look? Will we be willing to push past our boundaries and fear to believe that God is actually here with us? This is the God of the incarnation. The God who is present in our struggle to be human. This is the Queer.

I want you to know that I too saw the Spirit of God descend and remain on the Queer. I know God is Queer and I know the Queer is here. Do you? Do you have the courage to look out of your windows and see where God really is? I saw the Spirit of God descend and remain on the Queer.

"The Queer was outed in front of a caravan full of howling people on the side of the road...The next day...John outed the Queer again."

The Queer knows your struggles. The Queer knows what it means to be outed. The Queer knows what it means to be relentlessly questioned about preferences, habits, and plans. The Queer has incarnated into your struggle to shun normativitity and be the queer that God has called you to be. The Queer knows that anyone who leaves normativity behind is going to face the same persecution that the Queer did. God the Queer is with you in the struggle.

"What are you looking for?"

This is the question of human existence. We are all seeking and searching for logical answers. Is it possible that this is our problem? Is it possible that we have forgotten what it means to believe in something beyond ourselves? Perhaps the answers are to be found in giving up the search. Perhaps the answers are to be found in the embrace of mystery and love. Maybe it is time to cease striving and just love people. Maybe if we have the courage to cease striving and start loving people, the answers will find us.

Letting go of the normative and logical is the core of the message of the Queer Jesus.

"Can anything good come from the trashy riffraff of Ponder?"

Nathaniel made quite the ugly statement about the home of the Queer, calling the whole community of Ponder trashy riffraff. Nathaniel could not stand the idea of Ponder. Of course, Nathaniel actually speaks of Nazareth in the actual Gospel of John, but there is something to learn here.

Later, Nathaniel states, "My God! You are the Queer."

Nathaniel found God, the fullest expression of love, in the place that he hated the most. What does this say to us? Those areas, those people, those shops, those restaurants, those homes, those groups, and many other possibilities...the very places you hate the most might be the source of God for you, the fullest expression of love. Indeed, for Nathaniel love came from the most unlikely of destinations. We must follow the path of Nathaniel and keep our hearts open for such unlikely love to find us.

We have been challenged…questions have filled this sermon.

Do we have the courage to believe that it is the Queer amongst us that is taking away the sin of the world?

Do we have the courage to be a part of something queer?

Do we have the courage to be outed as queer like the Queer Jesus was?

Do we have the courage to cease striving and embrace the mystery?

Do we have the courage to open our hearts and look to the places and people we hate as a source of love and restoration?

The Queer Jesus calls the disciples in the last of these passages. This leaves us with a core overarching primary question: When the Queer looks at us and says 'Follow Me'…will we have the courage to move our feet?

I pray so.

19.

June 9, 2013

A Sermonic Eulogy for Ray Emory Hood

Last Thursday evening, I was on my way down to Livingston, Texas. I minister to a gentleman on Texas' death row and I was headed to the state prison. Somewhere along a lonely highway, I received a phone call. My mother informed me that my grandfather was dead. I cried softly. Later, one of my church members asked, "What do you believe in at this moment?" "Absence," I replied.

I am not interested in speaking like a minister at this moment. You see in this moment of darkness, I dare to speak like a human being. We can speak of God and religious things all that we want, but we fail to love our neighbor as our self if we don't acknowledge the pain that comes with absence.

In the midst of the pain, I didn't need verses of scripture…I just needed to remember a story or a version of it I read in a book by Peter Rollins.

There was a point in history where a woman named Regina, at just 30 years of age, made the decision to translate the Word of God into the obscure native language of her people. Regina saved her money to hire the scholars to translate and printers to print the copies. After 20 years, Regina finally had enough money…then an earthquake hit her small island. People were desperate for food and shelter. Regina spent all the money that she had raised on providing for the hurting. Regina fed the hungry and provided shelter for the homeless. It took everything she had to help the people and wiped out all of her savings. Desperate to translate the Word of God, Regina started over. Over the next 20 years, Regina worked odd jobs and strained for every ounce of wealth she could muster. Then, just as she was finally to the point where she could translate the Word of God, a plague hit her small island. People were lying out in the streets crying out for help. There weren't enough doctors or facilities. Regina spent all of the money she saved up to help the people receive the treatment they needed. Regina saved many lives. Once again, it took everything she had to help those around here. Now, Regina was 70 years old. Desperate to finish her life's ambition, Regina began to work again harder than ever before. Finally after another 20 years, Regina had collected the resources to translate the Word of God. Before she died at 91, she got to see the Word of God translated into the language of her people. It has been said that although Regina only translated the Word of God on paper once, she also translated it two other times for the people of her island.

This little story asks us to expand our minds as to what might be the Word of God. The truth is that sometimes the answers are not found in books. The truth is that books are only as useful as how they push us to live and love those around us. The Word of God is intended to be incarnated here with us. The truth is that everything that Jesus touches begins the process of becoming the incarnated Word of God until the restoration is complete. There are moments where we become the Word of God for others. Where we become the incarnation.

For me, my grandfather has consistently been the incarnation of the Word of God.

When I have wondered what the unconditional love of Jesus looks like, I didn't turn to a book...I turned to my grandfather. I ponder what it means to be married and devoted to someone for 72 years. I think about nursing staff having to ask my elderly grandfather to leave my grandmother in the hospital and him adamantly refusing. I allow my mind to imagine my 88-year-old grandmother sitting there night after night over the last few weeks of my grandfather's life...singing and telling him how much she loves him and simply not wanting to let go. The last words my grandfather ever spoke on this earth were to tell my grandmother that he loved her. I don't need a book to talk to me about unconditional love. I watched it lived. I watched two people love each other in ways I never thought possible. This is the incarnation of the Word of God for me.

When I have wondered what the generosity of Jesus was like, I didn't turn to a book...I turned to my grandfather. This is a man who loved everyone. Those the world called strange, my grandfather sought to love and touch. Those who needed a lift, my grandfather sought to pick them up. Those who were judged, my grandfather sought to save and love. My grandfather was changed by those he encountered and those he encountered were changed by him. This is the incarnation of the Word of God for me.

When I have wondered what the determination of Jesus looked like, I didn't turn to a book...I turned to my grandfather. From sun up to sun down, my grandfather worked on the farm and at the body shop. He worked hard to provide for my grandmother and his family. When he got sick over and over again, my grandfather pushed to survive. When he knew that the end of his life was approaching, he pushed to get out those final I love yous. My grandfather never gave up the fight. Even in the midst of death, my grandfather remained defiant. Love was always bigger than any obstacle or even death. This is the incarnation of the Word of God for me.

My grandfather was the incarnation of the Word of God for me.

John 1:1 states, "In the beginning was the Word, and the Word was with God, and the Word was God."

Those pieces of my grandfather that I saw...that I hold on to and speak about today...are the incarnated Word of God. Nothing my grandfather did right or well happened apart from the Word that is the incarnated God. I know that my grandfather has been restored and transformed to where he was in the beginning. I know that when my grandfather looked past my grandmother and out the window at the moment of his death...he met the Word and became the Word.

My grandfather was the Word of God in my life.

May we all become the incarnated Word of God in the lives of others.

May we be the translation that the world so desperately needs.

Amen.

20.

June 13, 2013

The Danger of Identity

In John 8:25, the religious leaders asked Jesus, "Who are you?"

Jesus was asked the same question of identity that we often are…and often the same question of identity that we ask our selves.

I sat with a young man at our church a few nights ago that had one question on his mind, "What am I?" The young man's response to his own question was direct and rather brutal, "I am gay. That is all that I am or will ever be. It doesn't matter that I am occasionally attracted to women. I need to learn how to fit into a gay identity." It was as if there were a few identities to choose from and he had to choose one.

Recently, I spoke on the phone with a 70-year-old female friend who was in a relationship with a woman for over 40 years that tragically ended with the death of the woman. After a few months, the recently widowed woman to the surprise of nearly everyone around her started dating a man about her age. I asked her if she considered herself to be bisexual or still a lesbian. Her response was priceless, "Why do I need a label? At my age, it's all just love."

This morning, I was contacted by a friend of mine who has always been attracted to women, but has now found himself at 40 years of age falling for a man. "Am I supposed to assume a gay identity or a bisexual identity? This is the only person I am attracted to right now, but I don't want to discount my past relationships. This guy is the only one that I want. Am I gay or am I bi Jeff?" My friend felt like he had to assume an identity immediately on the phone.

We are a people who push identities both on our self and on others. We need to know what box we are going to check. We need to know where you are going to fit. We need to know what we are and what you are.

The problem with such simplistic thinking is that we are living in a beautifully complex world made up of beautifully complex people where labels and identities always fail to describe the totality of who a person is.

When people ask me, "Who am I?"

I always respond that you are a queer child of God made in the image of a God who is queer.

The beauty of this statement is that it opens the space for everyone to be the totally unique non-normative child of God that they were created to be by a God that is totally unique and non-normative.

The problem with identities is that they force us to fit into new normativities, often without allowing us to be the unique person that we are. People should be able to love who they love, whether it fits into their assigned or assumed identity or not. To question their love based on the identity they have assumed or we have assigned them, is to not love.

Returning to John 8:25, Jesus responded to the question of the religious leaders, "I am who I told you I was from the beginning."

Perhaps we should start going by who we were at the beginning…a unique child of God made for unique purposes, who fight for the rights of all people to love who they want to love…for we never know when our assigned or assumed identities might fail us too.

Amen.

21.

June 16, 2013

"A Diaconal Ordination"

The church exists so that the love might be made known to the world. There is no more lofty an ambition than to give your life living, expressing, and teaching love. God calls all to the task of love. God calls some to the task of teaching others how to perform the task of love. It is for this reason that we gather this morning in this bar.

This is a peculiar space to be the site of a diaconal ordination. This is a secular space. Most would say too secular of a space. Most would say that God is located in churches with large pulpits and stained glass windows. These people would be mistaken in their assumptions about God's location. We are a church that exists to uplift the fact that God is often more present in the secular than in the sacred. God is undoubtedly with us this morning.

The office of deacon in our church is primarily a role of service to the people of the community. Our new deacon will be learning how to love people, commit to people, and fight for people. The next year will be a difficult journey of triumph and tragedy…such is the life of the minister. At the culmination of this year, after satisfactory completion of your diaconal course, you will be ordained a minister. Throughout this process and beyond, as your pastor and mentor, I commit myself to you.

I speak to you my translation of the words of Ruth to Naomi in the first chapter of the Book of Ruth:

Don't ever ask me to leave you, because I won't know how!
Wherever you need me, I will be there!
If you lose your way, I will help us find our way back.
I will walk beside you and rest where you rest.
Your community will be my community.
Your God will remain my God.
May God bring death and more if ever I fail you.

These are words of strong commitment. Some would even say that Ruth and Naomi were lovers. Perhaps, this is instructive of the type of commitment I want to make.

With our eyes closed, I want us to ponder the words of Ruth to Naomi before we lay our hands on our new deacon as a community.

Will you ever leave our deacon?
Will you be there when our deacon needs you?

Will you find and help her if our deacon ever gets lost?
Will you walk beside our deacon?
Will you rest when our deacon rests?
Will you be our deacon's community and welcome our deacon's community?
Will our deacon's God remain your God?
May death come for us all if we fail to love this one that God has called as deacon.

I invite you to come forward and lay your hands of ordination on our new deacon.

Amen.

22.

June 16, 2013

"The Water into Wine"

We continue this morning with my forthcoming publication, a modern queer translation of the Gospel of John, *The Queer,* in the second chapter...

The Queer attended the wedding of a friend in Argyle.

Today, we find Jesus or the Queer in the midst of a wedding celebration. Weddings are special times to celebrate the commitment of love. We as a people know a thing or two about weddings. We have all been to our fair share of these ceremonies. Unfortunately, we also know a thing or two about the denial of civil marriage to many queer folk in this country. It is difficult to talk about a wedding without thinking about the injustice of the denial of civil marriage to many queer folk.

I want it to be known in this space and to all who have ears that Jesus the Queer is with us in our struggle for marriage equality.

With this statement sealed by love for all of eternity, we move to the key elements of this passage.

Later on in the evening, after everyone was fairly drunk, the wine gave out.

Weddings are meant to be celebrations of love, thus is the reason that we still celebrate same sex weddings in Texas no matter what the laws of the state of Texas are.

During celebrations people often drink, in this case people were drunk. The passage reads that the wine gave out. I don't know if you have been to a party lately, but when someone says that the alcohol has given out then usually the people have had a tremendous amount to drink. The people were thirsty. They wanted more alcohol to celebrate the joy of love. The Queer complied.

The Queer ordered six large plastic barrels, capable of holding twenty to thirty gallons of water, filled to the brim and said, "Now draw out some water..." The catering manager was shocked and could not figure out where the amazing wine came from.

The Queer ordered a tremendous amount of water and made a tremendous amount of wine. The Queer gave as a gift at least 120 gallons of wine to people who were already drunk at this wedding celebration. That truth probably wouldn't sit well with some of our more conservative friends. They think Jesus never associated with alcohol. This passage seems to starkly speak otherwise.

The first recorded miracle in the Gospel of John is Jesus the Queer seeking to keep a celebration of love going.

Love is worthy to be celebrated above all things.

There were plenty of people who could have provided more water, but only the Queer could have provided more wine. We exist in a world where there are plenty of people who can provide more water, but few people to provide the sweet wine of love. Are we going to be a people who provide water or wine?

This queer event revealed the glory of the Queer and the mission of the Queer, love.

The mission of the Queer was and is to love.

Do we have the courage to connect with the image of God within us? Do we have the courage to connect with the Queer within? If we do, then we will boldly accept our mission of love…our mission to provide and be the sweet wine of love.

The disciples believed.

Love is believable.

When people see the bland water of everyday life changed to the sweet wine of love, they pay attention. When your life becomes about love, people notice. Do you believe in love? Do you believe in the way of the Queer? I invite you to believe in love.

In just a moment we will take communion, I invite you to taste the wine of love and take some with you as you leave this place to share with others…perhaps you too will find your self changing the water you find into wine.

Amen.

23.

June 23, 2013

"TELL THE TRUTH!"

In the second chapter of the Gospel of John verse 13, we find Jesus confronting a grave injustice. The money changers and sellers of sacrifices were cheating the people out of their money. Jesus responded by making a whip of chords, meaning Jesus had a little while to think about what happened next. In a rage, Jesus overturned tables and kicked all of the proprietors of injustice out of the temple.

The religious folk responded by asking Jesus, "What sign can you give us for doing this?" Jesus said, "If you destroy this temple, I'll raise it back up in three days." "How? It took 46 years to build the temple," they demanded. Jesus was talking about Jesus' body.

The religious folk wanted Jesus, but Jesus did not trust the people enough to give over the body.

In the second chapter of the Queer, we find the Queer in similar circumstances. The Queer went up to the Church of the Bible for a religious festival. Folks were everywhere trying to scare the shit out of people in order to get them saved, whatever that means. Hell and damnation were the chief tools of oppression. For the Church of the Bible, God was an often-sexist burly bloodthirsty homophobic American Christian man with a large penis. They persecuted everyone who did not subscribe to all the elements of this narrow doctrine.

Red with fury, the Queer slowly and methodically made a whip of electronic chords and went to work. In a righteous anger, the Queer overturned the sound system, ripped down the projector, tore down the American flag, and screamed of a God that loves all people. "Get this hate and injustice out of here NOW!"

The Queer declared, "This is my sign, destroy this church and I will raise it up."

Many started to believe. The Queer, however, did not trust them with the body of the Queer, because the Queer knew the destruction that people often inflict on the body.

These passages call out to us this morning. The words beckon us, "Who are you going to be in the face of oppression and marginalization? Who are we going to be as a church in the face of oppression and marginalization?"

We find Jesus confronting deep injustice. The money changers and sellers of sacrifices were taking advantage of some of the poorest people in the society. The poor people had to change their money and buy sacrifices at the door while the rich folk could simply bring their own. At the door of the temple was a line of class…those who had to use the money changers and sacrifice sellers and those who didn't. All of this was being done with the backing of the government. Jesus had a choice to make.

In the face of oppression, Jesus had to ponder, "Am I going to tell the truth?" We live in a world of grave injustice and we have to ponder, "Are we going to tell the truth?"

Are we going to tell the truth when people treat queer folk like shit?
Or are we going to care about our own wellbeing and comfort to the detriment of everyone else?
Are we going to tell the truth when factories with close ties to American retail stores burn down in Bangladesh and kill hundreds and hundreds of people?
Or are we going to keep wearing the clothes?
Are we going to tell the truth when Texas prepares to carry out its 500th execution of the modern age?
Or are we going to turn our heads?
Are we going to tell the truth when women are treated like shit all over the world?
Or are we going to remain silent?
When war breaks out all over the world are we going to tell the truth that the root of war is fear and insecurity?
Or are we going to fool ourselves into thinking that violence can accomplish peace?

The questions of truth begin to get closer to home…

Are we going to tell the truth when folks inquire about whom we love or are attracted to?
Are we going to tell the truth when our job begins to be endangered?
What about when we are told to stop our activism or lose our job?

I made that choice many months ago and lost my job.

Many of you think that that you can lie about yourself and that your deceptions won't hurt anyone.

I have brought our dear brother and noted mystic of the Civil Rights Movement, Dr. Howard Thurman, by way of an anthology of his writing (*Strange Freedom,* 148), to respond to such thinking:

"Deception has its genesis in fear wrought by precipitous and systematic violence…Deception practiced over time *however* becomes self-defeating and destructive to others…Deception and lying are never viable moral alternatives because they destroy the value structure of the one who deceives and lies. 'The penalty of deception is to become a deception'…Truth-telling underscores the fundamental dignity of human persons and highlights the equality of all people…For Thurman the *option to tell the truth* is the essence of individual freedom and each human being's birthright as a child of God."

The truth is what sets us free. The truth is what makes us whole. The truth is what draws us closer to God.

When we find injustice how are we going to react?

Jesus committed an act of civil disobedience. Jesus did not hurt anyone…but there is no question that Jesus did break the law to stop the oppression in the temple.

How far are we willing to go?

We all desire marriage equality…but the question ultimately becomes how far are we willing to go to make it happen? Are we prepared to spend a few nights in jail to protect and fight for the rights of all in our community?

What are the tables that we need to overturn? Instead of sitting quietly this morning, do we need to be working on a whip? Who do we need to be?

I pray that we will be a people who never stop asking these questions.

Jesus saw the injustice and heard the muffled cries of the oppressed.

I pray that we will be a people who never stop listening to the demands of the people.

Oscar Romero, in his 16th of July 1978 homily, said,

"The people of God, illuminated by their faith, look at their own aspirations, demands, and ideals. And with this faith they know how to discern what God wants according to the signs of the times. Clearly not everything that people demand is the word of God, but in the heart of the demands of our moments, there is much of God to be found…"

We find God in the signs of the times and the demands of the people. In the midst of such signs and demands, who are we to be? The people need truth and reaction to injustice. Are we willing to make the sacrifices it takes to be such things?

"Destroy this temple and I will raise it up!!!"

Jesus was talking about the body of Jesus. In this piece of the scripture, we find a deeper truth.

Jesus basically said, "You can't touch this temple." This unquestionably translates into our present age. Everyone wants to touch your temple. They want to change who or what you are. They want to destroy your temple.

You are all children of God made in God's image. The God that is queer beyond normalization. The image within you is uniquely queer. There is no one that can do anything to your queer image of God. No one can destroy it. If they try to destroy who you are, God will raise you up.

We are a people who do not believe in death without resurrection. So when you feel drug down and hurt by the pressures of society or you feel that death is near, know that you will soon be resurrected into a higher state of queerness and love.

Jesus did not trust the people with the body of Jesus.

Jesus knew what happens when you trust others with your body. They often name your body and call you what they want to. Don't trust anyone with your body. You are a queer child of God unlike anyone else...rest securely in that knowledge.

I am so tired of the attempts to create boundaries of identity and orientation that people are forced to exist within. I am exhausted by the attempts to name the body. We use the word queer because we are interested in queering such boundaries with the reality of the unique queerness of every individual.

Tell the truth! We are all queer.

Be who you are...that is where God is.

In conclusion, we tell the truth, refuse to not react in the face of injustice, we trust in the continual resurrection and rejuvenation of our persons, and ultimately protect our bodies so that we might be the queer that God has called all of us to be.

Perhaps it is the truth that will ultimately move us to one.

God is with us.

Amen.

-Fluker, Walter and Tumber, Catherine. *A Strange Freedom: The Best of Howard Thurman on Religious Experience and Public Life.* Boston: Beacon Press, 1998. Pp. 148.
-Wright, Scott. *Oscar Romero and the Communion of the Saints.* Marknoll, New York: Orbis Books, 2009. Pp. 121.

24.

June 26, 2013

The Religious Case for Queer Marriage

First of all, this is not a post about *gay marriage*...as I am not interested in any continuation of hints of sexism...rather I will be talking about queer marriage. Queer marriage is a broad construct that seeks the right of all people to marry whoever they love.

I found out recently that our church, The Church at Mable Peabody's, was recently kept from sponsoring a community event because the leadership said that gay marriage is a political issue and not a religious issue. Ultimately, the persons who blocked the church's participation said that religion plays no part in the determination of whether gay marriage should be legal or not. These persons have obviously not witnessed who has pushed for the passing of these state marriage amendments banning queer marriage equality all over the country. The main opponents of queer marriage equality are almost always religious people. Many of the main proponents of queer marriage equality are often religious people. Regardless, queer marriage is a religious issue for many if not most and to say otherwise is to be a dumbass.

I recently sat down with a queer couple that asked me, "Would Jesus approve of us getting married?" I can't fight for marriage equality if Jesus wouldn't approve of our relationship. I assured them that God is always on the side of love.

For this couple, queer marriage equality is a religious issue.

I was recently asked to participate in a couple's wedding ceremony. They told me how desperately they pray for the Supreme Court to overturn the laws that might keep their union from being recognized by the state. I told them that no matter what happens, God is always on the side of love.

For this couple, queer marriage equality is a religious issue.

I watched a couple on television not long ago, who are both female Episcopal priests in Maryland, that are legally married...unfortunately one is a citizen of Great Britain and the Defense of Marriage Act would not allow the spouse that is a U.S. citizen to sponsor the other for residency. They continue to pray to God for the overturning of our oppressive laws.

For this couple, queer marriage equality is a religious issue.

I recently read a story about two Islamic men who were nearly beaten to death for their forbidden love in Egypt by a group led by their local Imam. They fled to the United States and joined a progressive interfaith community in New York City. They described the community as helping them feel connected to Allah again and ultimately helping them to garner the courage to fight for the right to marry here in the United States.

For this couple, queer marriage equality is a religious issue.

In Chicago, two women raised and formed within Orthodox Judaism fell in love. Their community shunned them and they ran away. In their new home, they desperately desired for the state to not shun them like their religious community did.

For this couple, queer marriage equality is a religious issue.

I could go on and on with the stories of religion colliding with queer marriage equality, but I think it is sufficient to say that queer marriage equality is a religious issue because queer folk are statistically more often than not religious.

While I have no doubt that there are many other religious and spiritual ways to present a religious case for queer marriage, I can initially only speak as I am...an unabashed follower of Jesus.

In Matthew 22:39, Jesus commands Jesus' followers, "Love your neighbor as yourself." You cannot love your neighbor as yourself when you are taking away their benefits, denying them the right to be legally married to their spouse, levying tremendous extra taxes on them, making it difficult for them to adopt children, deporting their spouses, and on and on and on. The consequences of not having queer marriage are astronomical. Followers of Jesus and lovers of God cannot sit back and continue to treat their queer neighbors like shit. There is nothing loving about the treatment of queer folk that would be upheld by any religious or spiritual tradition. I love my queer neighbor and thus I fight.

In Matthew 25:45, Jesus states, "Whatever you have done to the marginalized you have done to me." Queer folk are consistently treated like shit in the United States. If you want to understand why I feel so confident in calling queer folk marginalized, all you have to do is look at the benefits that queer folk miss out on by not being able to marry, the rising hate crime statistics, the way that queer young folks are treated, the language our church has had to deal with from the community, and on and on and on. I will always stand amongst the marginalized...because that is where I was told to stand. I stand with queer folk and thus I fight.

In 1 John 4:8, the writer boldly proclaims, "God is love." This means everywhere that love is God is. Where love is not, God is not. I have witnessed unbelievably deep love in queer relationships. I have experienced it myself. Love is present in these spaces and that can only mean God is present in these spaces. Where love is God is and where love is not God is not. I want to be where love is, where God is. I support the love of queer folk and thus I fight for queer marriage equality.

The follower of Jesus cannot not support queer marriage equality. It is at the very core of who we are called to be as a people. We love our neighbors, we stand with the marginalized, and we proclaim a God who is named love. The only reason that I can think of for most followers of Jesus to not be in favor of queer marriage equality is fear. Fear is always the root of bigotry. The pertinent question for us right now is, "Are we going to follow Jesus or fear?" I choose Jesus. I choose love.

Everyone that reads this will not be a follower of Jesus or even religious for that matter, for you I ask a deeply spiritual question, "Do you believe in love?" We all try to keep faith in love. Love exists outside of us. Love is something we encounter. Everyone wants to meet love. What is the difference of love in queer folk? Do we believe that they are lying about love? Why can't we champion love? When we bolster love we bolster life. I stand with my queer friends and neighbors because I believe that no one has a monopoly on love and that love has been mislegislated for far too long.

I ask all religious and spiritual persons to stand with queer folk on the side of love.

Love is always a deeply religious and spiritual issue...so let us give both our heart and souls to this movement of truth.

Amen.

25.

June 26, 2013

"Speech at The Denton Day of Decision Rally"

Friends this evening I have a question for you…
Do you believe in the power of love?
Do you believe in the power of love?
Do you believe in the power of love?
I am Rev. Jeff Hood…Pastor of The Church at Mable Peabody's…a fabulously queer community. I arise tonight…as a Queer American…to celebrate…this unquestionably momentous time…love is winning. I believe that we are standing in a holy and sacred space…at a time to celebrate love defeating the evil of bigotry. I am with you to celebrate…but I am also with you to tell the truth.

You see this afternoon I wavered a bit about what the tone of this speech would be. I oscillated between two great paths within my spiritual tradition…whether I would be a celebrant or a prophet for this gathering.
I chose prophet.
There is no question that a major victory has been achieved. We have all worked very hard for this day. In striking down the Defense of Marriage Act and refusing to rule on Proposition 8 the Supreme Court of the United States of America partially affirmed a truth that we all know…that it is wrong to discriminate against people on the basis of orientation and identity. Notice I said, "partially affirmed." The federal government did not step in to stop the legal oppression and marginalization of queer folk that takes place by state governments all over the country. The truth is that the State of Texas can still legally treat queer folk like shit…denying queer folk many of the rights that are guaranteed to folks not deemed queer. Also do not let this large rally fool you into thinking that Denton, Texas is blameless. Just a month ago the Denton City Council refused to pass a resolution supporting marriage equality.

Tonight, I call on the federal government, the State of Texas, and the City of Denton to tell the truth of love and stop the oppression.

I also am here to apologize that there are not more religious leaders from our community on this platform. I don't have to think long to understand why they are not here. All I have to do is look on Facebook and see the comments that the parishioners of many of these churches are making. So on this day, I must also tell the truth about some of the religious leadership of this community.
If you want to find some of the local sources of oppression, you don't have to look far.

Tommy Nelson, the Pastor of Denton Bible Church, declared on June 14, 2012, "The idea of homosexual marriage is a moral and theological sleight of hand. It is not raised from any perspective of wisdom but from a concession to the humanism, perversion, and weakness of our age." (http://dentonbible.org/notes/dbc-response-to-obamas-support-of-same-sex-marriage/)

The Village Church currently sponsors gay recovery groups at all four of their campuses, including here in Denton.
(http://www.thevillagechurch.net/sermon/jesus-and-homosexuality/)
Matt Chandler, the lead pastor of the four Village Churches, said a few months ago that he was upset when evangelicals are treated like the "American Al Qaida" for opposing same sex marriage.
(http://www.religiondispatches.org/archive/sexandgender/6798/megachurch_pastor_we_re_american_al_qaeda_for_opposing_homosexuality)
To him I respond, if you don't want to be treated like the "American Al Qaeda" then quit acting like it!
There is no question that much damage has been done to queer folk in this community and others by these conservative spaces and others like them…but the story does not end there.

A few months ago, our church helped lead the community in purchasing an ad in the Denton Record Chronicle for churches to show their support for LGBTQ inclusion in their churches (http://revjeffhood.com/press/). Out of the over 70 churches located in Denton, there were eight ministries that signed, two of those were campus ministries. Three of those ministries have representatives here on these steps.
The parties that I was most disappointed in were all of the mainline or moderate churches in this town. There was tremendous fear that they might lose the support of the church hierarchy or part of their membership if they signed such a statement. They can do more and haven't. Such activity only allows the oppression to continue.

Tonight, I ask the religious leadership of this community to tell the truth and stand on the side of love…if you don't then you have no right to speak about a God who has called God's self love.

I also arise tonight for my twin sons Jeff and Phillip and the unborn child my wife is carrying. I want them to know that their dad loves them enough to fight for their right to marry whoever the hell they want.

Tonight, I declare that I will not stop telling the truth and fighting for a world where my children can be whoever God has created them to be.
There are many truths this hour.
We are gathering to celebrate marriage equality…but downstate in Huntsville, Texas a more somber occasion is transpiring. Kimberly McCarthy aged 52 is being

executed. This is the 500th modern execution in Texas. A broke down unjust system has claimed the lives of 500 people without shuttering.

Last night, women had to storm the Texas State Capitol in order to have their voices heard. Folks in power have refused to hear until forced to listen.

There are indeed many truths this hour…but this community gathered here has a special ability to share the truth of love. To turn the tide of despair into hope. To turn the tide of marginalization into inclusivity.

Jesus says in John 8:32, "The truth shall set you free."

You…the Queer folk gathered in this space…have an ability to share truth and free our world with your love.

Love is the only path to freedom.
I believe that we are the hope of love…we are the promise of tomorrow…if and only if we will continue to be the truth of today.

This is our hour to create the beloved community inclusive of all people that all of us have dreamed of.
Are you ready to love?
I feel the power.
Now go love somebody!

Amen.

26.

June 27, 2013

Remarks on SCOTUS Decision in Denton Record Chronicle

From the Denton Record Chronicle:
The Rev. Jeff Hood, pastor at The Church at Mable Peabody's Beauty Parlor & Chainsaw Repair in Denton, said Wednesday's Supreme Court decisions were ones affirming humanity and love.
Established March 31, the church membership is 95 percent lesbian, gay, bisexual or transgendered, he said.
"One of the things that I've encouraged our people and told our people is God is love ... and wherever love is, God is. I think today is an affirmation of love, and I think that's very spiritual," he said. "Ultimately, when we choose to love and we affirm the love of others, we're not only recognizing the humanity in them but the love in them, the God in them."

27.

June 30, 2013

"Daring to Love Beyond the Closet"

This is the story of Nicodemus...an establishment figure who dared to visit a man proclaiming love...the one called Jesus.

The Visit

Nicodemus was an establishment figure... a man of enormous prominence in both civil and religious society and governance. Think of it as being both a Roman Catholic Bishop and deputy mayor in the City of New York. Jesus was a religious radical that the establishment despised. The visit of Nicodemus and Jesus happened because Nicodemus dared to move past the boundaries of his identity. He dared to love and seek in forbidden ways. This visit would have never happened if Nicodemus had played by rules. This beautiful encounter transpired because Nicodemus was willing to step outside of his closet.

The Night

Nicodemus traveled by night. How many of you are used to traveling in the night looking for both love and answers? Quietly Nicodemus stepped toward something or someone that was named profane by all of those around him, the one called Jesus. The night can be a place of tremendous beauty and sometimes in the darkness we find answers. Sometimes it is only when we are there in the darkness and courageous enough to believe in the absence of God that we start to believe in the existence of God. Sometimes it is only when we are there in the darkness and courageous enough to believe in the absence of love that we begin to believe in existence of love. The night...the mystery...can hold many answers if we are willing to follow Nicodemus and step out into it.

BUT

Nicodemus told Jesus, "We know that you are from God but..." How often do we look at humans in this world and say "I know that you were made in the image of God but..."? I want to love my enemies but. We want to become open and celebrating of queer folk but. We want to provide for the hurting but. I want to quit hating people but. People have many buts when it comes to love. Like Nicodemus, people are often interested in affirming part of the message of God or love, just not the whole thing. Can The Church at Mable Peabody's be a church free of buts? Can we strive to be a place where there are no boundaries of but to love? Remove the boundaries! Tear down your walls! Love somebody!

Rebirth

Jesus tells Nicodemus that he must be reborn. Nicodemus needed big change. There is a need for rebirth in our lives as well. We must be reborn past the identities, labels, and boundaries that keep us from loving others and ourselves. We must be reborn into a space where we acknowledge ourselves as made uniquely queer in the image of God. Queer is the path to love as God loves…when we traverse it we are able to transcend the boundaries of normativity and live past hate to a place called love…where enemies becomes friends and love restores both our souls and our planet.

The Water and The Spirit

Jesus speaks of being born of both the water and the spirit. Nicodemus needed to be washed of all the rules and dogmas that kept him from knowing a God that actually loved him. Nicodemus was a victim of tremendous spiritual violence.

Many of you have been victims of violence and carry a tremendous amount of hate and anger in your hearts. What does it mean to be free?

The message of the water is the cleansing of all the burdens and hates we carry. You don't have to hurt or be angry anymore… Love is here to restore you. This is the message of Jesus.

The Spirit is a magical thing. It shows us how to love when we thought love was impossible. It whispers message of love, hope, and justice to encourage us to keep going. Unfortunately, many of you don't believe in such superstitious things.

Nothing is real unless you can prove it. If God plopped down in the middle of the room, you would look at her, it, or him and say, "My mind has no ability to explain you and therefore you are not real." When something mysterious knocks at your door, that might even be love or God, you slam the door and say, "No solicitations asshole."

In order to experience the enlightenment of rebirth, one must live past the provable and open their heart to mystery. God is there.

John 3:16

If the writer of 1 John 4:8 is correct and "God is love" then the scripture begins to look different. John 3:16 is probably the most famous passage of scripture in the history of Christianity. Imagine if it read, "For love so loved the world that love gave love's only begotten love that whosoever believes in love should not perish but have everlasting love." Or maybe it does and we aren't paying attention. When we begin to engage the message of Jesus as love, things begin to look different. Justice is a step toward wholeness for both the oppressor and oppressed. This broken world is in the process of being restored. Enemies begin to look like the path to the salvation of forgiveness and restoration. God becomes...more than our perception of the asshole or taskmaster in the sky telling us what to do...but on the inverse...love.

The Light

Are we willing to be the light of love? Are we willing to come out of our closets and boundaries to be the light of love the world so desperately needs? Love is knocking...

Amen.

28.

July 2, 2013

Learning to Fight for Life and the Rights of Women

I am surprised I am writing this piece. Honestly, I hate abortion. I feel that what happens during the procedure is a tragedy. I wish there was no reason for abortion to exist.

Unfortunately, this is not the world we live in.

We live in a world that fails to see the value in educating the young concerning contraceptives.
We live in a world where unwanted pregnancies happen consistently.
We live in a world where women are used, abused, and expected to suck it up and deal with the consequences.
We live in a world where women are raped.
We live in a world where women are molested.
We live in a world where medical crisis happen.
We live in a world of economic struggle.
There are millions of realities about our world that make abortion an unfortunate necessity.

I am horrified at the way that some in the legislature in the State of Texas have conducted themselves in the past few weeks. It has become increasingly apparent that many do not care about the opinions or rights of women at all.

Ultimately, I sympathize with some of their goals…I too pray and work for a world where abortion is increasingly rare…but to legislate against abortion is to devalue the health of women and force abortion underground. I desire to protect the right of women to deal with the world we live in as they see fit.

If our state is interested in reducing abortions, a good place to start is to quit treating women like mindless second-class citizens.

We must broaden sex education to include more options than simply abstinence. We must change our language. We must stand up to violence. We must push for equal pay for equal work. We must stand for equal education. We must change our systems. We must change our economics. We must change.

I find it unbelievable and evil that legislators in the State of Texas are willing to constrict the rights of women without having any of these conversations.

I am a recovering sexist who is learning how best to stand up for women. Like many of those pushing for restrictive legislation, I am also a follower of Jesus. The difference is that when I met Jesus...and realized that "Go and sin no more" included my sexism too...I changed.

I pray that our legislators will do the same.

Amen

29.

July 3, 2013
CAN WE BELIEVE IN LOVE OR LOVE OR LOVE

they display their god
and tell us to
trust him
but gods with testicles
can't be trusted
the incarnation
is more
than a penis
and the more
is the god in all

the god in all exists
far beyond
our laws
for our laws
aren't love
and love
can't be restricted
by our laws

CAN WE BELIEVE
beyond
what we see
perhaps
IN
a place
others call
make believe
or
are we
constricted
to
what we know
and constrained
to believe
only in below

can we
rise above
to a place
called

LOVE

if
we
dare
go
there
our
world
will
change
and
nothing
will
ever
be
the
same

perhaps
we
will
find
in
our
time

god

OR

LOVE

we
hope
we
dream
we
pray
we
believe

OR

LOVE

30.

July 3, 2013

GOD

i hear you whisper
don't have any fear
but i am scared and life is hard out here

i hear you talk
but not to me
only to the crazies who inhabit our tvs

i hear you call
don't stop you say
though i only really sense anything on the rarest of days

i hear you shout
prophet move the people
but they seem so confined to their imagined steeples

do i hear you
or
do i believe i hear you
or
am i crazy

i only know or think I might know the whisper, the talk, the call, and the shout
and i guess i will discover the truth after i turn the world inside out
for love

31.

July 3, 2013

PEOPLE

prayers are people
and people are prayers

only when we learn to love
do they realize that we care

it is not enough to speak about oppression
love is the only way for us to reach a peaceful destination

your boundaries and identities scare the shit out of me
because they leave you very angry and nowhere close to free

when are we going to realize that people matter
and to not believe so is to end up in disaster

when we destroy or dehumanize our enemy
we destroy or dehumanize ourself

because we fail to see the us in them
and the them in us

prayers are people
and people are prayers

32.

July 4, 2013

LIFE

what is this about
so you can collect amid constant doubt

what is this for
so you can put all you collect behind your door

why are we here
so you can work to collect all year

why do we continue
so you can collect and show it off at the latest venue

or perhaps there is more

what is this about
so you can give love despite your doubt

what is this for
so you can invite people behind your door

why are we here
so you can help people all year

why do we continue
so you can share more food off the menu

33.

July 4, 2013

TODAY

the waves crash
the rains fall
the birds coast
what is the meaning of it all

such a dreary day
the winds cut through me
what is there to do but pray

i sit and ponder your words trying not to hate
because I know there will be love to give at a later date

today is just a small violent storm and it will pass

34.

July 4, 2103

you and me

is it a hug
is it a grab

is it a word
is it a slander

is it now
is it deceit

tomorrow is today
are we known
or are we opaque

the hug
the word
the now
the shake

35.

July 4, 2013

history

the building of my prescriptives
is the building of my tolerance

i read books so that i might know
how you felt when they trashed you

the struggle to my listen
is the struggle to my hear

i record words so that i might hear
how you coped when you gave all and they shit on you

the divorces of my relationships
are the divorces of my sanity

i call your phone so I will know
how to handle it when they leave

the purity of my love
is the purity of my belief

i dream your response
so that i might know how love survives

the building struggle of divorces in love is the fulcrum of my peace
clarity is not for me

36.

July 5, 2014

THE HOSE

i got hot
i felt my face growing red
i couldn't figure out what to do
i was mad about something she said
i was out of sort when every local mechanic stopped to offer their initial report
i pushed to figure out a solution and called some friends
i hope I don't ever have to see this texaco station again

the car got hot
the steam careened over the car
the red light blink made me think
the temperature gauge was out of control
this was not a situation of which I was going to be able to take hold
the problem was a growing fright as i realized we weren't leaving tonight

phillip got hot
where is the bottle he said
as his face grew increasingly red
the only thing that pulsated was that large vein in his head
when he started screaming louder i was dead

jeff got hot
but only after a few
unfortunately sometimes he follows the lead of his brother, number two
when they both started screaming we didn't know what to do

emily got hot
i spoke harshly to her
she is my muse and I regret sometimes having a short fuse

the hose got too hot
it exploded

37.

July 5, 2013

THE SNAKE

i don't understand
why did you decide to take down that tree
your constant desire to work absolutely baffles me

the sweat fell
your desire for work
probably early on in life kept you out of jail

the snake bit
why did you decide to bite my granddad
he is one of the dearest friends i have

across the yard
you had to crawl
i know you thought you were losing it all

over and over again you screamed
why cant anyone hear me
why cant my wife just come near me

the broom hit the phone
and you grabbed it
your quick thinking kept the situation from growing more tragic

on the cold cement you lay
is today going to be the day
to god what would i say

consciousness is lost
as you close your eyes
and dream of a day when no one dies

bang bang bang
on the door upstairs
is someone sick here on the phone they sounded dead

there is no one sick here
were the words my grandma said
as my grandfather lay downstairs close to dead

we are going to take a look around
the lieutenant wanted to make sure they were no other sounds
then they started walking down

the growl of a dog
then the screams of a scared wife rang out
that my grandfather was very sick there was no doubt

get that dog out of here
the paramedics began to scream
but my grandmother stood there as if it was all a bad dream

the dog wouldn't move
so the paramedics utilized a trick
and rammed it with a back board to get to my granddad quick

sick on the concrete he lay
his blood pressure was extremely low
if he would survive they did not know

they started the compressions
and gave his heart much attention
they loaded him in the truck and drove fast

upon his arrival to the emergency room
the doctor stabbed him with needles
and he began to look less feeble

then anti-venom took
violently the body shook
things look better

the intensive care unit
tonight is your home
i am in Louisiana and know little of what is going on

are you going to live
are you going to be ok
are you going to say i love you on another day

i feel powerless
i can only sit
here at the Louisiana waffle house praying god saves you from this awful death pit.

38.

July 6, 2013

FRIENDS

they come pick you up
when the car breaks down
and you sit alone in some distant town

39.

July 6, 2013

hospitals

the hallways of hospitals are cold
death visits often

i like the music of the killers
they give me hope that death might be overcome

will it begin tonight

and the band played on

the road is dark

perhaps it is the music that will lead the way

40.

July 7, 2013

"Loving Justice Enough to Shut Up and Let Others Get the Credit for Achieving It"

In the third chapter of John, we find two baptizers, one named Jesus and the other named John the Baptist. Both had disciples and both were preaching justice as the way to love. A rabble rouser came up and challenged John the Baptist and his disciples, "Why is that guy Jesus over there baptizing more people than you are?"

Often when we participate in great movements of justice there are different types of questions that arise.

I love questions. I think that they are our chief tool in our pursuit of knowledge about our world and our self. I believe that there is nothing purer than an honest seeker. However, we also must be aware that there are questions that are not about seeking knowledge…these are the leading questions that seek to divide movements for justice.

These are the seeds of division.

The seeds of division ultimately ask us if we are going to care about ourselves more than the larger movement for justice.

The rabble rouser of Aenon was interested in dividing John the Baptist and Jesus by planting a seed of division and selfishness in the heart of John the Baptist.

It would be like someone asking you: Did you know that they are getting all the credit and you are doing all the work?

We must beware of such questions and questioners, because the seeds of division they sow can ultimately keep us from the justice we desperately want to achieve.

We've experienced tremendous victories for social justice as a church and larger community over the past few months.

We must beware of the seeds of division.

The desire to make ourselves increase can keep us from achieving further victories for justice.

Ultimately, John the Baptist stands united with Jesus in his reply, "I must decrease so that Jesus can increase." John the Baptist is saying that I must decrease so that justice can be achieved.

John the Baptist loved justice enough to shut up.

Do we love justice enough to shut up and let others get the credit for achieving it?

Amen.

41.

July 8, 2013

completion and reflection

the struggle to speak in ways that are familiar
the way of remembrance that was so clear
that moment of imagination when life was near

the victory of the breath
and the height of a song

the way of the struggle
to overcome fear
the way of the touch when my enemy was near

the causality of dreams
that pushes to survive
it all explodes before me
when i see the faith reflected in your eye

for you are the promise
for you are the love
for you are the truth

restoration begins in the explosion of reflection

42.

July 9, 2013

THE JUDAS REMIX

you called me to be your disciple
you asked me to watch all the money we took in
the other disciples were always jealous
because I was your man

we walked over country after country
to tell the people of god's great love
i was there for all the miracles
and saw things most only dream of

i saw you transcend racial boundaries
that I thought would never fall
i saw you give dignity to the oppressed
and in turn you gave dignity to us all

the eyes of the blind were opened
and they saw justice too
the legs of the lame were healed
along with the hearts of a few

i saw the man come out of the tomb
and i was amazed but not you
you just walked on in and hugged him
to express your love

the temple was stormed
and justice was served
this was an unimaginable feat
that love was something more magical than the rules we had to always repeat

when the waters got rough
we were terrified
there in the distance you appeared
i saw you first out of the corner of my eye

the thousands gathered hungry without any money
i felt threatened and thought i would fend them off with just my small weapon
but not you as you knew what to do
you opened your magical hands and fed five thousand with a fish or two

i saw the women come in to cook and to bless
then one poured perfume in her hair which became one expensive mess
i got in trouble for getting a little mad
but later you pulled me aside and lovingly told me not to be sad

when the palms started waving i knew it was approaching time
for the great martyr of love to finally die
just after the march you pulled me aside and told me to come with you
i came with understanding sigh

you told me what to do as the great lover of my soul
and i knew of my reputation the others would take hold
from the moment i came in i knew that this was the plan
I was to be the one to place you right into their hands

darkness has fallen and the time is right
there is no place for me to flee my plight
if i do not become a villain then the world is not saved
i love you Jesus was the last thing i said

i took the pieces and did the deed
i brought a legion of soldiers along with me
i kissed the man that i loved so much
and allowed my mind to wonder to the times when my body he clutched

they took you away and tortured you
i just couldn't take it anymore
although i knew this was what my life was for
you must remember it is very hard to kick someone you love through death's door

now, here i stand
right at this tree
a rope in my hand
so i can finally be free

i know everyone thinks what i did was betrayal
but I leave you with Jesus' last words to me
without you the prophecy fails

so tonight as the rope around my neck grows tight
i hope that someone somewhere will at least get my story right

i loved a man and he loved me back
and together we saved a world that was under attack

43.

July 10, 2013

The TriP

the lithium watches me from the cupholder in judgment
i know i need to take the pills to be functional
but what is the use of functional

the books stare at me in judgment
i know i need them to learn
but what is the use of knowledge

the road looks back at me in judgment
i know i need to move
but what is the use of movement

lithium, books, roads
they embody my life

functional, knowledge, movement
they represent my future

on this night though…shall i be…me.

44.

July 11, 2013

travel

are you the light
or
are you something else

are you a mirror
behind which lies the other side

reflect for me
will you please
be for me all that i need

i don't care what you are
i need you in this life to travel far

45.

July 14, 2013

"The Woman, Transgender Person, & George Zimmerman at the Well"

This morning we gather to meet each other in hopes that by meeting we might find community and in community we might find love and in love we might find answers somewhere in the dark mysteries of the universe.

We encounter Jesus meeting a Samaritan woman at the well. The Samaritan woman was of a marginalized identity. The disciples did not want to go to Samaria yet Jesus went and sought to transcend the boundaries of identity. In my version The Queer, I have The Queer encountering a transgender person to remind us that we still have work to do in order to continue transcending boundaries of identity.

Many of you will argue that this is not a necessary conversation…"I love everyone" you might say…but I think a quick discussion of the recent sins of one of the most prominent queer advocacy organizations in our country will help illustrate that we all have work to do.

According to Chris Geidner of Buzzfeed, in 2007 the Human Rights Campaign supported a trans-exclusive Employment Non-Discrimination Act. When confronted with the discrepancy, then president of the Human rights Campaign Joe Solmonese said, "there was no chance that bill was going to get signed into law." In March 2013 protests at the Supreme Court, staffers from the Human Rights Campaign asked repeatedly for transgender activists to take down their flags. One report says that a staffer or volunteer said, "Marriage is not a transgender issue." Ultimately, Human Rights Campaign Vice-President Fred Sainz said, "HRC regrets the incidents and offers our apologies to those who were hurt by our actions. We failed to live up to the high standard to which we hold ourselves accountable and we will strive to do better in the future (http://www.buzzfeed.com/chrisgeidner/with-apology-lgbt-rights-group-seeks-to-avoid-reopening-old). I am not just picking on the Human Rights Campaign, because the truth is we have all failed to live up to the high standard of love and should strive to do better in the future.

The high standard of love, "loving our neighbors as ourselves," is where we find ourselves this morning. Jesus goes to the woman at the well with love and destroys a boundary. The Queer approaches the transgender person with love and destroys a boundary. Who are we to approach with love this morning? What boundary are we to destroy?

Jesus tells us to "love our enemy." We meet this morning at a difficult hour. Last night the verdict in the trial of George Zimmerman came out and many of us were left disappointed. Trayvon Martin is dead and any semblance of justice seems to be fleeting. I looked on social media last night and thought I might find some insightful comments to help me know how to handle my disappointment. This is what I found, "Rot in hell Zimmerman." "Fuck you you motherfucking Zimmerman asshole!" "Fuck George Zimmerman!" "Fuck white people." "I hope George Zimmerman is eaten by wolves and left to rot." "Fuck white Hispanic people." "We are going to tear this motherfucker down tonight." "Watch out tonight because I'm coming for you!" "I am going to fuck up the next Hispanic or white person I see." These are just a sampling of the line after line of violent hateful words that I read. These words did not come from conservative folks they came from progressive folks.

And we wonder why we cannot communicate beyond the boundaries we have created... Jesus was told that the people of Samaria were to be seen as enemies. Jesus was told that this was a land of people like George Zimmerman. Can you imagine if Jesus had approached the woman at the well and said, "fuck you"? This would have turned out to be a much different story. You cannot love your enemy when the first words out of your mouth are "fuck you." We have to learn that in order to love we must first learn to not hate.

We learn not to hate by seeing the enemy in our self. Many of you in this room were disappointed with the verdict last night. Many of you have said hateful things about George Zimmerman because you have learned to love Trayvon Martin and your sense of justice has been violated. You are angry.

Have you ever considered that you killed Trayvon Martin?

Have you ever considered you pulled the trigger that ended Trayvon's life?

Most of you think I am talking crazy right now...but think about the way that we all constantly participate in a society that promotes violence to be a core value. We want to see, hear, and participate in death. The movies we watch consistently glorify killing and violence. We watch all types of programming about war. The television shows that we watch promote serial killers and violent police exploits. We want more gore more death and complain when there is not enough. The music we listen to promotes mafia aggression and gangster killings. We talk violently to each other. We love the stories that have someone carrying a gun and at the end they surprise and kill the bad guy. We all want guns as a result...and think we have to have them in order to protect ourselves. We want laws that allow us to carry anything, almost to the point of a nuclear weapon, in our back pocket. And we wonder why people are dying violently in this country... Daily we scream to the tops of our lungs...more guns, more violence, more cutthroat lyrics, and more people to kill in defense of what is mine. These are the same media and stories that produced George Zimmerman. It should be as hard to love George Zimmerman as it is to love your self...because you too participate in the culture that holds the gun.

Jesus offered the woman at the well living water. This living water is the substance that will make you never thirst again...love. You see love makes us whole...but we must learn how to love radically…for to love partially is to not love at all. We must love in a contemporary way that values each person in each moment.

Jesus approached the woman at a very special place, a monument of love from her ancestors, a well. We often construct monuments of love to the victories that we are able to accomplish. Unfortunately, too often we stay there and refuse to move forward. Can you imagine if the person you have asked to love you better…took you to a monument and said "this is a monument to where I once loved you best"? What the hell does that do? Love cannot be contained in monuments and we would do well to stop building them and love somebody. It is great when we accomplish things, but love is an occurrence of every second. Will you work to learn how to love day in and day out? Will you work to be made complete by love?

The restoration of earth is accomplished through love not hate. We are working towards a world where George Zimmerman is restored to love. We are working toward a world where Trayvon Martin never dies. We are working for a world where there is no longer violence or injustice. We are working toward a world where people and creation are made whole. We long for the restoration of love. We long for people to love and be loved.

The woman at the well and many of us are looking for love. It begins with the self. Learning to love who we are enough to move toward love can change everything…if we are willing. Learn to love your self and you will learn to love the community around you…for you will begin to see even in your enemies…love.

The woman is concerned that class boundaries will keep her from worshipping. Jesus tells her that the day is here when you can worship anywhere you want. You can love anywhere. True love knows no class distinctions. True love knows no boundaries. The day is here when you can love anyone and anywhere you want. Are you courageous enough to step beyond your fears and love? The woman says, "I know that this love is coming" and Jesus replies, "Look in front of you."

This is the day that love can reign. Are we ready to live lives electrified and restored by love? For many of us at this hour, it begins with George Zimmerman.

Amen.

46.

July 14, 2013

in and through you

i lived in you
yet you are closed to me

i am an outsider
and you cannot welcome me

i am a friend
but that looks different with you

i fought for your well being
although i was never sure you wanted it

i now pass through
however my prayers with you shall always remain
mississippi you are one wild beast i wonder how to tame

47.

July 15, 2013

"Prayer at Justice for Trayvon Martin Rally"

Pleasant evening, I am Jeff Hood, The Pastor of the Church at Mable Peabody's. I am a pastor and in times of difficulty pastors pray. So I come to offer you a prayer.

God, I come to you at this difficult hour to beseech you for justice.

Tonight, my heart is heavy for Tracy Martin and Sybrina Fulton. I pray that they might know the restoration of their lives in this life. May they feel the love that all of us have for them at this very moment. May it comfort them to know that we remember and are fighting for justice for their son, Trayvon, and the millions of others just like him who have died and are dying under the weight of oppression.

Tonight, I pray for an end to racism. May it begin with all of us gathered here examining the racism and privilege contained in our own persons.

Tonight, I pray for an end to violence, knowing that those who are now calling for violence are no different than George Zimmerman, who allowed his fear and anger to allow him to take the life of another. I pray for an end to the killing. I pray for peace.

Tonight, I pray for those who persecute and oppress that they might be restored to right thinking and acting. May we believe that we can meet them as humans and leave as coworkers in the restoration of our planet.

Tonight, I pray that an end to racism, classism, privilege, homophobia, sexism, and all the other factors that contribute to oppression, marginalization, and injustice will begin with the examination of our selves and continue until we revolution our communities.

Tonight, I renounce violence anew with the knowledge that justice only arrives when we have the courage to love.

So on this night, may we seek love for Trayvon Benjamin Martin.

In the name of the God whose name is love.

Amen.

*Not long after I prayed this prayer, an altercation broke out between people who were speaking at the rally and a gentleman and his friend on the courthouse lawn that were opposed to the language that was being used. The conflict got worse before everyone was separated. Trying to be a pastor, afterward I walked over and had conversations with the gentlemen who were involved in the conflict. Before I could speak to one of the gentlemen, he told me that he was sorry about what happened and that the only thing he remembered being said at the rally was my prayer. Perhaps there is something about love that pushes through hate makes people listen.

48.

July 16, 2013

AMEN

amen

you are a word
which speaks so much by actually saying so little
i ponder your mystery

the way you ring loudly from the throat
the way you slide softly from the lips
the way you whip violently around the tongue
the way

the truth when you say stop
the truth when you say thanks
the truth when you say love
the truth

the light you share in silence
the light you share in confusion
the light you share in darkness
the light

the way
the truth
the light

i don't know what you mean
but you mean so much to me
meaning in mystery is truth

amen

49.

July 21, 2013

"Remarks Upon the Retirement of Chief Jeff Hood : My Dad"

It is an honor for my family and I to be with you today to honor my father, the one you have known in recent years as Chief and Emergency Management Director Jeff Hood. For many years, we have served alongside my dad. In the early years, it was pretty cool to get to go the fire station, climb up on the trucks, and see the lights and sirens run. However as I got older, I can remember becoming aware that people died doing the job that my dad did. Then I remember hearing the preacher talk about "greater love hath no one than this, that they would lay down their life for their friends." Through my dad's life, these words became reality for me.

I can remember no stronger illustration of this principle of sacrificial love than the events of one fateful afternoon in 1991. On that day, Officer James Reonas lay shot multiple times on the front porch of a Clayton County home in a hostage situation. Under heavy gunfire, my father crawled up and placed his body on top of Officer Reonas. Taking pieces of shrapnel to his back, my dad helped Officer Reonas to an awaiting ambulance. Because Jeff Hood lives so too does Officer Reonas.

This is but one incident of many where my father has laid down his life for this community. Over and over again my dad taught us with his life what it means to love. On this day, my father need not be celebrated here beyond what he has been throughout his career…someone who believed in this community enough to give his life for it.

Friends may we all go and do likewise.

Amen.

50.

July 21, 2013

"God is Sweet. Love is Sweet. Now, go and be the sweetness…"

This morning we arrive back in the aftermath of a revelation of love. The woman at the well was granted sight of herself and the world around her. Jesus loved past the society of the time's barriers of race and class to actually see and restore a human being.

The events of the morning were so odd that the disciples were struggling to believe that Jesus was a real person. So often when we love in ways that are queer…people begin to wonder if we are real. Our society expects us to wear so many masks and normalizations that when we take off the mask and people find love…they struggle to believe it is real. The disciples got nervous and sheepishly requested, "Rabbi, eat something." You see the disciples wanted to know that Jesus to eat something so that they could test and make sure he was still real. You see they had never seen someone love another person like this. When was the last time someone wondered if you were a real person…just because they were amazed by how you loved?

Jesus replied, "I have food to eat that you do not know about." The sustenance of Jesus was the spirit of the living God found and sustained in the people that Jesus kept encountering. We too can feed off of love if we will take off our masks and allow ourselves real encounters.

Due to the woman's testimony, many of the Samaritans came to believe in Jesus. Many people were changed because Jesus took the time to love a woman. Will we allow ourselves the time to change the world through loving someone? What if one encounter can change everything? Would you take it? Would you speak? The world is curious…

After Jesus left Samaria, Jesus traveled to Cana in Galilee. A royal official ran out to meet Jesus and asked him to come and heal his son. Jesus replied, "Go and your son will be made well." The boy was healed because Jesus spoke. We all have similar power…if we will just have the courage to step out of our boundaries and speak a queer word… "I love you." "You are beautiful." "You are special to me." "Is there anything I can help you with?" "Can I help you get something to eat?" "Can I help you find somewhere to sleep?" "Would you like to sit down and chat for a little while?" "I have missed you." "I have never met someone like you before…you are amazing." On and on and on…

Friends…
We have the words of healing! We have the words of healing! We have the words of healing!

The boy was healed because Jesus spoke. I know many of you don't believe in miracles…but when you begin to speak healing words you will begin to see the miraculous. You will begin to see people made whole by love. The miraculous is the sweetness of life.

God is sweet. Love is sweet. Now, go and be the sweetness.

Amen.

51.

July 24, 2013

The Activist

are you fake
i don't know

is our fate truly hate
or is it love
a construct you seem to never dream of

are you fake
i don't know

is our goal to heal or to kill
think about it
to heal you must learn how to feel

are you fake
i don't know

with your words the oppressor you hit while you treat everyone else like shit

are you fake
i don't know

your emotions distract you from hearing your words as hollow
and then you wonder why no one will follow

are you fake
i don't know

are we all real people
or are you the only who gets to stand beneath your self-righteous steeple

are you fake
I don't know

if you want to love you must first start with self
unfortunately you try to put your shit high on the shelf

are you fake

i don't know

**you consistently call people privileged and not right
but how can you speak like that when you sleep with the same privilege tonight**

*are you fake
i don't know*

**i only know that i desire to bring us together not tear us apart
and i consistently wonder where is your heart**

yet still i dream

**can it all begin anew
here with me and you**

52.

July 25, 2013

exhaustion

exhaustion sets in on a long ride
every ounce of energy has gone

eyelids heavy with the weight of today
shorts stick to the itchy skin of the hour
the psychological trash of thoughts of dying creep of the moment

head needs shampoo
teeth need toothpaste
stomach needs food
yet we still ride

only two hours more until i walk in the door of sleep and forget this poem

53.

July 26, 2013

Is this what you call love?

YOU

you hit me
you hug me

you curse me
you praise me

you fight me
you embrace me

you hate me
you love me

who are you
i don't know
someone who claims to love me so

who are you
i shouldn't care
the way you act is not fair

who are you
i am gone
i shouldn't have called you anything for so long

your are me
and
i am you
but now i must tell you that i am through

54.

July 28, 2013

A Plea for Universal Healthcare

There was a pool in Jesus' day where folks who were blind, lame, paralyzed, and had other disabilities laid. The folks lay at this pool because every once in a while an angel of God would come down and stir up the water. The first one into the pool would be healed of their disability. This is a story of magic.

Most folks walked quickly by this pool. They didn't want to be bothered with the desperate needs of others. They were just too busy doing their own thing. I am sure you are familiar with such folks…

Jesus was deeply moved by the sight of the people lying their helpless and refused to not walk in. Jesus couldn't resist the opportunity to heal. You see Jesus believed in universal healthcare.

Jesus walked in.

So often the first step to healing people is to walk into the spaces where hurting people are. Often, the first act of magic is the courage to engage…the courage to care…the courage to love.

Jesus found a lame man at the pool who had laid there for 38 years. Each time he tried to get the magic of healing from touching the water…someone jumped in front of him.

Everybody kept jumping in front of him…
This man was desperate.
How many people are desperate in our community today and people keep jumping in front of them?

Jesus refused to walk by and not allow his heart to be moved by the injustice of sickness. Jesus engaged the man and declared healing words, "Pick up your mat and walk!"

The words and actions of Jesus healed.

How often do we have the opportunity to heal people with our words and actions?

When was the last time you said a healing word to somebody? When was the last time you healed a relationship or a community or our world with your words? When was the last time you offered to pay for someone's medical bills? When was the last time you sat down with your enemy to heal a broken relationship? When was the last time you worked for peace? When was the last time you saved someone's life financially, emotionally, physically, or anything else? Can we work for a world where everyone is loved, treated, and healed?

Some of you will say, "Jeff, this is impossible hippie dippy nonsense!" To that I reply, "It sure is if you sit on your ass."

Friends, we all have the power to heal if we are willing to put forth the effort. There is indeed magic in all efforts to heal a broken world. Can the healing of all people, all places, all things begin with us?

Do you believe in universal healthcare?

Amen.

55.

August 4, 2013

What does belief look like? Just run.

The great question of this hour is 'What does belief look like?'

We find Jesus this morning in John chapter 5 in the aftermath of a healing. The religious leaders are pissed that Jesus would have the audacity to heal on the Sabbath. The audacity of the healing was that Jesus left the boundaries of what one was supposed to believe and the rules that one was supposed to follow.

Jesus' leaving such boundaries allowed the lame to walk. Do you think the lame man cared what day it happened on? Can you imagine the lame man looking at Jesus and saying, 'Why in the world would you heal me on the Sabbath?'

Leaving the boundaries of religion or what was supposed to be believed allowed for a healing.

There are many of you who have been tremendously hurt by religion. Know that you have a tremendous amount in common with Jesus...who was consistently hurt and called into question by religion and the boundaries of his day. Yet Jesus consistently left boundaries in order to experience love and give healing.

There was the gift of love. Jesus loved the lame man and the religious rule keepers. Jesus sought to show them what belief looked like through love and action. No one is ever going to believe anything you or this community says until we learn how to love each other and love the community. You see the value of a spiritual community is not what teaching we can provide, but rather what love we can provide to each other and to the world.

What does belief look like? Love. What does love look like? You and me connecting with us and them. Surely you didn't think you could get to God without going through your neighbor did you?

To be quite honest, I do not believe that God or love can be experienced outside of community.

While Jesus gives a tremendous testimony of faith in the second half of chapter 5, I am wondering what the lame man was talking about right around this time.

We have a tremendous amount of skeptics in this room who will not allow themselves to experience anything that exists outside the boundaries of what they would call normal or scientifically provable. Can you imagine if that was the feeling of the lame man? Walking around and constantly asking himself, 'Am I really walking? Surely I am not really walking? I know I am not walking. I can't actually be walking.' This sounds ludicrous.

So too does it sound ludicrous when we spend our days questioning our healing experiences with love and God.

Belief looks like accepting what is.

Jesus gives a tremendous testimony in the face of long odds. Love is here to replace a system of broke down laws and judgments.

The Church at Mable Peabody's exists in the face of long odds. We exist to declare that love is here to replace the systemic broke down laws and judgments of the religious and non-religious alike.

Belief looks like replacing law with love.

Friends, together we have been granted the ability to walk...the ability to run. May we stop walking or running around...asking or thinking, 'Surely this is not real?'

Just be healed. Just believe. Just love. Just run.

Amen.

56.

August 7, 2013

the hidden danger of privilege

you confront me
and want me to see
that i am privileged

i agree with you and begin to work on myself
but if ever i disagree with you again about anything else

you assault me
you shit on me
you silence me
you hate me
you kill me
you dehumanize me
and much much more
as you call me privileged

these are crimes of hate of the highest order
and each time they make me wonder who truly had the privilege to begin with

so now i wonder how
we can help you begin to see your privilege now

57.

August 9, 2013

beau ties

beau ties remind us of days gone by when patriarchy most triumphed
perhaps they too like you can be redeemed

beau ties remind us of the clown that took advantage of kids in our youth
perhaps they too like you can be redeemed

beau ties remind us of aristocracy that chokes out the worker
perhaps they too like you can be redeemed

beau ties remind us of a joke of love we all have heard on a first or second date
perhaps they too like you can be redeemed

beau ties pop but the pop is usually directed folks the oppressed the wearer hates
perhaps it too like you can be redeemed

beau ties are difficult like the wearer whose oppressive is difficult to describe
perhaps it too like you can be redeemed

beau ties are sharp just like the tongue of the oppressive wearer
perhaps it too like you can be redeemed

beau ties are difficult to construct without hate like the constructions of the wearer
perhaps it too like you can be redeemed

beau ties take advantage of the marginalized and oppressed
or the desperate ones who need us the most
fortunately for all of us the beau tie wearer often fails to do anything well but hate
prayers for restoration of myself and the wearer of beau ties

this is not a poem about beau ties

58.

August 12, 2013

borders

humanity is here
why are there borders to fear

do we believe in the hope of connection
do we believe in the beauty of communion
do we believe in the impossible restoration of all peoples

why does fear keep up borders
what are their use

i can believe

how can i love you when there is a fence between us
how can i love you when there is a wall between us
how can i love you when there are guards between us
how can i love you when there is a dry arid death pit between us

what is being protected
why are you keeping us apart

i can love

is it possible for us to share
is it possible for us to live in community
is it possible for us to just be us

how will i ever know of possibility
why is there a border to such knowledge

i can struggle

what are you but human
what are you but friend
what are you but hope

how will i know you completely
how will i hug your neck

i can love

love knows no borders
restoration knows no boundaries
may boundless endless love come quickly
may it start with me

amen

59.

August 13, 2013

queer jesus

a queer jesus
how can it be
it is not possible
a manufactured jesus can only look like me

you pray aloud to the god you know
but what about for yourself so that you might grow
to understand that this queer is not about hand raising sentimentality
this is about a real jesus that exists in the middle of intersectionality

jesus
jesus
jesus

queer
queer
queer

please tonight wont you come near
i can no longer sit in this suffocating fear
that the world wont change
and all will just keep hating all the same

this is not about the battles you can win
this is about declaring injustice as sin

queer jesus end the fight
and show us the way to peace tonight

i don't need more ists or isms
to show me the way
i just need a world where people won't give a shit who is gay

queer jesus lead the way
in blurring the boundaries we have made
make the world whole
so that we might know
that it was true when you said you love us so

60.

August 14, 2013

"Feeding"

There was a multitude of people who were interested in what Jesus had to say. Now I say interested, remember that just because they were following Jesus doesn't mean they believed shit. They were interested or perhaps they were lost just following the crowd.

Jesus looked out at the people and knew that they must be hungry. Jesus felt that there existed a responsibility to feed the people. How are we to respond when we know people are hungry? Do we have the same burden to feed as Jesus did?

Jesus talked with the disciples about feeding the crowd and they complained that they didn't have enough money. I hear a similar rebukes often. The excuses run the gamut.

I wanted to feed the homeless but... I wanted to call the police when I saw the abusive racist man but... I wanted to confront that woman who was being a homophobic asshole but... I tried to get the courage to say that I am sorry but... on and on and on...

Indeed it is the buts that often get the better of us...as we spend more energy figuring out ways not to help rather than helping.

I am sure that most of the disciples really didn't want to feed the people and just made excuses. Do you?

There was one who stepped up. Peter remarked that a little boy just gave him five loaves and two fish. Jesus said to pass them out.

Now you know at this point somebody stood up and declared, "Now wait just one second, Jesus that is all the food that we have. What are we going to eat if we give it away?"

Ultimately, the food lasted to feed the five thousand. Sometimes we need the simplest lessons in life. We need to remember that when you begin to sacrifice and give your life for people things begin to multiply and people begin to be fed.

It is a beautiful story, but to stop here and not dig further would betray perhaps the strongest hidden beauty of the story...that which lies behind and beyond the text.

Out of all those five thousand people... you know there had to be some turds that were skeptical of Jesus and making hateful remarks.

I can hear them.

"Fuck Jesus what has he ever done for me?"
"Jesus is a fraud."
"You can't believe anything Jesus says."
"I bet Jesus is probably sleeping with all of those men."
"That Jesus doesn't care about anybody but himself."
"Jesus brought us out here and didn't bring no food...what a dumbass."

If what people who seek to love and serve people hear today is any indication, then people said these things and much worse.

I bet there were even people who were hungry and wanted to eat...but who complained about the taste of the food. Maybe there were people who got their fish and sent it back because they said it wasn't cooked correctly. After the miracle happened, there were probably people sitting there who went hungry because they were too busy trying to explain the physics of how the fish and bread multiplied. I bet there were some people in that crowd who later betrayed Jesus and stood by as he was crucified.

Jesus knew all of these things were going on and yet Jesus still fed them. You see when you become about feeding people...you don't just feed the ones that you like...you feed everyone.

Now for clarity sake, the story makes it clear that Jesus didn't hand out the food to everyone. Some people got a delivery from a distance. There are certainly times in life when people are so toxic that we have to get the food to them by having it delivered by someone else.

Regardless, the message of the story is to be about feeding people...even the ones that you don't care for that much.

The disciples made excuses and Jesus fed.

Will you be a feeder or someone who dwells on the shit that is always there?

Amen.

61.

August 15, 2013

"Queer Love or God Finds Us in Queer Spaces"

George Berry is a large man with a round face, stunning smile, and large eyes that beam through rather hip slightly oversized spectacles. I visit George as often as I can. He lives in another part of Texas and is unable to travel. During our last visit, George let down his defenses and told me that he was attracted to men.

"Jeff, I like butts man," is how he actually said it.

I immediately celebrated his comments and told him how much I appreciated his vulnerability and trust in talking to me about his sexuality. The conversation went deeper. The Spirit was present without question.

George began to speak of Tommy. The two met in a difficult space...but the two learned to love each other despite the many adversities. It was a forbidden love. The two were not supposed to be together yet for a time love prevailed.

Regardless of their love, the adversities of life and evil pulled them apart.

"I really did love him Jeff and I miss him...but he betrayed me," George concluded.

I was incredibly moved by the conversation. I pressed for more.

I asked him to describe how he feels now about himself and the space he finds himself in.

"No matter what, I always look at love and declare it is good," George replied.

The phrase reminded me of the way that God created and declared it is good. When I brought up this parallel, George declared, "Well ain't that what all this life is about? Trying to love how God loves. When we see love we need to just declare it is good. No matter whether it is hetero, homo, queer, or whatever...love is good."

George described love in a more beautiful and filling way than I could have ever dreamed. I left our visit dreaming of a world where people have the courage to love and accept people the way that George does. I dream of people having the courage to transcend their boundaries and actually see love...in order to boldly declare, "it is good."

This conversation was absolutely incredible yet there is something that makes it even more incredible, it took place with close to a foot worth of reinforced glass between us.

The truth is that George Berry is inmate #969378 and lives on Texas' Death Row.

Isn't it queer that often love and God incarnate seems to find us in those we attempt to throw away?

Amen.

62.

August 18, 2013

"I'm Here! Presence in the Storm, Parade, and in Life"

In life we consistently encounter storms. Some are big. Some are small. The truth for me is that I seem to always be walking into a storm, through a storm, or out of a storm. I think this is the case for any person who is actually living. I actually would argue that if you haven't seen a storm in a while then you probably aren't doing too much.

The disciples were in a boat in the middle of a lake in the middle of a raging storm that for all intents and purposes was going down really quickly. How many of you have been similar storms? Life is raging and you are going down. In the midst of this storm, Jesus appeared and declared, "I'm here." The storm calmed, the lightening stopped and the waves subsided...all with one phrase, "I'm here." How often do people simply need to hear that one phrase "I'm here" to calm their storm?

Yesterday, a few of us marched in the North Texas State Fair Parade. For most of the other marchers and floats, this was a time of joyous carefree celebration. This was not the case for me. I am privy to too many of the emails and phone calls that our church gets. I guess I know enough to be afraid.

One of the more difficult moments in the parade for me came when we were about to reach The Denton Square. There might have been upwards of a thousand or more people standing out there. This was the height of my anxiety. I saw a tremendous amount of unfriendly faces and I knew that the announcer was about to call out our name. I looked around at the people from our church that were marching with me and gave thanks for their presence. I didn't want to let anyone else know that I was afraid. The silence was deafening.

The announcer called out, "The Church At Mable Peabody's...a church for all people that loves all people." For a brief moment, there was silence. Then, scattered throughout the crowd there was intermittent loud applause, cheers, and words of approval. For me, these individuals were Jesus. In the midst of the storm of my anxiety, these individuals had the courage to say, "I'm here."

When I arrived home after the parade, there was a message on the church's website from a young lady. She wrote:

> "I saw your church in the parade this morning. I wanted to thank you for marching. In spite of the many storms in my life, it is nice to know that God is still speaking and standing with the oppressed."

For the young lady, by marching in the parade...The Church at Mable Peabody's loudly declared, "I'm here."

Jesus calmed the storm with mere presence.

May we never stop doing the same.

Amen.

63.

August 20, 2013

absence

you were here and now you are not
you were there and now you are not
you were somewhere and now you are not

in our everywheres we find our strongest reality
is god not more than sentimentality
but a presence that seems elusive
or perhaps conducive to our lives

shall we die this moment
first to ourselves
or shall we live and deny
the matter of our disaster

do we care about
the quiz that is
life

or is thine the glory
or is thine the power
or is thine the presence

your presence is elusive
it is simple not conducive
to being known in the chaos
of the modern age
and your absence seems to contribute to my rage

you are here and absent
you are there and absent
you are somewhere and absent
you are everywhere in absence

in absence is the presence of god

thus we trust
that love is the thrust

to the presence and power of love be the glory forever and ever

perhaps god is not so absent after all

amen

64.

August 25, 2013

martin's dream and us

fifty years ago...

the prophetic words rang out
because from a few rows back
one woman had the courage to shout
mahalia jackson declared "tell them about the dream martin"

justice was spoken like a song
and the people were given new courage to press on
the generation that heard the words started the race
and we are here to keep the faith

in this space the courage to love is undoubtedly here
because we are dedicated to pushing past fear

the beloved community might be near
because of our efforts to turn the world queer

we are the dream

amen

65.

August 25, 2013

Jesus in Drag

In the seventh chapter of the Gospel of John, Jesus is found in the midst of a verbal assault perpetrated by the family of Jesus. They were ashamed of who Jesus most authentically was. They were even more disturbed by Jesus' insistence on claiming his authentic or actualized self. Sound familiar?

So often in life when we begin to claim the queer within, there are attacks by those who live comfortably immersed in the evils of normativity and self-denial. The family of Jesus just wanted Jesus to just remain quiet and closeted. Jesus would not be Jesus if Jesus had stayed in the closet.

The Festival of the Tabernacles or Booths was going on in Jerusalem. Knowing that there might be violence perpetrated against Jesus, the family of Jesus dares Jesus to go. So what does Jesus do? Jesus ventures to the party in drag.

"When I am on that stage dancing and singing, I feel the authentic presence of God well up within myself. There is no time in my life that I feel more authentically who God has created me to be than when I am in drag," were the words relayed to me recently by a friend in drag. One has to wonder if Jesus felt the same.

The conundrum of authenticity haunts the reader of the Gospels. Jesus is persecuted and eventually killed for being authentically the queer child of God that Jesus was created to be.

Make no mistake dear friends...the only liberation that we can conjure up within the self is to be the queer that God has created us to be. You consistently speak of a desire to free the world from oppression, but you cannot free anything until you free yourself. Queer is the only way to be authentic.

The words of my friend in drag speak volumes. The person in drag in this talk represents the most authentic person. So this morning I invite you to find your drag and be the queer God has created you to be.

Amen.

66.

August 29, 2013

I Will Not Eat! A Pastor Responds to Potential Strikes on Syria

My heart is deeply troubled. The leader of the nation that I live in has started to contemplate dropping bombs again. I voted for the leader. I helped buy the bombs. Though I have no control over the decisions being made, I am responsible for what happens next.

The bombs will unquestionably escalate a conflict in Syria that has already claimed the lives of over 100,000. More people will die. There will be more pictures of children wrapped in white sheets and bullet-riddled bodies. Both sides in the conflict will be hardened and resist talks of peace. The violence will continue.

How can we tell other people not to kill while we drop bombs and kill? There is no such thing as a peaceful killer. If we strike, we will only be what we are...killers.

I am angry that Bashar al-Assad continues to perpetuate unfathomable violence against the Syrian people. I am angry that the Syrian rebels have engaged in heinous practices of violence in retaliation. I am angry...but I do not believe that further violence can ever bring about peace...only love can do that.

Though there is little I can physically do stop what seems like an inevitable military intervention, I choose to follow the examples of the prophets of old. In times of looming crisis they fasted and prayed. I choose to do the same. For the next three days, I will not eat and I will pray that all parties will choose love.

I will break the fast at communion on Sunday morning at The Church at Mable Peabody's.

I seek your prayers.

Amen.

67.

August 30, 2013

hungry

i dream of god
i ponder greek salad

i work for peace
i ponder shrimp souvlaki

i pray about hope
i ponder hummus

i grow angrier about war
i ponder fried rice

the interplay of food and god
the interplay of hope and hunger

hungry i seek love
love i seek greater hunger

hungry i seek god
god i seek greater hunger

hungry i seek peace
peace i seek greater hunger

hunger teach me to love in times of war
love teach me to be hungry in an age of apathy

i seek greater hunger
i am hungry for peace

I am hungry
for something to feed my...
soul
heart
mind
stomach
life

I am hungry

for something to feed my desire for...
god
hope
peace
justice
love

i get many appetizers
to let me know something else is coming
but i am ready for the main course

god
restorer of all things
come quickly

amen

68.

August 31, 2013

Remarks at The March for the Beloved Community

We gather this morning in the midst of impending war in Syria, economic injustice, skyrocketing rates of violence worldwide, and a relative state of injustice...yet still we gather. We gather because in this moment we choose to believe that God has created humanity for love and not for hate. We gather because over 50 years ago Dr. Martin Luther King, Jr. spoke of his dream of beloved community - a world community united in love. This morning we gather because we carry the dream forward. We work for a world where injustice and oppression are no more. A world where love has truly opened the door. We believe, in the words of Dr. King,

> Love is creative and redemptive. Love builds up and unites; hate tears down and destroys. The aftermath of the 'fight with fire' method which most suggest is bitterness and chaos, the aftermath of the love method is reconciliation and creation of the beloved community. Physical force can repress, restrain, coerce, destroy, but it cannot create and organize anything permanent; only love can do that. Yes, love-which means understanding, creative, redemptive goodwill, even for one's enemies-is the solution.

So, yes we gather for love. We gather to exhibit our love for each other. We gather to exhibit our love for our community. We gather to exhibit our love for the world. We gather and march...because we are the beloved community. So on this day, be who God has created this community to be...a beloved creation of diverse people showing the world a better way. Amen.

69.

September 1, 2013

Remarks Upon Ending My Fast For Peace in Syria

This very hour marks the third day I have gone without food to pray for true peace in Syria. While most fasts are silent, I have chosen for this fast to not be so in order to draw attention to the devastating consequences of further military intervention in Syria. President Obama has said that there is a need to bomb Syria in order to teach President Bashar al-Assad a lesson. This way of thinking is an age-old fallacy that is similar to the belief that hitting a child is going to teach them not to hit. You cannot make peace with bombs. Do we have the courage to end the ravenous cycle of violence? We break bread and drink wine today with the prayer that love will reign…and that on this earth no more bodies will be broken and no more blood will be spilled. We pray with all that we are that all we be awoken to the peaceful possibilities of love. Amen.

70.

September 1, 2013

Turn off the Swerve and Embrace Your Destiny

In the seventh chapter of John we find Jesus teaching at the Temple. Folks are murmuring about the bravery of Jesus to just go to the front of the Temple and start teaching. Some are murmuring that Jesus is a fraud. Some are murmuring that Jesus is exactly what they have all been waiting for. The illustration being that when we have the bravery to cross boundaries there will always be people who get frustrated...but there will also always be those who are liberated by our tenacity.

Jesus had a few steps to take before Jesus arrived at the pulpit. Jesus first had to walk through the door. Jesus then had to walk through the Temple. Then Jesus had to climb up in front of everyone. This is a long journey.

Between opening the door and arriving at destiny, Jesus had to take a few steps. We do too. Sometimes though we start swerving a bit on the road to our destiny. We believe that love is the answer, but sometimes we swerve toward other things. We believe in the pursuit of justice, but sometimes we swerve toward other things. We believe that human beings matter, but sometimes we swerve toward other things. We believe that authenticity and honesty matter, but sometimes we swerve toward other things. When we swerve we succumb to deception. We begin to lie to ourselves about what is real. Unfortunately, in the words of the great prophet Howard Thurman, when we start deceiving ourselves we become a deception. When we become a deception we can't go to where our destiny leads...because we heave deceived so much that we can't know for sure what our destiny is...but when we turn back toward love things begin to change and our destiny begins to come into focus once more.

On this day, may we choose honesty...may we choose love. May we walk the path that God has laid out for us. May we proclaim liberation to the captives. May we take our place in the pulpits of our world and proclaim, "love is here and love will never be silent."

May we never be afraid to follow God and allow love to lead the way.

Amen.

71.

September 4, 2013

generosity

i hate you
i don't know why
perhaps it is because a piece of you is embedded in my eye
perhaps in the eye of the beholder
there exists hate and love
and sometimes we choose hate
and sometimes we choose to not relate
if we continue on this path what exactly will be our fate
perhaps such choices give humanity an extinction date
will anyone learn to love at this tremendous rate
i hate you
i don't know how to stop
in you is me but i hate that part
i can't take it
it hurts to think about
it is easier to hate you
it is easier to be through with reflection
it is easier to not look at myself but rather to look in the opposite direction
i hate you
you me
me you
i
u
u
i
stop
generosity
love

72.

September 8, 2013

"Standing Against Patriarchy, War & the Self Takes Courage"

In the beginning of the eighth chapter of John we find Jesus in the middle of a scuffle. There is a woman thrown at the feet of Jesus. The Pharisees in all of their patriarchal glory have aggressively brought this woman in and said that they found her in the very act of adultery. The law says that the woman should be stoned to death and the Pharisees have the rocks at ready. Jesus is asked a pertinent question, "What should we do?" Jesus places his body between the woman and the Pharisees, writes in the dirt, and declares, "Let he who is without sin cast the first stone."

This is the story. Why does it matter? It matters because it defies our culture in three primary ways.

Jesus is a defender and lover of women. We are witnessing the acts of someone that was determined to destroy patriarchy and sexism. It seems that the message of Jesus with regard to women has been perverted ever since. Let me make something very clear. We are following the Jesus who gets down in the dirt with women and places Jesus' body between the woman and the death of patriarchy. Are we willing to lay our lives on the line to secure the livelihoods and rights of women? If we want to follow love and if we want to be who God has called us to be then we need to get down in the dirt with our sisters and secure their rights. We need to wake up and end the consistent blind participation in the patriarchy and oppression. We have got to put down our stones.

"Let the one without sin cast the first stone," are the words that Jesus speaks to directly challenge the Pharisees' assumed ability to judge. This morning we are wrestling with the conflict in Syria. Those who desire to go to war stand there holding their rocks or should I say missiles. There is no question that Bashar al-Assad is guilty of using chemical weapons in Syria...but those who think that the way to teach him not to use these weapons by shooting missiles at him are closely akin to those who think that they can teach a child not to hit by hitting them. We have not even arrived yet at the fact that the United States is not without its faults and responsibilities for grave injustices. "Let the one without sin cast the first stone." The message of Jesus defies our rush toward war and not toward peace. Life matters. Peace matters. "Let the one without sin cast the first stone."

In looking at the totality of our lives, there is a grave danger in always assuming we are the victim without considering ways in which we have been the perpetrator. We always want to rush to place our self in the space of the adulterous woman. We imagine the Pharisees standing over us and about to throw their stones at us. We are always quick to talk about the evils that have been perpetrated against us...but rarely are we willing to admit to ourselves let alone others that we have perpetrated tremendous evils against others. The primary sign of maturity is to come to terms with the fact that we will all be the adulterous woman and the Pharisees in our lives. We will all be victims and violators. Empathy for both parties within and without can take us a long way in finding peace and love capable of sustaining us.

It takes courage to defend women in a world that loves patriarchy. It takes courage to not fire missiles in a world that loves war. It takes courage to dig deep within and have empathy for the victim and perpetrator within and without. It takes courage to love. It actually takes your life.

Amen.

73.

September 10, 2013

messages

paragraphs in a novel
reveal my dreams
sentences in an article
challenge my truth
lines in a letter
prophecy of love
words in a poem
reflect my hope
novels in paragraphs
restore my dreams
articles in sentences
bring truth to challenge
a line of letters
speaks the prophetic love
poems in a word
springs forth hope

the power of god
the power of love
the power of tonight
the power of the morning
the power of light
the power of darkness
the power of the somethings discovered in syllabals
the power of messages

74.

September 14, 2014

eight-year-old commits suicide

eight-year-old commits suicide
those were the words in the newspaper i read
how can someone so young now be dead

the motivation was to leave the bullying behind
how does evil manifest in children so young
they are supposed to be outside playing and having fun

god i am pissed at you again
how could you have let some shit like this go down
and you expect me to wake up and preach about you in this town

i just don't understand
i cannot comprehend
the gravest of evils happen again and again

wait a second something just came to me
i can remember a time when i was eight
and on one of the other kids i leveled my hate

i can't believe it
i was a bully
it was because i didn't know myself fully

no matter the reason there is no excuse
the kids that commit suicide
do so because of abuse
i was the perpetrator once upon a time

when i begin to blame god for such tragedy
perhaps i need to spend some time thinking about my own agency
i am a killer whether I know it or not
i bullied other kids without even a thought

i am to blame you are to blame
the killing is collective
god just simple tries to show us the way through god's very name
love

there is no room for silence
we have been made to be love
when we learn to love each other we will create the world we have dreamed of

may my eight year old friend rest in the arms of love

75.

September 15, 2013

I Am The Light of The World

In John 8, Jesus saves the life of an adulterous woman by getting down in the dirt between her and the patriarchal Pharisees. Not long after, people are skeptical of who gives him the authority to do such a thing. Jesus responds in John 8:12, "I am the light of the world."

The scriptures consistently point us toward becoming more like Jesus...so what does it mean for us to be able to say in this life, "I am the light of the world?" What does it mean to be light for the world?

It means realizing that light is love and love is light.

Jesus transcended the dark terms of the oppressors and spoke of light to offer love...by doing such Jesus loved the oppressors. When we refuse to be defined by the circumstances thrust upon us by the oppressors, we are giving light to the oppressor...we are loving the oppressor. When we follow the example of Jesus and refuse to be defined by oppressor's terms and circumstances, we can boldly say to them and everyone else, "I am the light of the world."

The oppressor don't create light, we do.

Jesus got down in the dirt with the adulterous woman. When we get dirty in the pursuit of equality for all people, we are spreading light...we are spreading love. When we have the courage to stand for justice even at the threat of death, we are able to boldly say, "I am the light of the world."

The dirtiness of injustice don't create light, we do.

When we choose to be the unique queer God has called us to be, we are able to love boldly and say, "I am the light of the world."

The normative constructs of our world don't create light, we do.

Go and be the light of the world.

Amen.

76.

September 22, 2013

The Blind Man

Jesus was walking down the street and saw a man who was blind. The story that follows reveals much about human nature and the world that we live in.

Jesus places mud pies on the eyes of the man and tells him to go wash them out in order to enact the healing. Jesus healed him but he had to take the next step of acting out that healing. I encounter so many people who have the means to heal themselves of the sickness of hate and slander in their hearts but refuse...I guess you could say they would rather be blind.

When the man regained his sight, he went to claim his identity amongst many who should have had many reasons to celebrate the miraculous restoration of sight. Instead of loving the man and celebrating his miracle, the people questioned his very identity. The people declared, "That's not really you!" How many of us have encountered hateful people who claim...that's not really you? When you find love and freedom in who you are and who God has called you to be, there will always be those who want you to continue living as if you are blind. The people were blind and the formerly blind man just kept on seeing.

The formerly blind man was called before the Pharisees or the keepers of the normative boundaries of his day. How many of you have known a few of these folks who think they get to make the rules? Under Roman rule, the Pharisees were amongst the oppressed and ultimately they took on the role of oppressing everyone else. Pharisees and other oppressors come in all colors, genders, sexualities, classes, orientations, and so on...most speak of justice...but often their hearts are proven to be far from it.

These Pharisees of Jesus' day kept challenging the formerly blind man over and over again. They would not leave him alone. The formerly blind man's answer was always the same, "I once was blind but now I see." When they couldn't get more of an answer out of him, they grew angrier and angrier. Eventually they couldn't find anything else to do but make claims against the identity he claimed for himself.

The man tried to teach the Pharisees about love but was driven out of their sight. The anger that the Pharisees get when confronted with love betrays their motives. One quickly realizes that justice is a secondary concerns to controlling others. The formerly blind man however refused to have his eyes closed.

Jesus ultimately met up with the formerly blind man. The man encountered love and was changed. Jesus responds in declaration, "I have come to restore sight to the blind and to tell those who think they see that they are blind." There was a little creeper or troll Pharisee that snuck up behind them, "Are we the blind ones you speak of?" Jesus responds, "You tell the world how to see yet you are blind."

We carry on the mission and ministry of Jesus…the mission and ministry of love.

We seek to give sight to the blind whether they think they can see or not.

We are here, we will not be blinded, and we are not going anywhere.

Amen.

77.

September 27, 2013

Remarks from the Inaugural Denton Meeting of Pastors for Texas Children

This afternoon we pastors, educators, students, and social workers gather to express our concern about a lack of funding for public education in Texas. The voices and paths represented here are varied but our conclusions are the same...public education is at the forefront of issues of social justice. The local public school system remains one of the great forces in our society able to awaken the social conscientious of students and create a better world. I know because I experienced it.

Twenty-four years ago, I started first grade in Morrow, Georgia at Lake Harbin Elementary. On the first day, I was placed in Ms. Bellington's class. I walked in and sat down on a carpet with a bunch of other kids. I repeated the same routine for about two more weeks until one day I was called to the door and told that I was going to be switching teachers. I cried and then was led to meet Ms. Ellington, the first black teacher in the history of the school. This move was not without controversy, as my grandparents were very disturbed at the idea of me having a black teacher and offered to pay for me to go to private school. Resisting, my parents had the courage to keep me in the public school. During that time, I learned about the dream of equality of Martin Luther King, Jr., developed a deep passion for social justice, and experienced what it meant to exist in a diverse community. These lessons affect me to this day.

If not for public schools, I would not be the pastor or activist standing here today.

Knowing my experience, I cannot and will not be silent as a lack of public funding continues to decimate public schools. I join with faith leaders of goodwill and conscientious concern all over the state who are organizing to right one of the greatest social wrongs of our time...a failure to fund public education at an adequate level. I stand together with you for justice for all of God's children...because that is what Ms. Ellington taught me to do.

Amen.

78.

September 29, 2013

Jesus was a man under attack.

Jesus lovingly healed a blind man and the Pharisees simply didn't like it.

Jesus responded to them by extolling the virtues of both God and love. Jesus declared all loves without sacrifice to be partial loves. Jesus declares that love will never die. Jesus states that all are children of God. Jesus encourages them to believe in what they see happening all around them...love, miracles, and hope.

The Pharisees were enraged. These comments fit into none of their normative boundaries and identities. Jesus sought to push them into a queer space past their places of understanding, but the pull of the normative boundaries and identities were too much for most. For such pushing...the Pharisees prepared to kill Jesus. A crime of hate was brewing.

Jesus declared in retreat, "I have loved you...yet now you want to kill me?"

Jesus kept on teaching in retreat and many believed that love truly is the way.

79.

October 2, 2013

The Danger of Language

I met a young Jewish woman tonight. We were drawn into a conversation about energy, love, and the universe. The more we talked the more I found my spirit deeply connected to her spirit. I found her to be an inspired child of God...even the incarnation of Jesus for me in that moment. While I am sure she would describe it differently, it does not change the fact that I found hope, companionship, and God in an unexpected place. It seems that the universe draws such conversations together when we need them the most. When I arrived back to the car, I found myself curious as to why others can't cross boundaries and replicate the miracle of a God without boundaries that I experienced? The answer for me has consistently been the danger of clinging to language.

The danger of clinging to language is the danger of allowing language to keep one from truly making contact with the self, God, or anyone else...because we simply can't get past words.

I have seen many people never get to God because they make idols out of words on a page...yet when we allow words to shift, change, and sometimes dissipate we eventually realize that true being comes from allowing the self to transcend the boundaries of language.

What language can describe the totality of the beauty of two lovers' first kiss? What language can describe the totality of the amazement of a newborn baby? What language can describe the totality of God? I want to have more experiences like tonight that are largely beyond the power of language to describe.

May we move past words and become more human in the process.

Amen.

80.

October 6, 2013

A Church Under Attack!

Like every Sunday morning, I arrived early at Mable Peabody's Beauty Parlor and Chainsaw Repair Shop to set up for church. The musicians were inside and I was outside unloading my car. I had my back to the parking lot when all of a sudden from behind me I heard repetitively, "Fuck You Faggot!" I turned to see three young men pointing and snarling at me from their car. I stared long and hard enough to give the young men time to see my resolve then went inside. I tried to forget what happened. I returned to the door about ten minutes later and there were a bunch of broken bottles right next to my car. Even though I saw those same bottles in the hands of the guys I saw previously, I convinced myself that they were there from the bar the night before. I had a sermon to preach and a church to guide. After church, I walked out to my car and there were shards of glass carefully leaned up against my back tires to puncture the tire when I backed up. One of our folks stated quite clearly the feelings of everyone present, "We are a community constantly under attack."

These words have rung true in my mind. It doesn't matter what our church does...we will be attacked. Our love makes us a target and vulnerable.

During the service surrounding these events, I taught about Lazarus and believe that Jesus has much to teach us about being attacked for our love. In the eleventh chapter of John, Jesus decides to go see his sick friend Lazarus. The disciples begged him not to go, as they knew they were under attack. When Jesus chooses to love his friend Lazarus and go to him, the disciples felt that they were traveling to their deaths. I guess in many ways we are all traveling to our deaths, it is just a question of what we are going to stand for as we travel.

Jesus arrived. Lazarus was dead. Jesus wept. Some scholars have speculated that Lazarus was Jesus' lover. This is a secondary question for me, as I am most interested in the quality and quantity of Jesus' love. Jesus loved Lazarus with all the love that Jesus could muster and that is queer enough.

Even though Jesus knew it would lead to more attacks, Jesus raised Lazarus from the dead. Love is proven to be more powerful than death. Love is proven to still be love even when it is under attack. For this, the religious folks decided to kill Jesus.

The incident at the church yesterday was just a brief reminder that we are consistently under attack. Our love is going to make us vulnerable. So what do we do? I pray that we will continue raising people from the dead.

Amen.

81.

October 7, 2013

faggot

faggot

these were the words three dudes screamed at me
i was at church and thought i was free of such bigotry

i walked back inside to swallow my pride
i knew i had a church to guide

during the service I was a little distracted
i was wondering if their anger would prove to be protracted

i concluded the service and walked out into the light
thankfully no one was there who wanted to fight

i looked under my tire to find glass pushed against my back tire
the pain in me was burning like a fire

i stopped to pray
there was nothing much else to say

i count myself lucky to have had the privilege to be lead
to a place where i have the same word jesus would have had hanging over my head

faggot

82.

October 13, 2013

National Coming Out Day

This morning we sit firmly between the juxtaposition of safety and risk. Since we opened the doors of this church, we have consistently dealt with such juxtaposition. Last week, I had a few guys scream "fuck you faggot" at me and later put glass underneath my tires. This week we had a religious man roll up on a motorcycle and become rather confrontational with some of our folk who were standing outside smoking. Although we work hard to keep all of you safe in this space, make no mistake that the work that we engage in is risky business. There is risk involved in daring to promote a queer way of looking at the world. We dare to confront bigotry and homophobia. We dare to confront normalized identities and categories that accomplish nothing but division. We dare to stand for total love. We dare to stand for total inclusion. We dare to out ourselves as queer in a world that often seems hopelessly closeted...and by God we dare do it with the cross of Jesus in the middle of our space every Sunday morning. This is not just risky business...this is downright scandalous.

We are not alone in the creation of scandals.

In the twelfth chapter of John, Jesus creates a scandal. Let me paint the scene for you. Jesus raised Lazarus from the dead. Now, Lazarus sits at the table. When was the last time you had dinner with a formerly dead man? Then, to take things even further, Mary pulls out her perfume, pours it all over Jesus' feet, and whips her hair back and forth to make sure the perfume is rubbed in. So we have a dead man and a pretty sensual woman sitting at the table...and then we find out that some of the motley crew of disciples that Jesus ran around with were also in attendance. This was one scandalous interaction. Many folks on the outside, including pastors and other activists of the time, talked about what was going on in the house. I think you all refer to such talk as, "talking shit."

Regardless, many of the same folks who talked shit about Jesus' scandalous meal were also there to greet Jesus as Jesus came out in Jesus' own way on the way into Jerusalem. As everyone waived rainbow flags and Jesus rode in on the back of a longhorn at what might have been the first Pride, we also meet all of the actors who less than a week later at the very least will refuse to stop and at the very worst will participate in a hate crime that ends in the death of Jesus. In the crowd Jesus knows that those who hold rainbow flags in one hand and a knife behind their back in the other are worth the risk...the risk of love. Whatever these folks held and whatever creature Jesus rode in on, the point is that coming out to love was not just risky for Jesus...it ultimately lead to death.

Jesus declared love to be the destiny of Jesus...and love takes risk. When we come out to love we are dying to the perceived safety of closets...we are awakening to ourselves so that we might destroy the need for closets and bring the universal inclusive change that can come if we all live as exactly the queer that God created us to be.

You see we are a church that declares that all are in and none are out. We are here to save the church. We are here to save the world. We are here to save ourselves.

Jesus beckons the people, "Believe in God...Believe in Me." When you come out, you are declaring to the world that who you are is exactly the image of God that you are created to be. You are a reflection of God. You too are able to say boldly, scandalously, "Believe in God...Believe in Me." So on this day take hold of your life and do not allow anyone to define the queer that you are and will always be. So on this day...follow that old queer Jesus...come out to love...come out to freedom...come out to hope...come out to light...may there never be a need for any closets again.

Amen.

83.

October 15, 2013

Liturgy From The Wedding of Two Brides

Dearly beloved, I welcome you to this a most momentous of occasions. On this day, we gather to witness and bless a marriage. We partner with a God that declares God's self to be love...so in the name of love, I invite you to participate in the joining of these two women together in a ceremony that is as old as time itself...marriage.

The union of these two women in heart, body, mind, and soul is intended by God for their mutual joy and affection. Marriage is a beautiful thing and it is not intended to be entered into lightly...but reverently.

Into this mysterious union of love these two women now come to be joined. If any of you can show just cause why these two should not be married...either speak now at this very instance or hold your words and judgment forever.

Do either of you know any reason why you should not be married?

No

Will you have this woman to be your wife? Will you love her, comfort her, honor and keep her, in sickness and in health; and forsaking all others, be faithful to her as long as you both shall live?

I will

Will you have this woman to be your wife? Will you love her, comfort her, honor and keep her, in sickness and in health; and forsaking all others, be faithful to her as long as you both shall live?

I will

Will all of you witnesses who are here in support of these two women do all in your power to uphold them in marriage?

We will

Who gives this woman to be married to this woman?

Her mother and brother

Who gives this woman to be married to this woman?

Her mother and I

May the words of the Apostle Paul in the 13th chapter his first letter to the Church at Corinth speak to us at this most beautiful hour:

> *If I speak in the tongues of mortals and of angels, but do not have love, I am a noisy gong or a clanging cymbal. And if I have prophetic powers, and understand all mysteries and all knowledge, and if I have all faith, so as to remove mountains, but do not have love, I am nothing. If I give away all my possessions, and if I hand over my body so that I may boast, but do not have love, I gain nothing. Love is patient; love is kind; love is not envious or boastful or arrogant or rude. It does not insist on its own way; it is not irritable or resentful; it does not rejoice in wrongdoing, but rejoices in the truth. It bears all things, believes all things, hopes all things, endures all things.*
>
> *Love never ends. But as for prophecies, they will come to an end; as for tongues, they will cease; as for knowledge, it will come to an end. For we know only in part, and we prophesy only in part; but when the complete comes, the partial will come to an end. When I was a child, I spoke like a child, I thought like a child, I reasoned like a child; when I became an adult, I put an end to childish ways. For now we see in a mirror, dimly, but then we will see face to face. Now I know only in part; then I will know fully, even as I have been fully known. And now faith, hope, and love abide, these three; and the greatest of these is love.*

Let us pray.

God of love you have created us in your image. In these your children may your lvoe shine forever as their love grows forever. *Amen.*

I ask that you repeat after me.

In the name of love, I take you to be my wife, to have and to hold from this day forward, for better for worse, for richer for poorer, in sickness and in health, to love and to cherish, as long as I have breath.

I ask that you repeat after me.

In the name of love, I take you to be my wife, to have and to hold from this day forward, for better for worse, for richer for poorer, in sickness and in health, to love and to cherish, as long as I have breath.

Could I have the rings?

Bless these rings as a symbol of love and the vows made on this day. *Amen.*

I ask that you repeat after me.

I give you this ring as a symbol of my vow, and with all that I am, and all that I will ever be, I honor you in the name of love.

I ask that you repeat after me.

I give you this ring as a symbol of my vow, and with all that I am, and all that I will ever be, I honor you in the name of love.

Now that these two women have given themselves to each other by solemn vows, with the joining of hands and the giving and receiving of a ring, I pronounce that they are married now and forever in the eyes of God.

That which love has joined together let nothing come between.

Let us bow our heads for a blessing.

You are amongst my dearest friends and I love you. I pray that love will always go before you, be with you, and be behind you in all that you do. In the name of the creator, redeemer, and sustainer. *Amen.*

Friends...It is my pleasure to introduce to you this majestic couple.

You may each kiss your bride.

Interlude

Before you depart...a quick blessing.

You have witnessed this day a love that dares exceed boundaries and limits. May you too be strengthened to depart this place so that you might know the height, depth, and width of love. *Amen.*

84.

October 17, 2013

Peace

I have heard much talk of peace over the past few months. As someone who seeks peace, any talk of peace should be comforting and encouraging that the world is moving in a positive direction. Rather than comforting and encouraging, I have found recent talk of peace to be downright scary.

I have found many people's ideas of peace to be nothing more than disguises for violence. Over the past few months, there was a real push for military intervention in Syria. "We need to bomb them in order to make peace," explained some of the hawkish politicians. I encountered a pastor with a gun on her hip the other day. When I asked her why she carried a gun, she replied, "I have a duty to God to help preserve peace and order." I talked to a man recently about disciplining his child. "I have to hit him in order to teach him not to hit," he explained. In a counseling situation, I talked to someone who was having a conflict with someone and she described that the only way to make peace was to bash the person into submission. I read recently about monks that flog themselves in order to find peace with God. I don't think I want too much to do with that God. Over the last few months, I have consistently had conversations in which peace is disguised as violence.

It seems that we are a culture that has little conception of how violent we are. The movies we watch, the games we play, the way we handle conflict, and the way that violence pervades the whole of our lives has brought us to a place where we don't understand what violence or peace is anymore. We seem to think that peace is about power and violence is the means to get us there. We fail to see the violence within much less the violence without.

Just last week, I was visiting my friend Will Speer on Texas' Death Row. Will has committed heinous acts in his life and does not hide it. There is a tremendous amount of honesty in our relationship. On this visit, Will talked to me about the murder of his mom in 2007 at the hands of his stepfather. While on Texas' Death Row, Will became a victim of murder. So are we to treat him as a murderer or a victim? Maybe we are all both? In the midst of our conversation, Will explained to me about how violence is a core part of who our society has created him to be. I immediately thought...doesn't this describe the way that all of us were raised?

The ones who are quick to call Will Speer a monster are the same ones who buy their toddlers superhero underwear and ultimately teach their kids that fighting is the way to achieve peace. The ones who call out for the death of murderers often fail to examine the ways that their economic decisions are making them mass murders of persons in sweat shops around the world. The truth is we are all incredibly violent...perhaps it is time we start spending less time describing others as monsters and locate the monster in our self.

Make no mistake, there is a need for justice when wrongs are committed...but we must decide if we are pursuing justice in vengeance and violence or love. There is a big difference and the route we take will determine our own destiny. Will we be a people of peace and love or vengeance and violence? I pray that God guides us to a place where we never forget that peace and love does not include vengeance and violence.

Amen.

85.

October 20, 2013

Betrayal, Love & Feet

In the thirteenth chapter of John, the closer Jesus gets to the inevitable moment of execution, the more we discover hate bubbling below and above the surface. In these hours, Jesus teaches us many things. We learn that to respond to hate with anything less than love is to live as something less than God. Jesus was prepared to love those who hated Jesus until the very end and beyond.

Judas was getting ready to betray Jesus and Jesus had inklings that such betrayal was coming. How does Jesus respond to having a potential charlatan in the room? Jesus loves him more.

Jesus did not take the safe route. Jesus loved even when Jesus knew that it was not safe. This does not mean that Jesus intentionally placed Jesus' self in danger...in fact Jesus retreats at various points in scripture...but it does mean that Jesus took the risk to love in dangerous times. When we dare love, we are participating in the risky business of God. I do not encourage anyone to stay in dangerous or toxic relationships, but let us never forget that loving someone is always risky. We can never know how things might turn out, but we can choose how we are going to live...we can choose love.

Have you ever wondered if you had the option of viewing a roadmap of where the betrayers would be marked throughout your life, would you take a look and avoid them? I can't speak for you, but I can speak for me. I have experienced many moments of betrayal throughout my life and I would not avoid any of them. I have had many opportunities to love people in this community over the last six months and not all of these relationships have ended well...but our love cannot be dependent on or taken hostage by the emotions or reactions of others. We must love for the sake of love. This is the business of God.

In the midst of hate and coming betrayals, Jesus washes the feet of all of the disciples present. This is the dirty God...the one that gets down in the dirt to wash people's feet. These folks probably had not had their feet washed in some time. Their feet were probably really stinky. I would imagine that there were multiple bunions and warts present. I would even imagine that there was probably some donkey or camel shit thrown in there for good measure. Yet Jesus goes to washing or loving with no concern for the dirt, bunions, warts or even shit that might get on Jesus' hands or person. This is the shitty God that dares to get down in the shit with us. This is the God that dares to stoop down and wash feet even when he might get kicked in the teeth. This is the God that pushes past caution and loves all of us dilapidated and broke down creatures.

When the time comes for Jesus to wash Peter's feet, he says, "No, I am just too wounded and too dirty to have my feet washed by you." Jesus takes this moment to teach that it is out of our washing that we are healed and learn how to heal others. Unless we allow ourselves to be cleaned, then we are not going to know how to clean others. I pray we will not resist the cleansing so that we might discover who we are clean.

Jesus looked at the disciples and said, "You have called me so many things and bestowed on me so many honors, but all I want to do is wash your feet." This is the call of a God that is far queerer than our ability to grasp...to wash people's feet. May we go through life not seeking titles, honors or anything else...but rather be willing to get down in the shit with people and wash their feet.

The passages end this morning in the juxtaposition where they began, between betrayal and love. Jesus reveals that Judas will be the vessel of betrayal. Jesus loves Judas anyways. Everyone assumes that Judas is the primary betrayal, but then Jesus reveals that Peter will betray Jesus also. So who is the primary betrayal? Perhaps the point is to understand that we will all at one time or another be betrayed and betrayers in this life. Perhaps the point of the text is to illustrate that no matter the circumstance we must humble ourselves to be love...we must humble ourselves to be feet washers.

Amen.

86.

October 27, 2013

Things Grow Queerer or From Mable Peabody's to My House to Beyond

Let us not delay in stating the obvious. We are meeting this morning in my house. We find ourselves in this space after many conversations about the need to find a new space to meet on Sunday mornings. Though our parting with Mable Peabody's was quite amicable, we are still meeting this morning at a critical juncture.

This morning we are able to feel the power of Peter's words to Jesus at the end of the 13th chapter of the Gospel of John, "Where are you going?" Many of us are looking at each other and asking a similar question, "Where are we going?"

A few verses later, Jesus does not reply with specifics. Jesus simply says, "Do not be afraid."

In times of uncertainty, it is easy to be afraid. In these moments, we desire clear certain paths and often they are not to be found. So where are we to go? Jesus asks us to go that place beyond fear and create our own path of love.

How do we get to that path beyond fear? Jesus responds, "I am the way, I am the truth, and I am the life."

This verse is used to consistently pummel those who don't believe that only Jesus is the way, the truth, and the life. I think such an interpretation is a failure to move beyond fear and to the path of love. If we follow the path of love and are slowly made to be like Jesus, then we too should be able to declare, "I am the way, I am the truth, and I am the life." Thus, through love, we too become the way, the truth, and the life.

Jesus affirms such a message later in the chapter, "Those who love me will love others." The reaction should produce action. Those who long for the way, should be the way. Those who long for the truth, should be the truth. Those who long for life, should be the life.

Jesus tells us to believe a higher love is coming. I invite you to be that higher love. When you get to the end of the way, then make your own path. When you get to the end of your truth, then be the truth the world needs. When you get to the end of your life, then be life for others.

The message of Jesus is that the path of love is the path that is not easy...but rather the path filled with risk and danger that takes us to places of love and hope that we can only dream of.

We have some decisions to make as far as our name and location, but I think we are on a good path when we are blazing our own queer trail of love.

I conclude with the words of Jesus to the disciples at the end of the 14th chapter, "Get up, let's go."

87.

November 2, 2013

death penalty penalty death

i dreamed of love and justice
execution
is
dead
said
the
fairy
of
texas
i
couldn't
believe
the
words
proceeding
from
the
window
of
the
lexus
then
i
opened
my
eyes
and
awoke
from
my
stupor
i
knew
it
was
just
another
liberal
dream

i
got
up
and
rubbed
my
eyes
and
then
i
knelt
to
pray
i
received
a
vision
that
said
it
was
wrong
to
kill
not
matter
what
the
state
says
love
is
beyond
political
ideology
god
pushed
me
to
work
with
all
to
restore
justice
and

to
all
may
morality
and
justice
be
restored
but
how
to
speak
death
penalty
penalty
death
how
is
there
any
room
for
love
or
grace
left
death
penalty
penalty
death
how
can
the
morality
of
murder
be
contingent
on
who
carries
it
out
death
penalty
penalty

death
life matters even in Texas

88.

November 2, 2013

tears

tears let go are classless, colorless, genderless, orientationless, and many other lesses
to say otherwise is to not understand the construction of a tear
tears are primarily water and once released they stand on their own
they do have a human origin but proceed elsewhere as they fall
to the ground to create life once more
the tears move from life to life
tears illustrate the cycle of life
our tears connect us to everything
even you

89.

November 3, 2013

Energy = God?

What do you believe God is? I think most people think about God as a being. Some might even think God as a human. I think there are even those who think that God has a penis. I feel like I have talked to many of them who refer constantly to God as he. Regardless, this morning we find ourselves thinking about Jesus as the electricity of life and God as the source.

What does it look like to think of God as less being and more energy? It's a shocking way of thinking about things isn't it? You see energy keeps us going while powering movement and change. The renowned scientist Albert Einstein once said, "Energy is never created or destroyed." Perhaps this is a more realistic way of thinking about eternity. Maybe we are pieces of energy that cannot be created or destroyed. Maybe God is the source of all energy that cannot be created or destroyed.

What is energy for the human? I don't know about you, but the actualization or hope of love is what keeps me going. I love love. Love is electric. Love moves the world and moves me. How is energy created? The answer is through friction or difference. The Queer creates energy. The Queer creates life. The Queer is God.

What does it mean to stay electric? Jesus tells us that if we abide in love then we abide in God. To abide in love we must learn to love our self, our community, our world, and all that is beyond. To learn to love begins with learning to love difference or queerness in yourself and in the universe around you. Queerness is from God. The Queer is God. In order to stay electric, you must connect with the Queer within.

Have you ever considered that we are the source of energy or the source of God for people? If we look like everyone else, how can our queerness be heard? God is the source of all love and queerness. Whoever hates the Queer hates God. Whoever hates the Queer hates God. You cannot deny the Queer within or the Queer within others and love God. Jesus says, "They will hate without cause." There are plenty who hate the Queer within and without without cause.

Perhaps it is our job to tell the world that the Queer lives...in us and in the universe.

I want you to know that when they kicked us out for our queerness they kicked God out. Don't forget the Queer is God and God is the Queer. When you kick out the Queer, you kick out the church. We the gathered Queer are the real church. In this church, we will not stop proclaiming this message. Where love is is where God is. We will not stop proclaiming the hope...the Queer...within us. May the electric queerness of God and life guide our efforts to set us free and queer the world.

May the divine electricity of a queer love beyond identity and boundaries that sets us free be within, without, up, down and all about.

Amen.

90.

November 5, 2013

Pastors for Texas Children and The Fight for Neighborhood Schools

In the Christian creation myth, God creates humanity. Upon creation, God invites humanity to go and name their world. In the midst of the naming story, it becomes obvious that God educated and guided humanity on what to do. Throughout time, it has been the human responsibility to continue to educate and guide younger generations in the task of naming creation. The question is...are we continuing in the task of educating and guiding our children in equipping them to name their world?

This morning, I sit around a table with other Statewide Steering Committee members of a new organization called Pastors for Texas Children. The organization is a collection of over 500 Texas faith leaders who have joined together in the last six months to stand for neighborhood schools. About an hour ago, the Statewide Steering Committee dedicated itself to organizing an additional 4,500 pastors before the 2015 Texas Legislative Session. I am proud to sit around the table with this amazing group of passionate people who refuse to allow local schools or the last bastions of public good to fall to privitization.

Also this morning, there are school board elections taking place all over the country between pro-neighborhood schools candidates and pro-privatization candidates. Right outside of Denver, Colorado this morning in the Douglas County School District, venture capitalists Koch Brothers, through their political advocacy group American's for Prosperity, have spent hundreds of thousands of dollars seeking to elect a local school board that is pro-privitization. Make no mistake...there is much money to be made in education. Texas is a very attractive option for the forces of privitization. Imagine these companies gaining an ability to make a buck off of millions upon millions of Texas children.

So why should pastors care?

We choose to push because we believe in the mandate of Jesus in Matthew 25 to the least of these. We push because we know that if neighborhood schools are shutdown the people who will suffer the most are the disadvantaged. Education should be a right not a privilege. We push because we know that if schools are privatized then there will no longer be the centers of diversity that can be resources to promote inclusion in all of our communities. We firmly believe that our children should be used for profit.

I participate so that my sons Jeff and Phillip might have a public place to go to school that educates them because they are human not because they are wealthy.
Amen.

91.

November 10, 2013

The Risky Queer Path of Love

We begin this morning with Jesus immersed deep in thought. There is a crime of hate coming, but wasn't it always. Jesus was simply too queer for a world that demanded neat identities and boundaries.

This morning there are many of us who feel similarly. We know that to challenge the acceptable identities and boundaries that we are placed in is to open our selves up to crimes of hate. We have all experienced the vulnerability that Jesus is experiencing. We know the feeling of impending crimes of hate.

Just this past week, we were reminded of what our society does to the Queer. The skirt of Sasha Fleischman, an 18-year-old gender-neutral high school student in Berkely, California, was lit on fire by 16-year-old Richard Thomas. Sasha suffered 2nd and 3rd degree burns. Richard has been charged with attempted murder and a hate crime, which carries the possibility of a sentence of life with parole. Our hearts break for Sasha and Richard, knowing that these events transpired because our society hates queerness and taught Richard to hate too. Even with the knowledge that society can be so dangerous, Sasha choose to love Sasha and not lie to the world about who Sasha is. Sasha refused to live within the presumably safe space of inauthentic closeted identities and boundaries. I am moved by the courage of Sasha to live honestly in unsafe spaces and I pray that we will follow.

Jesus has much to teach us about notions of safe space. Jesus did not live in a safe space, but Jesus chose to keep going on the risky queer path of love. Jesus was ready to sacrifice Jesus' life so that life might be born anew and people might know love.

If we are going to truly experience life and love, our journey will not be safe. For life and love are inherently risky. If we decide to challenge the demanded and oppressive identities and boundaries of this world, there will be pain in the journey away…but in the journey away there is real freedom and love to be found.

The path that we choose as a community is not safe. There are no maps or safety nets on how to be a queer church. Journeys without clear paths are always dangerous. No matter the cost, however, we have chosen to be the queers that we are and go where the Queer leads. Sasha and Jesus did too.

When Judas plants the kiss in the park, Jesus had a choice. Do I take the risky queer path of love or the safe path of closeted normativity? Sasha and Jesus chose to be queer. May we go and choose likewise.
Amen.

92.

November 12, 2013

The Prayer

In 1993, a jury in Harris County convicted Jamie Bruce McCoskey of kidnap and murder of Michael Keith Dwyer. In addition to these crimes, McCoskey was also accused of raping Dwyer's fiancé. The sentence was death and that sentence is to be carried out in Huntsville, Texas today at 6pm. I don't know Jamie Bruce McCoskey. I only know the convictions and evidence that everyone else knows, but I do know God and I know that you can't love your neighbor as your self while killing them.

Tonight, I will stand on the Denton Square and pray. I will pray because it is wrong to kill, no matter who is doing the killing. I will pray for peace, so that all eyes might be opened and all hearts turned to justice. I will stand with a few friends and pray that the people of the State of Texas discover what it truly means to love our neighbor as our self.

Amen.

93.

November 18, 2013

The Crucifixion of Jesus, Transgender Day of Remembrance & Crimes of Hate

In our journey through the Gospel of John, we find ourselves today experiencing Good Friday in November. When I consider that we will also commemorate Transgender Day of Remembrance this week, it doesn't seem all that out of the ordinary. For what we are talking about today is a crime of hate that was predicated on a hatred for queerness. The events that led to the passion of the Christ has occurred and continues to occur over and over again in the dehumanization and murder of transpersons all over the world. The characters and situations show up over and over again.

The only person that could have saved Jesus from the hate crime he was about to experience was Pilate. In the midst of mob hatred, Pilate declared the events unjust and washed his hands of responsibility. How many Pilates do you know? I regularly encounter people who consistently seek to wash their hands of injustice and act as if they are innocent. Just because you didn't pull the trigger, doesn't mean that you are not responsible for murdering someone or their character or their livelihood or their hope. So often we don't intervene when transphobia is going on because we are trying to protect our status, our jobs and our lives. The lesson of Pilate is that when you wash your hands and look away...you are exactly what your souls tells you you are...guilty of the hate crime that you failed to stop.

The crowd screamed for death. Make no mistake, Jesus was and is queer in a world of hate. These people did not want to kill Jesus because he was a safe normal person. The folks wanted to kill Jesus because Jesus was the queerest thing they had ever encountered. Societies have consistently sought to kill the Queer. If you choose to be who you are in our world and stand up to the demanded normativities of all sides, they will come for you too.

Jesus is humiliated, beaten, tortured and dehumanized before Jesus is killed. In those final moments, Jesus speaks a word of forgiveness. This week as we remember the victims of transphobic hate crimes, may our prayers not be too far from those who perpetuated these crimes. For if we can follow the example of Jesus and find it deep within to forgive even the most heinous acts of transphobia, then love will win and we will begin to see the society of equality that we so desperately want to see.

Love begins within, moves to shape without and pushes until we all arrive at a world where all people are allowed to live as exactly that which they were created to be...queer.
Amen.

94.

November 19, 2013

Stop the Damned Drilling!

I will admit that environmental issues have never been one of the driving forces of my ministry and spiritual activism. While I have a deep respect for those who fight for the environment, there are just a plethora of other issues that have drawn my attention over the past decade. Tonight was different.

I live in Denton, Texas. Denton is a beautiful city with a real community feel to it. I have noticed lately the large drills that seem to be popping up in weird locations around town, near houses, apartments, the football stadium, playgrounds and a whole host of other sensitive areas. When I heard that a City Council meeting was going on tonight to talk about the issue, I decided to attend. In the reports of citizens, I listened to resident after resident call for a moratorium on drilling inside the city limits. In their unique pleas, each resident revealed something about their lives to illustrate their concern for the issue.

One pregnant woman delivered an impassioned plea for the health of her unborn baby. In the midst of her pleas, I imagined listening to my 40 weeks pregnant wife Emily ask a similar question, "Jeff, how are we going to protect our baby from this drilling?" The issue of drilling in Denton became very real for me in that moment.

I had to leave the meeting not long after the citizen reports, but there is a part of me that is still there...asking and praying "How are we as a family going to protect our children from this unnecessary drilling?"

My mind has consistently traveled tonight to Jesus' command to "love your neighbor as your self." I don't see how you can "love your neighbor as your self" and allow drilling next to their house! I don't see how you can "love your neighbor as your self" and allow drilling within walking distance from where they go to school! I don't see how you can "love your neighbor as your self" and drill near where kids play on the playground! I don't see how you can "love you neighbor as your self" and allow drilling that is ruining lives through sickness and oppression! I know that many of the council members considering a possible moratorium and those who own/manage the energy companies profess to be Christians. So as a minister, I will ask in the words of Jesus...

Can you please "love your neighbor as your self" and stop the damned drilling?

Amen.

95.

November 25, 2013

The Courage to Feel a Resurrection

What a stunning Easter in November! It is freezing, sleeting and possibly snowing outside and there is little indication of the vibrant warmth of Spring that we usually associate with Easter, but we have come to the end of our journey through the Gospel of John and so we press on into the resurrection story.

Mary Magdalene arrives at the tomb or the coffin or the grave or whatever you want to call it to find the body of Jesus missing. It is in this moment out of pure exacerbation, Mary Magdalene cries out, "They have taken my Lord and I do not know where they have laid him." I have always loved this phrasing...as it speaks directly to our time and the battle for the resurrected Jesus.

I hear many people who claim that Jesus hates gays, lesbians and nearly everyone else except them and their friends. They have taken my Jesus and I do not know where they have laid my Jesus.

I hear many people talking about how Jesus is shutting people out and closing doors. They have taken my Jesus and I do not know where they have laid my Jesus.

I hear many people say that Jesus wants to bomb and execute people. They have taken my Jesus and I do not know where they have laid my Jesus.

I hear many people talk about how Jesus wants you to get yours and get rich without a care for anybody else except yourself. They have taken my Jesus and I do not know where they have laid my Jesus.

I hear many people talk about how Jesus wants to give us power over people so that we can control them. They have taken my Jesus and I do not know where they have laid my Jesus.

Later, Jesus appears to the disciples and shows them the wounds to prove it is Jesus. Thomas misses it. Even later still, Jesus appears to Thomas and lets him place his hands where the nails and spear went. In that moment of feeling, Thomas is awoken to the truth and power of God.

The problem with much modern talk about Jesus is that people are trying to prove something and not feel something. The resurrection of Jesus is too mysterious and beautiful of an occurrence to be proven.

People ask me all the time… Do you believe in the resurrection? I always have to ascertain what they are asking me. If you are asking if I would have had a Polaroid camera could I have caught it on film, the answer is that Polaroid cameras didn't exist back then. If you are asking if I would have had a high quality digital camera could I have pulled it up on my computer, the answer is that such things didn't exist back then. The only evidence we have is that something magical happened that transformed the world and me.

I am not interested in rules, proofs, boundaries, logic or anything else…I am interested in feeling something.

Jesus loved Thomas enough to be vulnerable with him. Jesus let Thomas touch the wounds. Together, they felt something. If you want to get past the boundaries and normativities of this life, you are going to have to be vulnerable enough to let yourself feel those who you want to touch and those who want to touch you. Through vulnerability you get fed and feed others…you feel something.

At the end of our passages today, Jesus asks Peter an infamous question, "Do you love me?" After some back and forth, Jesus replies, "Feed my people." If you want to feel, then you have got to feed somebody. If you want to love, then you have to feed somebody. If you want to experience the resurrection, then you have to feed somebody. You can't feel without feeding and they can't feel without you being fed.

The beauty of the resurrection is the pieces of the resurrected Jesus we might find in loving each other. For in the feeling and the feeding, we find salvation.

The resurrection of Jesus is something to be experienced not proven.

Amen.

96.

November 27, 2013

if god be in / a queer rhyme for our time

if god be in the sky
then what good is such a god for those who can't fly
if god be in the ocean
then what good is such a god for those who can't swim
if god be in silence
then what good is such a god for those whose minds can't stop creating sound
if god be in truth
then what good is such a god for those whose lives are lived in spaces of grey
if god be in music
then what good is such a god for those who can't hear
if god be in a book
then what good is such a god for those who can't read
if god be in heaven
then what good is such a god for those who are presently living in hell
if god be in the united states
then what good is such a god for those who live in india
if god be in identity
then what good is such a god for those who have no identity

if god be in the sky then the sky is god
if god be in the ocean then the ocean is god
if god be in silence then silence is god
if god be in truth then truth is god
if god be in music then music is god
if god be in a book then the book is god
if god be in heaven then heaven is god
if god be in the united states then the united states is god
if god be in identity then identity is god

all of these musings are rather silly you see
because the truth of the rhyme is that god is with me
not just me of course
but where i and you are
not in some distant faraway other land
if you want your constructed god to be there then let god be there
but if god is queer then god is always here

97.

November 30, 2013

Jesus has AIDS

World AIDS Day.

In the end of the 25th chapter of the Gospel of Matthew, Jesus mentions taking care of the sick and judges the nations based on a simple premise, "what you have failed to do for the least of these you have failed to do for me." Jesus consistently incarnates or becomes the sick, mistreated and vulnerable. According to the World Health Organization, over 35.3 million people worldwide are currently living with HIV/AIDS, an estimated 1.6 million people died of HIV/AIDS in 2012, 1 out of every 20 persons in Sub-Saharan Africa has HIV/AIDS and HIV/AIDS is the world's leading infectious killer (http://www.who.int/features/factfiles/hiv/facts/en/index2.html and http://www.who.int/mediacentre/factsheets/fs360/en/index.html). The ongoing HIV/AIDS crisis has created a world in which Jesus has AIDS. I believe that Jesus liberates us to love through our encounters with the sick, mistreated and vulnerable. On this day, may we not fail to remember that our salvation and liberation lies with those with HIV/AIDS.

Amen.

98.

December 1, 2013

The Calling Past...to Birth

This morning we begin our adventure into a Queer Christmas. In the initial scenes of the Gospel of Luke, a priest named Zechariah and his wife named Elizabeth are blessed with a child named John (later John the Baptist), who ultimately becomes the great forerunning prophet of Jesus. This being a parallel queer version of the story, I would like to introduce you to Bob and Tommy who ultimately have a daughter named John, who becomes the great forerunning prophet of Jesus. Let us journey into the magic of these queer events...

Bob was in the living room of his house praying and all of a sudden a light overcame him. The angel Gabby appeared and declared that Bob and Tommy were going to be blessed with a daughter named John. Bob gets scared and starts making excuses.

Now, I am really not concerned about whether you believe in angels or not. The magic and mystery always seems to take care of it's self anyways. What I am most concerned about is the way you respond to life-giving information or light. So often we respond like Bob did and tremble in fear. We refuse to believe that something magical and fantastical could even happen to us. I think a large part of leading a life of light is surrendering to love and light. No excuses...just love. No excuses...just light.

Even though Bob was unable to speak when he left, he was so full of light and love that he was blinding. When was the last time you had such an affect on people...you shined of light and love so brightly that you blinded them?

Bob was able to tell Tommy on a tablet that a daughter named John was on the way. The two squeezed and shook with glee. Everyone else present thought they were crazy.

When you start embracing love and light regardless of the circumstance, people are going to think you are crazy. It is crazy to love your neighbor as your self. It is crazy to love your enemy. It is crazy...and sometimes crazy is good. Sometimes that which people call queer or crazy actually changes the world.

Not too long after, Marina, a social worker with Child Protective Services, called Bob and Tommy to ask if they were interested in adopting a girl named John, even though she didn't meet any of their identity criteria. Bob and Tommy screamed in unison, "Yes!" Our society consistently judges and prescribes identity to people, but the God that we are talking about today asks us to move beyond identity to see the intrinsic individual value of all people. We are asked to love our neighbor as our self no matter what the identity of the neighbor is. Like many of us, Bob and Tommy had certain ideas about identity and God called them past such ideas. Today, God is still calling us to the same.

This season of birth beckons us to birth of light and love.

Amen.

99.

December 5, 2013

The Birth of a Child & The Changing of a Name : A Living Tribute to Nelson Mandela

"You are the light of the world." -Matthew 5:14

Jesus spoke these words in the infamous Sermon on the Mount. Throughout my life, these words have signified what I have tried so hard to be...light. I have constantly sought light.

Early this morning, I jumped into a birthing pool in our living room to hold my wife Emily as she labored to give birth to our third child. In the midst of the pushing and throes of labor, Emily pulled a baby out of the water. I took one look at him and thought, "You are the light of the world." We call the light Quienly.

This afternoon, Quienly experienced problems keeping a high heartbeat and we were forced to transport the light to the hospital. As I worried about my child, I was watching over our twin sons when I heard on the news that the great light of peace and love Nelson Mandela had died. I mourn.

I mourn Mandela because he had the courage to move from violence and vengeance to the belief that forgiveness and love are the only real way to peace and justice. Mandela demanded an end to identity-based domination and called for all people to be respected as individuals. In pushing for a Rainbow Nation, Mandela asked a people to forgive the unforgiveable acts that had taken place during Apartheid. In so doing, Mandela used forgiveness and love to guide us all toward peace and justice. Nelson Mandela was and is the light of the world.

On December 5, 2013, Quienly is born and Mandela has died.

This evening, I arrived at the hospital to check on my wife and child. My wife and I discussed are mutual love and admiration for Nelson Mandela. We decided that this was an occasion that could not be missed. We called and had the birth certificate changed.

Dillard Quinley Hood is now Quinley Mandela Dillard Hood.

May the young Quinley Mandela continue to be the light of the world just like his namesake.

Amen.

100.

December 6, 2013

**i waited and we found
a story of us**

i waited for you
we met in a strange place
i waited for you
we found love
i waited for you
we found truth

i waited for you
we met something new
i waited for you

we found new life
i waited for you
we found change
i waited for you
we found movement
i waited for you

101.

December 8, 2013

The Baby of Belief

In Luke 1:39-56, a baby named John leaps inside of Elizabeth at the sight of Mary and then Mary praises God for the baby growing inside her named Jesus. In John 1:1, Jesus is called the word that was, is and will be God. These passages both describe beautiful divine mysteries and reveal speak of the word, truth, love and hope.

In our lives this morning, let us listen for the word, truth, love and hope. Words help us to experience truth. Jesus was the truth and can help us understand truth. The word was necessary to reveal the truth. In truth we find love. Love cannot be false for it is the truest entity to ever exist. Love grants us hope. Love grants us the courage to continue.

We learn these lessons from a baby named Jesus this morning.

Lately, I have been celebrating a baby too.

Over the last three days, I have experienced the first few days of life with my son, Quinley Mandela Dillard Hood. In Quinley Mandela, I see and hear astounding words that don't need to be spoken or written, I know the truth that radiates from his being, I feel deeply a deep love that just exists and I experience an abiding hope that is simply beyond explanation.

This is the message of Gospel of Jesus Christ coming from a baby...beautiful words beyond comprehension, radiating truth in being, deep love that simply exists and hope beyond explanation.

In this season of birth, may we open our hearts and believe.

Amen.

102.

December 15, 2013

Birth and the Queer

Toward the end of the first chapter of the Gospel of Luke, we find Elizabeth and Zechariah about to welcome a son named John. You can substitute the names Bob or Elaine for Elizabeth or Zechariah or take away names and make the people whoever or whatever relationship status or sexuality you want, but the fact remains that these were individuals about to welcome a child into their family and just like in all cases of birth, adoption or any other way of bringing a child into a family many were curious as to what the child would be like. There were questions.

We are culturally a people who often demand answers and certainty in the midst of questions. When John was brought into the family, friends and neighbors assumed that the child would be named the culturally appropriate Zechariah after his dad, but Elizabeth and Zechariah said no and departed from the normative expectations of others to name the child John. When we follow God, sometimes names change and don't seem to fit, but let us not forget that we serve a God whose perfection always arrives out of the queer.

John or John the Baptist is proclaimed to be the one who will prepare the way for Jesus the Christ. The one with the queer name...who will only become queerer...is actually called the preparer of the way for the queerest of them all.

Elizabeth and Zechariah refused to succumb to normative pressure and staked their claim in a queer space in naming John.

When questions of identity come our way, will we stake our claim in the normative expectations of others or in being the queer individual that God has created us to be?

Elizabeth and Zechariah blessed their child with difference so that John might make a difference. You cannot make a difference until you are willing to be different. You cannot change normative constructions of hate and fear until you are willing to embrace the queer.

Who or what will we decide to be?

When queer things begin to happen, sometimes doubt slips in. How many people know about self-doubt and insecurity this morning? When people begin to question who or what we are, it is easy to self-question and retreat to the safe spaces of normativity.

In the second half of our Christmas story this morning, Joseph is struggling with the fact that Mary is pregnant. He knows that he didn't get her pregnant and figures that she must have cheated on him. You can insert any impossible pregnancy into this situation (including same-sex couples or individuals) and understand the picture. Things grew queerer and queerer...and Joseph flipped out.

An angel appeared to Joseph and let him know that the queer was actually God.

In the next week we will be talking about the birth of Jesus...and as the story grows queerer...let us not forget that the queer is God.

May we all embrace the queer in this special time of year.

Amen.

103.

December 15, 2013

An Invitation to Birth

***A Sermon Delivered at the Interfaith Peace Chapel**

Is there any doubt that birth is the theme of this time of year? My wife Emily and I welcomed our third child Quinley into the world just last week. We will celebrate the birth of Jesus in a few weeks. It seems that everywhere we turn there is talk of birth. Tonight will be no different. The only difference is the birth I invite you to experience and celebrate will be your own.

When we talk about birth we are talking about a beginning. Tonight I invite you back to the beginning. When we talk about birth we are talking about the perfection of a new creation. Tonight I invite you to think of your self as a perfect creation of God.

John 1:1 states, "In the beginning was the Word, the Word was with God and the Word was God." The Word can be understood as a perfect construction that is completely non-normative. That which is perfect is always queer. The Word can be understood as the Queer. "In the beginning was the Queer, the Queer was with God and the Queer was God." Let us go back to the beginning. Let us go back to the perfection. Let us go back to the Queer.

The God that is non-normative and queer or perfect beyond normative constructions created human beings in God's image. At our birth we were created by God to be queer like God or completely perfect in our unique non-normative self just like God. Perhaps the call of Jesus is a call back to this moment of queerness or perfection.

In the third chapter of John, Jesus meets an earnest seeker of God and salvation named Nicodemus and tells him that he must be born again. The phrasing "born again" has taken on many negative connotations due to the often-problematic evangelism of many Christians, but I think the phrasing need not be lost. When Jesus calls Nicodemus to be born again, Jesus is calling Nicodemus back to that queer place of perfection. Perhaps Jesus is saying...you are created perfectly and uniquely queer in the image of loving God...return to your birth and be what God has created you to be...queer. Now is the time to be born again.

The question for the baby in Bethlehem was always: Will this be the Queer the world has always longed for? The question today remains: Will we be the Queer the world so desperately longs for? The invitation to return to birth is the invitation to return to your truest being...your queerest being...and offer the world a way to love and justice.

In this holy time of year, may we have the courage to be hear the call of the baby in Bethlehem to be truly born...perhaps again...queer.

Amen.

104.

December 16, 2013

Phil Robertson and the United Methodist Church

Though I find it dreadful and disgusting, this whole Phil Robertson/Duck Dynasty controversy over the past week has not been all that shocking to me. In fact, I grew up with Phil Robertson. Not literally of course, but I have always known people like Phil who make hateful homophobic and bigoted comments and claim to be speaking the words of Jesus. In southern culture, it seems like churches founded on hateful homophobic and bigoted comments are as prevalent as kudzu or mosquitoes.

If I wanted to follow God, I knew I had to leave behind these hateful homophobic and bigoted religious spaces.

A few years ago, I graduated from the United Methodist Church's Candler School of Theology at Emory University and considered very seriously pursuing ordination in the United Methodist Church. I met with countless pastors, district superintendents and others to discern my call. In our meetings, we kept on hitting a roadblock. I simply would not commit to being silent in my support of queer people. The United Methodist Church and I ultimately parted ways.

If I wanted to follow God, I knew I had to keep leaving behind hateful homophobic and bigoted religious spaces.

I heard a really nasty hateful homophobic and bigoted statement this past week...it simply stated, "The practice of homosexuality is incompatible with Christian teaching"(http://www.umc.org/site/apps/nlnet/content3.aspx?c=lwL4KnN1LtH&b=4746363&ct=3169111). Phil Robertson didn't say these exact words...though they don't sound too far from what he did say. The words are actually from the United Methodist Church's Book of Discipline. Pennsylvania United Methodists used the words of the Book of Discipline this week to defrock (or to take away the ministry credentials of) United Methodist Pastor Frank Shaefer for the offense of performing the marriage of his son to his partner.

A few months back, I performed my first same-sex wedding. It was a beautiful and holy affair. God was in attendance. If I had stayed the former course and done so as a United Methodist minister, I would be in the same position as Frank Shaefer.

I know many United Methodists ministers who claim to be loving and inclusive of all people. With such in mind, I consistently inquire how any of these ministers can remain in a church that keeps consistently perpetuating injustices against queer people (which is sometimes their closeted self)? The answer often revolves around money...including talk of salaries, pensions and the economic power of the institution. I try to remind them every time of the rich young ruler in the scripture who stopped following Jesus because he had a salary, pension and perhaps the economic power of the institution to think about.

Regardless of the direction I would like to tell many of my United Methodist friends to go (straight to a truly inclusive religious space), I don't think that there is much difference between what many in the United Methodist Church are trying to do and what Phil Robertson does...claiming to exclude God's children in love. I want no part of it...because God is not involved such a project.

Amen.

105.

December 19, 2013

demons

many tell me they do not believe in demons
it is hard to believe in disbelief
it seems the more we try to disbelieve in demons
the more we really start to believe

i refused to believe in demons
then someone rapped and killed a child
and i changed my mind

i saw demons not in me
but in the rapist and killer
that was the monster or demon

i guess i wanted to point at them
so as not to blow the cover off the demons of hate i hide

me or you you or i us or them them or us or everyone

demons hide deep within
they are sneaky little things disguised as friend

if we are going to love our neighbor as our self
we better start with our enemy
that one we construct to be the most demonic of demons will not do
for the real demon is in me and you

how we going to love the demon when we can't love our self?

can i get an amen?

106.

December 21, 2013

Response to Being Given the 2013 Fort Worth PFLAG Equality Award

I accept the Fort Worth PFLAG Equality Award on behalf of all people who hunger and thirst for justice and righteousness. It is a truly humbling moment to be recognized as an activist and minister. These are not professions and paths one chooses for status and recognition. Nevertheless, I thank you from the deepest regions of my soul.

What an honor to be chosen for this award by PFLAG Fort Worth. You are an amazing group of people whose work inspires me and countless others. I always cherish the moments I experience in your presence.

Throughout this past year I have felt called by God to accept a deeper prophetic role in the struggle for queer equality. From protesting outside the homophobic Denton Bible Church to posting demands for open doors on the doors of every church in Denton on Ash Wednesday to writing for and granting interviews to national religious news outlets to founding and leading the only explicitly queer church I know of to leading our church to place two ads in the Denton Record Chronicle calling for queer equality to countless rallies, writings, interviews, conversations, protests and other actions, I have certainly accepted a deeper prophetic role. I have no doubt that God has lead me in all of this work...because to be honest...everything that has happened has truly been beyond my wildest dreams.

There is no doubt that God gets the credit for all of this, but on a human level I know and you need to know that none of this would be possible without the love, support and constant encouragement of my wife Emily. There is also no doubt that my little boys Jeff, Phillip and Quinley also daily provide fuel and propel my drive to make the world a better place. The Rev. Dr. Steve Sprinkle at Brite Divinity School has served as my mentor and friend throughout my work this year and I don't think any of this would have happened if it had not been for him. Lastly, I wanted to thank all of those who have been or continue to be a part of our church in Denton...without all of you none of this would have happened.

With God at my side, I can promise you I will keep acting up until we reach that day when all of humanity will no longer have to hunger and thirst for justice and righteousness and we can all be the queers we were created to be.

Amen.

107.

December 22, 2013

Bethlehem & The Way

Over two thousand years ago in a stable filled with shit, Mary cried out with loud labor pains. While all the shepherds and angels were singing in the fields outside of town, Mary was pushing out a baby. If she was anything like my wife Emily, I know there were moments that she wanted to stop. Yet Mary pushed through and gave birth. In an instance...Mary's pain turned to joy...for in her arms rested perfect hope, justice, peace and love.

Later on in life, Jesus talked about being the way. I often think about the way when I think about birth. It is almost as if each birth reminds us that the only way forward is through perfect hope, justice, peace and love. The difference is that Jesus embodied these constructions perfectly. We can call Jesus God because Jesus showed us that God is perfect hope, justice, peace and love.

I think that the baby in Bethlehem came to do much more than provide regulations...I think the baby came to provide transformation...through perfect hope, justice, peace and love. I believe that God uses the baby in Bethlehem at this time of the year to call us back to the way...the way of perfect hope, justice, peace and love.

Blessings on your way.

Amen.

108.

December 24, 2013

Embrace the Incarnation: A Christmas Message

On the way to church tonight, I drove past many churches large and small filling up with people. I would imagine that most of the pastors of these churches will begin their sermons with some variation of, "Over two thousand years ago in a town called Bethlehem a child was born..." Throughout my life, I have heard similar Christmas Eve sermons. Surprisingly, I never grow tired of them. For me, there is something quite magical about calling the attention of modern people to a specific moment in historical time and space and declaring that God was incarnate in a baby named Jesus in Bethlehem.

When you begin to tell the story of historical incarnation...all types of skepticisms arise. It offends modern sensibilities to think that a virgin might give birth. It is ludicrous to imagine the skies filling up with angels to proclaim the newborn God. It is crazy to imagine God taking the form of a human. I am not quite sure that most of you gathered here tonight because you believe such things or even because you want to believe such things. Honestly, I believe many of you came tonight because you thought there might be some love and hope here on this Christmas Eve. I think you were hopeful that there might be an incarnation for you.

I believe in incarnation. I have seen it throughout this year. Whether it was the beauty of performing the wedding of two beautiful women in our church last October or the camaraderie I experienced staying out all night Christmas shopping with one of our church members last night or the long productive counseling sessions I have experienced with so many of you or the embrace of my wife, I have been witness to the incarnation of God. God is love. When we experience love we are experiencing the incarnation of God. Is it too difficult to believe that love was present in that manger there in Bethlehem 2000 years ago? I saw the birth of my third child three weeks ago and it is not too hard for me.

If you want to debate the miracles claimed in the Bible, all you have to do is turn on your television and there will be countless prognosticators and pundits to join you. I don't think that will get you any closer to what you came here tonight to experience. I don't have all of the answers. Truthfully, there is no need for answers when you are living in the presence. I only know that God is love. I have experienced it in you. Tonight, you do not have to be afraid or search any longer...just look at the light of the candles all around and follow the light.

Embrace the mystery. Embrace the love. Embrace the incarnation.
Amen.

109.

December 30, 2013

Beyond The Language of G-O-D

This morning we celebrate and remember the visit of the wise men or wise persons or wise women or wise folks to the home of a young Jesus. The wise folks came from the east or from deeper into what we now call Asia. They followed a star in the sky with a firm belief that there was going to be something mysterious and amazing at the end of their journey.

Most nativity scenes would have you believe that these wise folks were present there with the shepherds next to the manger right after the birth of Jesus. This was not the case. Many scholars believe that the wise folks arrived to meet Jesus as late as three years after his birth. If the star appeared in the sky right when Jesus was born…then the wise folks traveled for multiple years. How far then did these wise folks travel? Could they have come all the way from Thailand or Cambodia? Could it be possible that they were Buddhist monks? Some of this is mere speculation I know…but I have often dreamed of what it means that the wise folks came from the east.

While backpacking in Cambodia a few years ago, I had a beautiful encounter. I encountered a Buddhist monk while walking along a dirt road. We talked and walked together for hours. Though we were using different words in these deeply spiritual conversations, I could not help but wonder whether we were talking about the similar things. In these moments, I began to wonder if language was keeping me from deeper experiences of the divine.

When the eastern wise folks encountered Jesus…do you think that words were sufficient to describe what they saw? It seems to me that the spark of divine that the wise folks sought and we continue to seek was and always is beyond language, name or description. This is the divine that exists in the unexplainable beauty of wild untamed moments of hope. This is the divine who is love so loving that the divine exists beyond love. This is the divine that exists beyond…

When the wise folks looked to the star and started their journey they sought the divine beyond all the language they could muster and beyond their wildest dreams…may we be wise and go and do the same.

Amen.

110.

December 31, 2013

eschatology

universal universal
perhaps this is simply a dress rehearsal
maybe all of these people who thrust hate into my time
are really just pawns in a game of divine
there is much juxtaposition you see
because between the alive and dead lies me

i exist
i am real
i am a human who knows how to feel
but in the universal where do i fit
i need to know i matter in the midst of this fucked up trip

my friend there is no need to let love slip away
for i do believe the queer has something to say

the queer in you is the queer in me
the universal context of a queer theology

theology is poetry and you must learn to rhyme
for it certainly helps to pass the drudges of time

peace or death
how many days do we have left

111.

January 5, 2014

The Baptism of Quinley Mandela Dillard Hood

This is Quinley Mandela Dillard Hood...a child of the living God.

On this day we have gathered to pour water over the head of this child as an outward symbol of an inward grace that has sealed his name and person in love for all time and beyond.

Quinley you were and will forever be created by a God that loves you.

Quinley you were and will forever be redeemed by a God that loves you.

Quinley you were and will forever be sustained by a God that loves you.

Quinley on this day I baptize you in the name of the God that created you, in the name of the God that redeems you and in the name of the God that will forever sustain you.

This is Quinley Mandela Dillard Hood...a child of the living God.

Amen.

112.

January 5, 2014

The Year of Living Dangerously: The Dangerous God

Welcome to the year of living dangerously! On this day I begin with a dangerous question...What type of God will we give Quinley? What type of God will we give to this tiny baby that we have just baptized? The answer to this or that question is the same answer to the question...What type of God will we give our self? For surely our highest wishes for this baby here should also be our highest wishes for our self. When we think about this tiny body, we want to give this child safety. When we think about our self, we want to give our self safety. Indeed in our culture safety is the top priority. That is what we think we want. Unfortunately or fortunately depending on where you sit, this sermon series is not entitled the year of living safely. I propose that we give to Quinley and to our self a God of love. Love is inherently risky and therefore dangerous.

In 1 John 4:8 the writer states clearly, "God is love." A God of love is an incredibly dangerous God. We see this lived out in the life of Jesus. You see we are not gathered this morning to pursue a safe God. The God that we talk about this morning was tortured...was lynched...was executed...was the victim of a hate crime.... and without question died. This sermon is not going to be a sermon that encourages us to pursue danger for the sake of danger...or to stay in dangerous places or situations for the sake of staying in dangerous places or situations...but rather this sermon is going to be about pursuing love for the sake of love and recognizing the inherent risk involved in love. Let us not teach safety as the primary objective in life to Quinley or our selves...but rather let us teach love.

After the death and resurrection of Jesus in John 21, Jesus asks an incredibly pertinent question to Peter three times, "Do you love me?" In many ways, the question of the divinity of Christ rests in the question of the divinity of us. The question of love is always a divine question. Throughout life we are consistently meeting the dangerous God of love that begs of us, "Do you love me?" We are consistently asking the question from our own person, "Do you love me?" This question comes from the God within...the God in whose image we are made. We want to know about love.

Let me expound on a few ways that we can take a risk on love.

This morning God is calling out to us from deep within to ask, "Do you love me?" The very body cries out, "Do you love me?" Will we dare take the risk of loving our bodies? Will we dare take the risk of loving our self? The big secret of love is that it begins with you. In Mark 12:31 Jesus commands us, "Love your neighbor as your self." While this passage is about loving your neighbor, we can't forget about the self that is included in this command. You see it is impossible for you to love your neighbor as your self if you can't learn to love your self. The dangerous God calls us to take the risk of loving our self. Every day our very body, soul and spirit calls out, "Do you love me?"

Within our relationships, God is asking the same question, "Do you love me?" Many of you this morning are in the midst of difficult struggles with people that you love and there are questions that you do not know how to answer. I think that God only asks us to know the answer to one question, "Do you love me?" I invite you to take the risk of love...even if it is for the hundredth time. Now of course sometimes it might be better to send your love through an email or through the US Postal Service or perhaps through a prayer...but do say yes to love.

In Matthew 28, Jesus states that he will inhabit the least of these or the marginalized amongst us. It is important to remember that the voices of the struggling and oppressed are the voices of God. The cardboard signs we pass that say things like "will work for food" or "help" are actually saying..."Do you love me?" The signs on the shelters and difficult spaces seeking to help people find a way out of oppression and marginalization are actually saying..."Do you love me?" Many of the neighborhoods that we passed on our way to church this morning are crying out..."Do you love me?" Throughout the world those that are oppressed politically, spiritually and economically are asking..."Do you love me?" The question of whether or not we will work for justice is a question of love. How will we respond to the needs of our world? The dangerous God asks that we bind our lives to the marginalized and oppressed. The great question of God calls us to do more..."Do you love me?"

Just this past week, I read a report that the leader of North Korea Kim Jong-Un executed his uncle by feeding him to 120 hungry dogs. There are all sorts of people all over the world destroying the lives of millions if not billions of people. In your personal lives, there are people who have wronged you or committed evil against you to the point that they have become your enemies. Jesus in Matthew 5:44 commands those that love God to also love their enemies. Today God is calling to us from the person of Kim Jong-Un and asking..."Do you love me?" Today God is calling to us from those we hate in this life and asking..."Do you love me?" The love of the dangerous God does not extend just to those we like or those who ask for it...but also to those we hate and think to be the most vile of creations. It is dangerous to love our enemies...because we give up the right to hate. God is calling to us from the mouths of our enemies..."Do you love me?"

There are many places that we might hear the great question of the dangerous God..."Do you love me?"...but today I conclude that we must take up the task/risk of making the answer to the question always yes. I know many of you came to a queer church this morning expecting a queer message...well in a world of hate the message of love is always as queer as it gets. The dangerous God calls to all of us this morning..."Do you love me?" I pray that we will teach Quinley with our lives to live dangerously...to follow the dangerous God...and to always say yes to love.

Amen.

113.

January 5, 2014

Gloria Evangelina Anzaldúa, Jesus & the Space Between

In our first gathering as a church, we spent time wrestling with what it means to be created queer in the image of a Queer God. We explored what it looks like to birth the Queer from within following the example of Jesus. We dreamed of what it looks like for the Queer Spirit to guide us in queering the world. We are a new church learning and experiencing many new things. Today, we will discuss the space from which the Queer is found…that space from which we transcend temporal normative boundaries and experience the divine in and outside of our self.

I want to share with you a reading from renowned Chicana feminist queer thinker Gloria Evangelina Anzaldúa from *this bridge we call home: radical visions for transformation*:

> "Bridges span liminal (threshold) spaces between worlds, spaces I call *nepantla*, a Nahuatl word meaning tierra entre medio. Transformations occur in this in-between space, an unstable, unpredictable, precarious, always-in-transition space lacking clear boundaries. *Nepantla* es tierra desconocida, and living in this liminal zone means being in a constant state of displacement--an uncomfortable, even alarming feeling. Most of us dwell in *nepantla* so much of the time it's become a sort of 'home.' Though this state links us to other ideas, people, and worlds, we feel threatened by these new connections and the change they engender."
>
> [Gloria Evangelina Anzaldúa & AnaLouise Keating, Gloria Evangelina Anzaldua's Preface "(Un)natural bridges, (Un)safe spaces" in *this bridge we call home: radical visions for transformation* (New York: Routledge, 2002)]

I have found the space that Anzaldua calls n*epantla* to be similar if not the same to the space that I call queer. This queer space is a bridge between spaces that lacks clear boundaries and can ultimately be the space from which we transcend boundaries. Existing in this precarious space of between means that we must claim identity based on who we are as an individual. The queer person or every person is created queer beyond identity and boundary. In order to discover the queer within and without we must travel to these border spaces beyond boundary. I believe that it is in these spaces of between that we find God. Jesus made a habit of existing and traveling in these spaces.

In John 4, Jesus meets a Samaritan woman at a well and asks her for a drink of water. This might not sound too revolutionary to you...but this was a very queer encounter. The Samaritan woman could not believe her ears...for Jews did not associate with Samaritans...you can go ahead and substitute black and white or male and female or brown and black or brown and white or gay and straight or whatever sometimes opposing constructed identities you like. Jesus pushed down the boundary and began a conversation that had eternal ramifications...because Jesus was willing to be at the border and the Samaritan woman boldly refused to leave the space. Boundaries were eliminated as Jesus and the Samaritan woman existed beyond ethnic borders and dwelled in a space of love and justice called queer. This was not the first or the last time that Jesus revealed the Queer.

In Matthew 14, Mark 6 and John 6, the disciples of Jesus see a figure walking across the Sea of Galilee in the midst of a storm. Jesus called to the disciples and Peter got out of the boat and walked on water toward Jesus. In the space between the natural and the supernatural, Jesus called to Peter and they both stood in a queer space. Unfortunately, the space became too frightening for Peter and he began to sink. The danger of running away from that which we are afraid is that we often lose our footing in the space called queer. In the queer space between the natural and supernatural, Jesus calls all people to get out of the boat and find the queer within and without as they walk on water. Jesus was not afraid to step into the storm and nor should we be...for it is in those spaces of fear that the divine is revealed. I believe that Jesus teaches us to push into and past fear...and thus reveal the queer.

Jesus was not afraid to be...queer...and nor should we.

Amen.

114.

January 9, 2014

Empathy is An Act of Imagination

Empathy is a challenging word. What does it mean to attempt to take on the feelings and pain of another? I was sitting at an event in Dallas tonight when someone declared empathy to be an act of imagination. I was moved by these words and wondered where I lack imaginative empathy. I think it is true that if we begin to empathize and thus struggle with others then we are able to free our self from the self. Those who remain trapped in selfishness are trapped by their own lack of imagination. Maybe empathy can break down barriers and we can help those whose minds and hearts our blocked. Maybe together we can imagine our hearts changed toward those we hate and who hate us... the enemies...so that peace might be known now in a world of hurt. We pray that we might gain the imaginative power to empathize with our neighbors and our enemies as freely and graciously as we empathize with our self...in the name of the Creator, Redeemer and Sustainer.

Amen.

115.

January 11, 2013

1 Corinthians 13:13

in the end these three remain

faith
fullness of finding
assuming no answers
intensities of impossibilities
total transformations
highlighting the hidden

hope
heal the hate
opposition to oppression
past power
equalities for everywhere

love
laugh the loudest
opportunities for the other
victorious vastness
effective beyond earth

but the greatest of these is

love
last
of
varied
earths

116.

January 13, 2014

I am, Ground of Being and the Courage to Be: A Dangerous Proposition

The dying can really teach the living the power of being. Then again, I guess we are all dying whether we grasp it or not. Perhaps in this moment of time, we might all be better served if we were dying. For in the realization that we are dying, we gain an ability to truly live. This is a sermon about pushing past fear to a space of being.

The great theologian Paul Tillich spoke of gaining the courage to be. In a world that encourages normalization that creates masses of posers and imposters, actually being you or having the courage to be is a very countercultural and dangerous act. But being is of utmost importance to the spiritual journey. Tillich often speaks of having the courage to pursue the God that is beyond God. I think the journey to meet that God starts within. I am channeling Tillich when I say...when we have the courage to leave all behind and reach the ground of our being...then we shall meet that which is the ground of all being.

It is interesting that throughout scripture God is the most self-actualized of all. Numerous times God simply describes God's self as "I am." I believe that God calls us to the same boldness. To the boldness of "I am."

In John 14:7, Jesus declares, "I am the way, and the truth, and the life." Jesus claims exactly who Jesus is and we are called to do the same. Why are we so frightened to simply be who we are? Why do we live frightened? The answer is that we value safety over being. We would rather be safe than real. This is not the life that Jesus has called us to.

In Mark 10: 17-27, Jesus encounters a rich young ruler. The ruler asks about eternal life. Jesus tells him that the rich young ruler knows the commandments. The rich young ruler claims that he has kept all of them. Jesus asks him to sell all that he has and give the proceeds to the poor. The rich young ruler turned from following Jesus, because he was very rich.

The rich young ruler treasured the safety of his possessions more than he valued true being or being with God. When we cling to that which makes us safe rather than that which makes us most fully alive...we are no different than the rich young ruler. We often can't know who we are because we are clinging so tightly to everything else or all the illusions. How many of us would rather be safe than have the courage to be...to follow God...to be real? This morning...I invite you to let go and embrace your ground of being. I invite you to speak the words of God and declare, "I am." I invite you to be and God will join you there.
Amen.

117.

January 13, 2014

Stay Awake With Me

It is a beautiful thing to be gathered here with you this evening around the light of candles. It feels like we are staying awake together.

With torture and execution looming, Jesus is in anguish in the Garden of Gethsemane and requests that the disciples stay awake in Matthew 26. When Jesus needs the disciples the most, the disciples keep falling asleep. Ultimately, the disciples just can't stay awake and it adds to Jesus' anguish.

In this queer space that we are attempting to create together...a space where everyone can be exactly who God created them to be. The great question is will we stay awake?

When we are tempted to turn back from who and what God has made us to be...will we follow God or we turn away from God and follow our own path? Will we stay awake with God?

When we open our mouths and express who we are as individuals...and people are disturbed by our lack of normativity...will we stand beside each other as the insults and violence flies? Will we stay awake with each other?

When we begin to open up to each other in this space and become disturbed by what someone else has said...will we have the courage to sit with that person and try to understand where they are coming from? Will we stay awake with them?

When the world is spiraling out of control...will we have the courage to stay awake and be the voice of justice?

When we begin to open up and express who we are...will we have the courage to push past what others might think of us? Will we stay awake with our self?

I pray that this will be a space where we serve our self, each other, our world and God with eyes wide open. If we stay awake...it will be dangerous...but God is there waiting to join us in the task of love.

In time, God will lead us through the fear to a space called queer. God is calling us to stay awake.

Will you stay awake with me?
Amen.

118.

January 16, 2014

Jesus the Atheist : Beyond the God of Theism : A Response to "A Year Without God" former pastor Ryan J. Bell

Back in college, I went on a few dates with a woman that I assumed was a Christian...as it is statistically safe to assume that just about everyone you meet in Auburn, Alabama is a Christian. After a fewc dates, I began to talk in flowery language about my dedication and love for Jesus. This woman looked at me like I had lost my mind and replied, "You know I am an atheist." I freaked out. I drove as fast as I could to get her home, out of my car and out of my life. As she left the car, I apologized and told her that I just couldn't date an atheist. I got home and prayed that god would forgive me for spending romantic time with one of his enemies. Before my world began to widen and my heart softened, the only way I knew to interact with atheism was to run like hell or something like that.

Over the past few weeks, I have been following the journey of former Christian pastor and professor Ryan J. Bell, who in announcing his "A Year Without God" (or his year to leave God or Jesus behind and try out atheism) has made a major splash in the news (http://religion.blogs.cnn.com/2014/01/08/pastor-learns-the-price-of-atheism/). When I first heard Bell interviewed, I was struck by his sincerity and courage in stepping away from the safety net of traditional theism and I began to ponder his chosen journey. Unfortunately, I have come to the conclusion that Bell's sincere experiment fails at the misguided binary where it began. I don't think that the true follower of Jesus is ever a theist.

The god in the biblical Book of Deuteronomy commands the Jews to slaughter the Canaanites. I am an atheist when it comes to a god that would command genocide. The god in the biblical Book of Leviticus commands the stoning of gay men. I am an atheist when it comes to a god that would command the stoning of anyone. The god in the Letters of the Apostle Paul condemns homosexuality, promotes the sexist mistreatment of women and gives guidance for a humane human slavery. I am an atheist when it comes to a god that would bless such statements. Throughout the centuries, the Christian Church has claimed that god encourages, promotes and gives blessing to sexism, classism, genderism, racism, homophobia, slavery, war, intolerance, hate, violence and a whole litany of evil practices. I am simply an atheist when it comes to such a god. I am in good company.

Jesus commanded us to love our neighbor as our self not to commit genocide. Jesus commanded us to love our neighbor as our self not to stone gay men. Jesus commanded us to love our neighbor as our self not to exclude homosexuals, oppress women or enslave our neighbors.

Jesus commanded us to love our neighbor as our self not to oppress and commit injustices against our neighbor.
So I guess Jesus was and is an atheist too.

Jesus sought and found the divine that was and is beyond a traditionally constructed god...the indescribable uncontainable God beyond god. Jesus pushed aside numerous traditions and demanded more...even daring to command a love beyond traditional concepts of love. Jesus was an atheist with regards to the limited constructed gods of theism...and I think we should dare to be the same.

Surprisingly in leaving theism, perhaps Ryan J. Bell is now more a follower of Jesus than he ever was before.

Amen.

119.

January 18, 2014

A Prayer from the Dr. Martin Luther King, Jr. Parade in Dallas, Texas

God we gather to honor the legacy of your son...the great purveyor of peace and justice Dr. Martin Luther King, Jr.
On this day, let our minds and hearts be not far from Dr. King's eschatological notion of a Beloved Community...that magical and majestic space where all people are ushered into a community of love and justice
But also let us not fail to realize that such a Beloved Community begins deep within us
We must learn to love our neighbor as our self
Even more we must learn to love our enemies
Even more we must learn to love our enemies as our self
For in loving our enemies as our self we begin to realize that our enemy is most often within our self
The Beloved Community begins within
Let us realize that we are the racism and prejudice we wish to see overcome
Let us realize that we are the mysogyny, sexism and patriarchy we wish to see eradicated
Let us realize that we are the classism and economic inequalities we wish to see made right
Let us realize that we are the homophobia and genderism that we wish to see eliminated
O God may we be brave and humble enough to realize that we are just as much the source of evil as anyone we try to hate
So in the spirit of Dr. Martin Luther King, Jr. let us love our enemies as our self and...as we clean up our own lives...may we see the fruition of peace there in the Beloved Community...where we can join all of humanity in declaring that we truly are free of evil at last
We pray these things for our hardened hearts who often fail to see our culpability in the crimes against humanity we wage every day
In the name of Jesus of Nazareth who Dr. Martin Luther King, Jr. so majestically served

Amen

120.

January 19, 2014

The Year of Living Dangerously: Loving Your Enemy or Jumping in the Gelatin Dessert

The nation will stop to celebrate the life and legacy of Dr. Martin Luther King, Jr. tomorrow and on this day I intend for us to do the same. Dr. King spoke often of a beloved community...a place of economic and social justice where people are reconciled to each other in love...this morning we are going to talk about how the journey to that space of beloved community begins with the enemy and ends with you or me or us. I intend to honor the legacy of Dr. Martin Luther King, Jr. by focusing on one of the chief teachings of the Jesus that he served...loving your enemy.

We live dark spaces of injustice that are often not all that different from the space of injustice that Jesus experienced in the last few days of Jesus' life. Just like Jesus, many of the greatest social prophets of our time have been silenced and sometimes killed. Nevertheless, I want to concentrate on three principle actors from the last few days of Jesus' life to illustrate the principle of loving your enemy...Judas, Peter and the actions of Jesus.

We all have our enemies. On many days, I believe that I might have been blessed with more than my fair share...but I digress. It seems that the more you speak out and demand change in the way that populations act and think...the more you have to worry about the Judases of the world. The more you push the slack of inaction and indifference the more you have to worry about those that you love the most revealing a knife from behind their back. When you challenge the status quo there will be Judases. Perhaps it is even true that the number of Judases you have in your life is indicative of the level of work that you are doing and the good you are accomplishing. Many of us know the feeling of standing at the height of our success... and then looking around the room knowing that everyone else has knives behind their backs and not knowing who is going to stab you first. How do we remain to be love in such circumstance?

After taking some coins for his work, Judas betrayed Jesus with a kiss...in order to let the gathered government officials and authorities present know exactly who Jesus was. A kiss is intimate. Jesus could have smelled the breath of Judas. How many of us have been betrayed by those we love? How many of us have been to hell and back with those we expected to love us forever? How many of us have gone on a journey of a love that seemed indestructible and brought back nothing but broken memories? Love can sometimes be a dangerous thing...but it also our salvation.

We could sit here for a long time and talk about Judas' faults...but let us also remember one key point...if God is love...then the actions of Judas should not overwhelm the outcome for Judas. Ultimately, Judas commits suicide by hanging. Obviously, the grief of Judas was great. In such a situation or even in any situation, I cannot imagine a God that asks us to love our enemies to not keep such a command.

I know many of you do not believe in heaven...but I ask that you appease me for a second. I want you to imagine going to heaven and meeting Jesus. Then all of a sudden a few people walk up and then some more...and they all seem vaguely familiar. Jesus says I want to introduce you to a few of my enemies that I have loved and reconciled with. This is Judas. This is Adolf Hitler. This is Jeffrey Dahmer. This is the person that oppressed you. This is the person that abused you. This is the bully. On and on and on...until we begin to realize that the love of God must be big enough to change the hearts and souls of us all. I believe in a God whose love is that big. Let us join God in the process of dreaming about the potential for loving and being reconciled to our enemies.

On the same night of Judas' kiss came Peter's cut...you see Peter was a macho man and when Jesus was being arrested...Peter fought back. Peter pulled out his sword and sliced off the ear of Malchus...one of the government officials present. Jesus healed the ear and told Peter, "Those who live by the sword will die by the sword." The more I think about this series of events...the more I think that we too cut off people's ears and destroy our own lives as a result. You see when we monsterize someone and hate them we silence them by refusing to listen to anything they say and then we damage the relationship so that they no longer are willing or can hear what we have to say....we cut off the ears. When people cannot talk or hear each other then the relationship is damaged beyond repair and then the death of love comes quickly. I think that our task is the task of Jesus. Our task is to heal the ears of people so that they might learn to hear the love of those they thought were their enemies again. When you love your enemies...you become a healer and not a slicer my friends. This interaction also reminds us that we cannot love our enemies with weapons in our mouths or hands...our mouths and hands must be used for healing.

When Jesus hung on the cross...blood dripping from all the wounds and abuse the body of Jesus endured...Jesus looked out and asked God to forgive all of those who put him through this hell. The ultimate example of love is to love those who are oppressing, abusing and killing you. This is how you fight for justice...you love your way out of oppression. May we live like Jesus and believe that love can heal the world.

Now all of this sounds beautiful, wonderful and all...but the message of loving your enemies doesn't stop at those we call other...it ends with us. Thomas Merton in his brilliant essay "The Root of War is Fear" writes, "So instead of loving what you think is peace, love other men and love God above all. And instead of hating the people you think are warmongers, hate the appetites and the disorder in your own soul, which are the causes of war. If you love peace, then hate injustice, hate tyranny, hate greed--but hate these things in yourself not in another." Only when we learn to love our self will be able to love our neighbors and enemies as our self. Forgive your self and have grace for your self so that you might forgive and have grace for others. To paraphrase Merton's "The Root of War is Fear" once more, "It is as if the entire world is walking around with a gun in their hand and no one knows if they are going to shoot their self or someone else first." This morning I invite you to put down your guns. We talk so often about the shooting massacres that have happened all over the world...but we fail to talk about the massacres of hate we perpetuate in our own lives and souls every day. Stop the shooting and put down your guns. You can have peace within and without no matter the circumstance if you will root your self deeply in God and love. Let us go to that space...

Imagine you are in a giant tub full of gelatin dessert and the gelatin moving all around you is love. It is oozing into all of your pores and it has just engulfed you. The feeling you get from it is absolutely electrifying... it is the most amazing thing that you can imagine. You cannot figure out where the source of all of this love is coming from and then you realize that all of your enemies are around you...but the difference is they are no longer your enemies they are the source of all of this electric love and you their electric love. Your former enemies are so close that you can feel the warmth of their love and they you. Everyone is electrified because they chose love and not hate. This is an imaginative representation of a world that begins to gel in love...a world where loving enemies and pushing for reconciliation is valued above all else.

When we begin to love our enemies we quickly find that many of them reside within our own person. So on this day let us start to love our enemies...may we look to them as a representation of what lies within and may we choose love for both.

Amen.

121.

January 19, 2014

Gone to Mixing

Yesterday, I marched with the Texas Coalition to Abolish the Death Penalty in the Dr. Martin Luther King, Jr. Parade here in Dallas, Texas. As the parade got congested and slowed almost to a stop, I took the opportunity to get a different experience and leave the parade route to enter into the areas where people were watching the parade. As I was standing on a sidewalk, a woman came up to me and asked, "Are you from New York?" Taken aback, I replied, "No ma'am. I am not. Why do you ask?" "Well sugar here in Dallas the whites and blacks don't mix. Where exactly are you from?" she pushed. "I grew up on the Southside of Atlanta," I offered. "That explains it. You are ahead of the game...you really know how to mix. Well, it was a pleasure to talk to you...and oh yeah...keep on mixing," she said as she smiled and walked away. This short conversation spoke to me in a way that a million sermons have not. There is much truth to be found in mixing.

When we are brave enough to go to those queer spaces of borders and boundaries...we find that it is in that space that mixing occurs. When we get to mixing we find ourselves able to transcend borders and boundaries that have held us back from our self and those we call other. We leave group identity behind as we mix with others to create higher communities that value the unique differences of individuals above all else. My talk tonight is about mixing.

When we decide to get mixed up in the work of God we often find our persons in strange spaces that transcend what we know or what is known. When we cling most tightly to only want we know or what is known and refuse to allow room for mystery...it is difficult to mix with God. In order to mix with God we must be willing to travel to that space between the earthly and the divine...into the unknown or mysterious...that space where God is beyond name and being. I pray that we will be willing to mix into our lives a belief in love beyond love or the God beyond God...or simply mystery.

The dream of Dr. Martin Luther King, Jr. was that all individuals would go to mixing. If God is in all of us or if we are all created in the image of God, then there is something quite divine when two people cross boundaries and borders to come together...images of God crashing into one another...creating mixed up mosaic representations here on earth of the divine.

When we move to those borders or spaces of between we meet people who are strangely familiar...perhaps because they were made in the image of God too...even though they are another identity, orientation, nationality, color or anything else you might call other...and we can both hear in that space a strange voice calling us to get to mixing. That voice is the voice of love...the voice of the originator of mixing...the voice of God. If we are to be the beloved community then we must get to mixing.

Certainly we cannot finish any talk about mixing without talking about those we think are our enemies. If we are children of God, then we are all bone of bone and flesh of flesh of each other. What if we began to see our self in those we hate? What if we started to get all mixed up and love our enemy as our self? What if we followed the example of Jesus and offered grace no matter what the crime? What if we really got to mixing with our enemies? It seems like they wouldn't be enemies for long...ultimately they would become a part of us and us a part of them. My God think of the possibilities if we just got to mixing.

Jesus was not afraid to mix. Thus is the message of that queer notion of incarnation...when God comes to earth and gets all mixed up in what is going on down here. What does it mean for us to be incarnational? It means for us to be the queer individual that God created us to be...and then to go and start mixing with the other images that all around us...until we reach that community in which all of God's queers are able to be called and call each other beloved.

...and all the people shouted...

Amen.

122.

January 22, 2014

Love Your Neighbor: The Case of Edgar Arias Tamayo

Take a long look at this man. His name is Edgar Arias Tamayo and he is a native of Mexico. Mr. Tamayo was convicted of killing Houston Police Officer Guy Gaddis with three shots to the back of his head inside of a police cruiser. No matter what you think about him or the crime he was convicted of, it is important to remember that Mr. Tamayo is a child of God.

Tonight, Mr. Tamayo was granted a last minute reprieve from the United States Supreme Court to halt his execution in the State of Texas. Without the reprieve, the State of Texas would have executed Mr. Tamayo around 6pm. There is no guarantee that Mr. Tamayo will not be executed tonight...especially if the Supreme Court denies Mr. Tamayo's appeal before midnight. In the uncertainty of this moment, I thought I would take this opportunity to write a few words about my neighbor.

Thousands of years prior to the life of Mr. Tamayo perilously dangling between life and death, a man named Jesus of Nazareth gave a simple command, "love your neighbor as your self."

Today, based on Mr. Tamayo's lack of access to Mexican legal counsel assistance, which is guaranteed in a provision of the 1963 Vienna Convention on Consular Relations, his lawyers along with the Mexican government argued for his execution to be halted. Tonight, there are many who would argue that those of us who reside in the State of Texas failed to love our neighbor as our self by not guaranteeing or demanding Mr. Tamayo receive the legal representation that he is legally entitled to under international law. Those who would make such an argument would of course be correct...but there is a simpler truth to be found.

The truth is that if we are to love our neighbor as our self or love our enemy then it is quite logical that we should refrain from trying to kill them. Those who lead and the large majority of those who inhabit the State of Texas claim to be Christians...yet every time someone is executed in this state we disobey a basic command of the God that we claim to serve...to love each other...even those that are deemed unlovable.

For many tonight the case of Edgar Arias Tamayo is clear, a man from Mexico should be executed for killing Houston Police Officer Guy Gaddis. For me tonight the case of Edgar Arias Tamayo is clear as well, we are called to love our neighbor not to kill them.

May it be so.

Amen.

Update: Edgar Arias Tamayo was executed by the State of Texas on Wednesday Jan 22, 2014 at 9:32pm. May the grace and love of God be with him for all of eternity.

123.

January 25, 2014

North Texas Fellowship of Reconciliation: A Beginning Benediction

In the folk religion of Japan, it is often the case that the stranger to the village brings truth, love and divinity. The stranger the village is often suspicious of brings life changing surprises and revelations. And so it is, on this day we gather in a strange place to seek to accomplish strange feats desperately desiring to be guided by that still small voice of the stranger. In this moment, may we not be afraid to listen to the voices of the strangers in our midst. May we not be afraid to follow the voice of the stranger leading us to strange places. May we not turn back when the voice of the stranger calls us to do strange things. Let us follow the stranger. In the founding of the North Texas Fellowship of Reconciliation, may we be known as strangers that are bold in our commitment to love and justice. In a world of violence and oppression, let us listen to and follow the stranger as we become strangers in the midst of the strange people we are called to be.

Amen.

124.

January 27, 2014

The Year of Living Dangerously: ...on the Bible

Since the various early councils to construct a cannon or scripture, the Bible has often been a tool of great evil. This morning, let's do a quick run through of some evil things that the Bible says. In addition to these initial passages, all of the further passages I read will be from the New Revised Standard Version of the Bible.

On homosexuality:

Leviticus 20:33: "If a man lies with a male as with a woman, both of them have committed an abomination; they shall be put to death; their blood is upon them."

On genocide:

Deuteronomy 7:1-2: "When the Lord your God brings you into the land that you are about to enter and occupy, and he clears away many nations before you—the Hittites, the Girgashites, the Amorites, the Canaanites, the Perizzites, the Hivites, and the Jebusites, seven nations mightier and more numerous than you—and when the Lord your God gives them over to you and you defeat them, then you must utterly destroy them. Make no covenant with them and show them no mercy."
Deuteronomy 20:16-18: "But as for the towns of these peoples that the Lord your God is giving you as an inheritance, you must not let anything that breathes remain alive. You shall annihilate them—the Hittites and the Amorites, the Canaanites and the Perizzites, the Hivites and the Jebusites—just as the Lord your God has commanded, so that they may not teach you to do all the abhorrent things that they do for their gods, and you thus sin against the Lord your God."

On slavery:

Exodus 21:20-21: "When a slaveowner strikes a male or female slave with a rod and the slave dies immediately, the owner shall be punished. But if the slave survives a day or two, there is no punishment; for the slave is the owner's property."

Ephesians 6:5: "Slaves, obey your earthly masters with fear and trembling, in singleness of heart, as you obey Christ..."

On the oppression of women:

1 Timothy 2:11-14: "Let a woman learn in silence with full submission. I permit no woman to teach or to have authority over a man; she is to keep silent. For Adam was

formed first, then Eve; and Adam was not deceived, but the woman was deceived and became a transgressor."

1 Corinthians 11:3: "But I want you to understand that Christ is the head of every man, and the husband is the head of his wife, and God is the head of Christ."

On the death of rape victims:

Deuteronomy 22:23-24: "If there is a young woman, a virgin already engaged to be married, and a man meets her in the town and lies with her, you shall bring both of them to the gate of that town and stone them to death, the young woman because she did not cry for help in the town and the man because he violated his neighbor's wife. So you shall purge the evil from your midst."

Obviously, these passages are pretty heinous. The words combine to create a world where oppression of others is expected and commanded by God. There are many who would quibble at the exact meaning of the above and many other evil passages of scripture and try to explain away based on context and original language, but for me it is hard to explain away genocide, homophobia, sexism and other obvious evils contained in the scriptures. So how in the hell do we interact with scriptures every Sunday morning and produce a space as inclusive as we currently sit in? The answer lies in our hermeneutical approach to scripture.

The word hermeneutic refers to how we interpret the scriptures. Our main hermeneutical approach in this space is love. I believe that the scriptures exist to educate us on the ways of love or the ways of God...for in the words of 1 John 4:8: "...God is love." Jesus encourages such a hermeneutical approach in Matthew 22:36-40: "'Teacher, which commandment in the law is the greatest?' He said to him, 'You shall love the Lord your God with all your heart, and with all your soul, and with all your mind. This is the greatest and first commandment. And a second is like it: 'You shall love your neighbor as yourself.' On these two commandments hang all the law and the prophets." Love is the message of Jesus. Jesus even demands in Matthew 5:44: "Love your enemies." If love is the core of the message of Jesus and Jesus is the core of message of God then we have to assume that that which falls out of the message of love is not a part of the message of God to us in scripture.

On homosexuality, using the hermeneutic of love...I do not believe you can love your neighbor as your self and deny their sexuality. I believe that God is for love.

On genocide, using the hermeneutic of love...I do not believe you can pillage and eradicate entire races of people in a loving way.

On slavery, using the hermeneutic of love... I do not believe that you can love your neighbor and enslave them at the same time.

On the oppression of women, using the hermeneutic of love...I do not believe that you can treat one sex different from the other and do so in love.

On the double victimization of rape victims, using the hermeneutic of love...I do not believe that you can lovingly kill someone for being raped.

On all the other evil contained in the Bible, using the hermeneutic of love...I believe there are passages and stories in scripture that are not loving and in turn are not of God.

Scripture exists to magnify the God who calls God's self love.

Love is the hermeneutic we must employ.

There is tremendous beauty in the Bible...but such beauty can only be found through reading the text through the lens of love.

Before I conclude, there will be those who read this sermon online in the next few days and get disturbed...perhaps even disgusted. I want to send them a message...I love you more than I love a book...which is why I feel the need to tell you...if the first words out of your mouth are always Leviticus says and not I love you then you don't understanding what the word of God is for. The word of God is for helping us love God and others...if it keeps you from doing either then perhaps you need to put it down for a little while.

May love not just be our hermeneutic for the Bible...but also for all that we encounter.

Amen.

125.

January 28, 2014

The Terminal

Not all that long ago, I spoke on the phone with a friend of mine back home in Georgia. After a few moments, my friend informed me that her beloved grandmother had terminal cancer. After a few moments of tears and grief, I declared, "Well, I guess the truth of the matter is that we are all terminal."

Life in the physical sense is always terminal. The truth is that we all die. Death is a known quantity. However, I think the bigger question is: Will we all live? It seems that most people waste their lives with things that matter very little to them or others. It seems that most people simply don't live they just exist. If our disposition to life is ever going to change then we must arrive at the terminal. If we are to truly live...If we are to fill life with life...then we must remember that life is terminal and we must put meaningful life into the time that we have...we must arrive at the terminal.

We have spoken often about the need to leave behind the identities, borders and boundaries to go to the borderland where we can be the queer that God has created us to be. That borderland between all the identities, borders and boundaries imposed on us is the terminal that can take us to other places. The terminal is a place of transit that can take us to higher places of living. When we realize that all of these categories, binaries and dualisms that we try to keep up are all fading away, we gain the freedom to transcend them and be the unique queer that God has made us to be. In the realization that life is terminal and so are all these useless categories...we start to learn how to live as God meant us to live...as us.

I believe in resurrection. If we dare go to the terminal...that place of transit...I believe that Jesus can resurrect our lives and bring us to a place of true living.

Jesus challenges us as such in Matthew 6:30, "And if God cares so wonderfully for flowers that are here today and gone tomorrow, won't God more surely care for you?"

Have courage my friends...let go...you will be cared for...and embrace the terminal.

Amen.

126.

January 29, 2014

The Beginning: North Texas Fellowship of Reconciliation

On the 30th of December 2006, I collapsed to the floor of my room in tears. I knew I wasn't supposed to be crying. I was a few weeks away from beginning my first semester at The Southern Baptist Theological Seminary in Louisville, Kentucky. I was supposed to believe that God brings about absolute vengeance and retribution...yet there I was on the ground crying. I had never known Saddam Hussein, but I did believe he was a murdering genocidal dictator. So as the world cheered his execution, why was I crying? I guess I was crying because I was just bold enough to believe that when Jesus declared that I should love my enemies...he also meant Saddam Hussein. This was the moment I began to believe that violence has no place in the life of the follower of Jesus. Since that moment, my commitment to love and reconciliation instead of violence has only deepened.

When I tell people that I am committed to non-violence and peacemaking, the conversation always immediately turns to the "What would you do if someone came into your house with a gun and threatened your family?" question. I respond in the only way I know how, "I am not a situational ethicist." These words highlight my firm belief that our situation cannot dictate our ethics. We must decide before the situation comes what we believe to be truth and not allow the situation to tell us what is truth. Jesus told me to love my neighbor as my self and to love my enemies. That is my truth. I cannot live out that truth and commit violence. Love is truth and I am committed to it.

The North Texas Fellowship of Reconciliation draws persons together from different faith backgrounds who have come to the conclusion that violence is spiritually incompatible with love and peace. In the blogs and essays that will appear every week on northtexasfor.com, members of the North Texas Fellowship of Reconciliation will seek to respond in a non-violent way to the most pressing social justice issues of our time. We are all painfully aware of the cost of violence and we are simply no longer willing to wage it. For us, love is truth and we are committed to it.

in expectation of a brilliant peace,

Rev. Jeff Hood
editor and organizer, North Texas Fellowship of Reconciliation

127.

February 2, 2014

Phillip Seymour Hoffman, Us and the Denial of Death

Phillip Seymour Hoffman was found dead earlier today with a needle in his arm and emptied bags of heroin littered around him. The temptation will be for all of us to distance ourselves from his death by arguing that we live so much cleaner than he did. If we succumb to such temptation, we will not be the alone. It seems that all of us try to turn our heads and immune ourselves from death.

The death of Hoffman is a tragedy. Hoffman was brilliant and one of the greatest actors of our time. We should all be devastated. Unfortunately, we don't have the time or energy to feel such emotion. We had to get to the Super Bowl.

After multiple mindless hours of watching the Seattle Seahawks destroy the Denver Broncos, we will all go to bed and wake up in the morning to go to the jobs that help us mindlessly pass through our lives. Forget actually living, there are simple too many other things to do.

The greatest tragedy in the death of Phillip Seymour Hoffman is that most of us will refuse to allow it to teach us that life is short and death will come for all of us. I pray that we will stop living as if death is never coming and fill each day with all that we are.

I will miss Phillip Seymour Hoffman.

I don't want to miss you.

Amen.

128.

February 3, 2014

somewhere to lay my head

jesus had nowhere to lay her head
mary had nowhere to lay his head
peter had nowhere to lay her head
martha had nowhere to lay his head
john had nowhere to lay her head
elizabeth had nowhere to lay his head
you othered me
now i too have nowhere to lay my head

129.

February 3, 2014

being and healing: responding to the call

John the Baptist called out from the wilderness to make a way for Jesus. You see it is important as we begin to make our way through the Gospel of Mark that John the Baptist is the fulcrum of the entire story. John the Baptist sets the stage. John the Baptist made the way from the wilderness. John the Baptist called out Jesus' name.

This morning as we begin Black History Month, I am reminded of my upbringing on the Southside of Atlanta. As a young man one Sunday, I remember sitting at a large predominately black church and being moved beyond words when the pastor looked straight into my eyes...yea perhaps even my soul...and loudly declared, "somebody is calling your name."

We all have our own John the Baptists that are walking around...those voices that are calling us to our destiny. Jesus was moved to be Jesus because John the Baptist was calling his name. John the Baptist brought Jesus to his destiny.

Will we listen to those voices that are calling us to our destiny? Will we listen to those who call out our name?

Perhaps an even greater question is...when we call the names of others will we call their names to call them to their destiny or will we call their names to slander and hurt them? There are many who cannot hear their name being called to higher and greater things because they drowned out such words with all the shit they keep talking about everybody else. Are you going to be a life giver or a life taker?

There is nothing queerer than to love people and help them live into their queerness.

John the Baptist baptized Jesus and the heavens opened up. Jesus accepted exactly who God created Jesus to be and the heavens opened up. If you will respond to the call of God to simply be who God created you to be and live into your destiny...then you will have the otherworldly experience of the heavens opening up. Do you want the heavens to open up in your life? Respond to the call of God to be who God has created you to be and live without the fear of not being normal. Be my friends just be you. God is there.

After Jesus accepts Jesus destiny...just like when we start to accept our own purposes and destiny...there was and will always be the temptation to turn back. I am sure you have heard such words...you are never going to make any money doing that...your major will never get you a job...that sounds crazy...you might as well go ahead and get divorced...go back to the places that are safe. Don't turn back! Don't turn back! Don't turn back my friend! We all need you to be you. We need you to be who God has called you to be.

If we keep going, we will begin to realize that there is a crowd of people who are following us. When we have the courage to be, there will be many who want to know the secret of our being. Jesus began to collect disciples after Jesus responded to the divine call to be, embraced who he was called to be and pushed through the temptation to turn back. Can you imagine if Jesus had turned back? Jesus pushed through to become and became exactly who the people needed Jesus to be. Where are you at right now? What are you becoming? Who's following you?

The entire end of the first chapter of the Gospel of Mark is filled with healing. The healing comes from being. The evil spirit shouts out, "I know that is you Jesus! Leave me alone." Jesus confronted evil by simply being. I want us to live in such a way that all the evildoers in this world are convicted in their evil at our mere presence. I think this can happen when we have the courage to be and live into who God has called us to be. Later, Jesus heals a leper. Leprosy was the social stigma of the era. Will we be the people who heal the social stigmas of our era by being who we are called by God to be and encouraging others to be the same? Will we be the destroyers of social stigmas? Will we be the ones who heal in love? Will we open doors for all people and invite them in?

Do you choose to live in a way that heals your self and others? Do you choose to be?

It begins with listening to those who are calling your name, accepting your destiny, pushing through the temptation to not be and joining in the restorative healing of all things.

Do you choose to live in a way that heals your self and others? Do you choose to be?

Go in love. Go in love. Go in love. Go in love.

Amen.

130.

February 3, 2014

the ice pellets on the head of God: reimagining church

The weather is difficult this evening. We slipped and slid a bit on our drive down. The wind, rain and ice are brutally cold. This does not seem to be a night where we could experience a good conversation outside much less the divine. However, I think Jesus is found out in the elements on nights like tonight.

Imagine Mary and Joseph as street people. Imagine Mary birthing Jesus behind the same dumpster that earlier the family had dug around in for food. Imagine pellets of ice hitting the newborn Jesus' head.

In Matthew 25, Jesus declares, "What you have done to the least of these you have done to me." I want to be with Jesus. I want to be with the least. I think both Jesus and the least are out there freezing their asses off tonight. Will we go and be with them? Will we brave the elements to have an encounter with the divine?

In just a second, we are going to discuss what it looks like to become a church without walls that happens out there amongst the people. I have increasingly come to a place where I believe we miss Jesus because we are afraid to leave the safety of the walls and boundaries we have created. Now is the time to   May God grant us the courage and strength to be where God is.

Amen.

131.

February 4, 2014

air: who in needs it anyway? / a short tale from the city with the worst air quality in Texas...Denton

Denton is tied with Houston as having the worst air quality in Texas. Tonight, I sat through a Denton City Council meeting during the course of which I heard citizen after citizen speak about physical ailments caused by poor local air quality. The cause of the pollution is no mystery...there is drilling or fracking all over the city. The top agenda item at the Denton City Council meeting tonight was about a 30-day pause in new drilling. This sounds ok at first hearing...but the problem is it does nothing to alleviate the suffering of those who already have these drills so close to their houses or the rest of us who have to keep breathing this horrible air. Most of us in the room wanted a moratorium on all drilling in the City of Denton. We didn't get it. We got a 30-day pause that means nothing and will probably be ignored by the drilling companies. Denton is tied with Houston as having the worst air quality in Texas. air: who needs it anyway?

Source:
Why Denton's Air Quality is the Worst in Texas
http://blogs.dallasobserver.com/unfairpark/2013/11/not_ready_why_does_denton_coun.php

132.

February 5, 2014

Suzanne Basso. Take a second and repeat that name. Suzanne Basso.

Suzanne Basso was sentenced to death for the 1998 slaying of Buddy Musso. The body of Buddy Musso was found in a ditch lacerated, covered in bleach and scrapped with a wire brush. There is also evidence that Suzanne Basso made herself the beneficiary of Buddy Musso's insurance policies and Social Security benefits. Tonight at 6pm, Suzanne Basso is to be given a lethal dose of chemicals and put to death by us...the citizens of the State of Texas.

Suzanne Basso. Take a second and repeat that name. Suzanne Basso.

Is it possible...even after all the crimes she was convicted of...Suzanne Basso is still a human being created in the image of God and loved by God just like the rest of us? Tonight, those whose hearts seek vengeance will have to answer no, turn their eyes away and call Suzanne Basso a monster, possessed and other silly names out of storybooks to dehumanize her and assuage their consciences. Those have the courage to state the obvious fact that Suzanne Basso is a human being created in the image of God and loved by God just like the rest of us, they will have to join me and look directly into the eyes of Suzanne Basso and know that the State of Texas will turn all of us as citizens...whether we look or not...into murderers tonight. Whether our hands are there or not...it will be all of us who push the needle into the arm of Suzanne Basso...it will be all of us who force chemicals into the body of Suzanne Basso...it will be all of us who watch the life slowly drain from the eyes and face of Suzanne Basso...it will be all of us who dispose of the body of Suzanne Basso.

Suzanne Basso. Take a second and repeat that name. Suzanne Basso.

Suzanne Basso is a beloved child of God.

Would Jesus execute her?

Go and do likewise.

Amen.

133.

February 6, 2014

Remarks to Fort Worth Pastors for Texas Children

We gather around this table this afternoon because we believe. We believe that children are important. We believe that local schools are important. We believe that local schools are the last entity or institution that exists purely for the common good. We also are gathered because we believe that the local school is under attack from outside forces that seek to privatize it for financial gain. I am not willing to say that the people who seek to accomplish the task of privatizing local schools are evil...but I can tell you that the destruction of the only entity in our community that exists for the kids with both the least and the most is flat evil. I can tell you based on my own experiences.

The church did not teach me about the value of diversity. The local school did. The church did not teach me other religious traditions. The local school did. The church did not teach to believe in and fight for the equal rights of all people. The local school did. In my youth, the local school taught me many of the things that I could have never learned from the conservative church I grew up in. The local school often does what the church often cannot...introduce the child to the diversity of a massive world.

In Matthew 25, Jesus states quite clearly that the least of these amongst us are Jesus. Do you think a private school is going to spend the tens of thousands of extra dollars to educate impoverished children with special needs? Do you think that private schools are going to send buses out to the projects to transport children to their schools? Do you think that private schools are going to provide free and reduced lunch? I could go on and on. The local school is the only entity that can protect the children that would fall into the category of the least of these. The local school is the only entity that can protect the Jesuses amongst us.

No one at this table has any problem with private education. The problem that we all have is when you take money from the children who need it the most and put it in the hands of someone trying to make a buck off our kids. We are a group of people dedicated to loving our neighbors as our self by providing quality education and opportunities for all of God's children regardless of their socioeconomic status or anything else. We are Pastors for Texas Children.

Amen.

134.

February 6, 2014

Islam, Rihanna & the Surprise of Belief

There are many days I wake up and know that I am going to be a little crazed today and perhaps for a few weeks or months if it lingers. My brain simply feels different. I act and think differently too. I was diagnosed with Bipolar I Disorder a few years ago. In my condition, I often oscillate around in an aggressive mixed state of hopeless depression and uncontrollable mania. In these mixed states of mania and depression, much of my thinking centers on God, the problem of evil and relationships. If God is good or love then why is there so much pain? Can I trust anyone to love me and not hurt me? If we are just going to die then what is the point of living? Would I be better off if I never talk to another person again? There are many others, but you can probably imagine the damage that can be done by not being able to come off of these or similar questions for weeks or months could do. Regardless, I presently do pretty well thanks to a little miracle drug called lithium that keeps my symptoms under control. I still experience these mixed states of mania and depression, but they are much more subdued than the times that I am not on lithium. Throughout this past week, I have experienced a subdued time of depression with flashes of mania.

In my doubts, I have to preach to my self. Last Wednesday the State of Texas executed Suzanne Basso, I was pretty depressed (http://revjeffhood.com/the-case-of-suzanne-basso-would-jesus-execute-her/). I told my self you must believe that love will win in the end. I decided to go and get a bite to eat at my favorite restaurant down the street. While there, I had a long talk with the owner and his son about Islam. The beauty of the way they talked from an Islamic perspective about Jesus and the need to love all people moved me deeply. Their faith pushed me to believe again.

After a slow snowy day of driving and depression to Dallas and back, I picked up my twin sons from their little school. I was planning to take them home…when I got a call from my wife to come over and join her at her classmate's house. I went over to the house and the first thing I noticed was that the wife of my wife's classmate was in a burqa. I sat down and began to talk. My friend described the pressure that is felt by women having to make their bodies and persons look a certain way and that she was glad she could wear a burqa and not have to worry about it. We moved on to faith and the way that the couple described their conception of God as a loving uniter of all people pushed me past my preconceived notions of what a family would be like where the wife and mother wore a burqa. Their faith moved me to a deeper place of belief.

Before I went to bed last night, I was preparing for our church service this Sunday when I heard Rihanna's unmistakable voice come over my computer. "Now we are standing side by side as your shadow crosses mine what it takes to come alive...We found love in a hopeless place." The words of "We Found Love" moved me to tears. I realized that in this hopeless place called earth, I found and shared love and faith in places that were unexpected and surprisingly found Jesus once more too. My Islamic friends and I might call our religious symbols and the personification of love different things and that is ok...but love is always an unmistakable substance...and the love they spoke into my life was the love that I needed. As my shadow crossed the shadows of friends new and old...I was healed. I believe.

Amen.

Source:
"We Found Love" lyrics
http://www.directlyrics.com/rihanna-we-found-love-lyrics.html

135.

February 9, 2014

The Paralytic Church, Queerphobia & Frank Schaefer

Do any of you believe in healing? Do you believe that Jesus actually healed a paralytic in a house full of people? What if someone rolled into this space in a wheelchair this morning to ask for our prayers and walked out? There are many of you who would explain it away at all costs. You simply could not handle the thought that a real healing might have actually taken place. I want to remind everyone that it will be difficult for you to be healed if you don't believe in healing. I want to remind everyone that it will be difficult to change our culture if we don't believe in healing. I want to remind everyone that it will be difficult to change the wider church if we don't believe in healing. Do you believe?

The most beautiful group of people in this story from my vantage point are the friends of the paralytic who take the time to lift him up, carry him to the house where Jesus is, lower him through the roof and make sure he gets to see Jesus. There are many of you sitting in this room this morning who have had a difficult week....you have been down on the mat... and you have needed friends and sometimes they have answered or sometimes they have not. I want to make sure that this is a church full of mat carriers....when people are down on the mat...I want us to pick them up and take them to places of healing. I know an entity that is down on the mat this morning...the church.

The church is paralyzed with queerphobia. The church is terrified of anything that is different or not fitting within normativities. Our church exists because we have decided to not play by the rules of the institutional churches that have oppressed so many for so long. We have decided to set up shop outside the gates of what the institutional church calls normative. We have dared call ourselves queer. The church is on the mat this morning and I believe churches like us are the only spaces that can take the institutional church to spaces where real healing can take place...at the very feet of the God who calls God's self love. Are we going to be mat carriers for the church this morning?

Not long after the healing of the paralytic, the disciples of Jesus picked some grain on the sabbath. This might not sound like that big of a deal to you, but during this time to do any work on the sabbath was a direct violation of Jewish laws about the sabbath. The Pharisees confront Jesus and Jesus responds, "The sabbath was made for humanity not humanity for the sabbath." This parallels the religious world that we find ourselves in this morning.

I think there is a big question that the church needs to hear... Is the Bible made for humanity or humanity for the Bible? The Bible says thou shall not kill...but the Bible is the number one murder weapon used against queer folk...to kill our spirits...to kill our minds...to kill our bodies. The Bible says to love your neighbor as your self...but the Bible is the number one weapon used to deny love to queer folk. The Bible says that Jesus is united with the least of these...but the Bible is used over and over again to take Jesus away from queer folk. The Bible says that faith, hope and love will remain but the greatest of these is love...but the Bible is used to say that the love of queer folk is not deserving of the title of love. I am tired of folks who believe that humanity was made for the Bible not the Bible for humanity. If God is love...then our only question about anything should be is whatever we are examining love or not? That is the fundamental question of our faith. If it is not love...then I don't care what chapter or book you found it in...it is not the word of God...period.

Tonight, I get the opportunity to interact with Rev. Frank Schaefer...the defrocked Pennsylvania United Methodist minister who has made national news in recent months. Let me tell you all what crime this man committed to get defrocked or to lose his ministerial credentials...Schaefer performed the wedding ceremony of his son. The local annual conference of the United Methodist Church took away Schaefer's credentials to be a minister because Schaefer's son married a man. Which one sounds like love to you? A dad performing the wedding ceremony of his son or a church taking away the ministerial credentials of someone for performing the marriage ceremony of his son? The answer is of course obvious to us...but not to those church folk who are paralyzed by queerphobia.

I will be there tonight at the Cathedral of Hope to support Frank Schaefer and all ministers who have the courage to pursue a church that is founded in and on love.

May we never stop carrying the mat where the paralyzed church lay and being the partners that it needs to get to that place where it meets Jesus again and finds love anew.

Amen.

136.

February 9, 2014

The Wise Men...Reinterpreted or The Lack of Wisdom in the Wise Men

Have far would you travel to meet God? The idea of incarnation is that God is present where we are. It seems that the answer to the aforementioned question comes easy in the light of a true belief in incarnation of God with us. I don't think you have to travel far at all to meet God. I believe you just have to open your heart.

The birth narrative of Jesus would not be complete without the so-called wise men that traveled far to meet God. For some time, I have thought that they wasted their energy and would later ruin the lives of many people for not waiting on the incarnation of God where they were. The message of God as told through the life of Jesus is that God is coming to us where we are. So why did the wise men feel the need to travel so far? Maybe the wise men were not so wise after all.

The wise men stopped to see King Herrod in Jerusalem. The visit of the wise men with King Herrod later in the story leads to the death of thousands of infants under the age of two in and around Bethlehem as King Herrod tries to make sure he has killed Jesus (who had already escaped). I would imagine the mothers whose babies were slaughtered in front of their eyes would not call these wise men wise at all.

The actions of the wise men and King Herrod reminds me of what is presently going on in Bethlehem. Wise men and rulers of nations keep talking about liberation for the Palestinians...but by consistently exalting their wisdom and committing atrocities...a people continue to grow more oppressed and degraded by the minute. The same situation occurs over and over again throughout the world as people are oppressed and degraded and told that wise men and other rulers of nations are doing the best they can. When those of us whose hearts are soft for all people ask questions and demand answers, we are told to just listen to the wise men. In our current context...those of us who consistently question the patriarchy, classism, queerphobia, racism and other ills affecting our churches are consistently told to just listen to the wise men. I am tired of wise men. I do not want to hear from those who are running around claiming wisdom...I want to hear from those whose hearts are rich in love and hungry for justice. You do not have to travel far to gain such richness and hunger my friends...you just have to learn to love your neighbor as your self...you just have to learn to love the least of these...you just have to open your heart to love and justice and learn that God is here with us.

I no longer pray for wise men. I pray for people who will open their hearts where they are.
Amen.

137.

February 11, 2014

The Journey to Abolition: Remarks to the Dallas Texas Coalition to Abolish the Death Penalty Prayer Breakfast

"Jesus hung on a cross for a long time and had plenty of time to abolish the death penalty...but you know what...he didn't." These types of arguments and similar words filled the pulpit of the Southern Baptist Church of my youth. I was taught that the economy of God revolved around vengeful wrathful and the constant exchanging of death for death.

I had never cried at a movie before...but the depiction of the relationship between Sister Helen Prejean and Matthew Poncelet in *Dead Man Walking* moved me to tears and changed my life. The questions swirled in my head. Is it possible that someone on death row is really a child of God? Does the commandment of Jesus to love our neighbors and our enemies extend to death row? Why was it that Sister Helen Prejean and Matthew Poncelet at different points looked so much like Jesus to me? I tried to ignore the questions...but they kept gnawing at me...and in my heart I knew the answer to all of them.

In time, I grew. The hesitancies I had to opposing the death penalty faded. I became an activist when I encountered the case of Troy Davis. I knew that a black man accused of killing a white police officer named could not have received a fair trial in Savannah, Georgia in 1991. There was little untainted direct evidence Davis to the killing of Officer Mark MacPhail. Two weeks after my wife and I were married we stood outside Georgia Diagnostic and State Classification Prison in Jackson, Georgia with hundreds if not thousands of others praying that somewhere someone would do the right thing. I knew persons on the Georgia Board of Pardons and Parole. I thought surely they would do the right thing. They did not. Troy Davis was executed and declared dead at 11:08pm on September 21, 2011.

I never wanted to move to Texas. I thought then and think now that Texas is the capital of guns, egos and unnecessary violent death. I feel like the violence is only perpetuated by the State of Texas' insistence on leading the nation in executions. Quite simply... I believe you can't teach folks how to kill by killing. I became involved with the Texas Coalition to Abolish the Death Penalty or TCADP not long after we moved here two years ago and I have been involved in the work of the organization ever since. I presently and proudly serve on the Board of Directors of TCADP.

One of the relationships that informs my activism on the death penalty the most is my relationship with Texas death row inmate Will Speer. Once per month, I make the long journey down to Livingston and spend a few hours with Will. In those moments, I interact with a child of God. I have learned that loving your neighbor extends far beyond your neighborhood. Will has taught me that the best argument against the death penalty is one that Jesus gave us...love your neighbor as your self. It seems obvious to me that one cannot love their neighbor as their self and execute them. I invite all of you to a life of spiritual activism. I invite you all to help us abolish the death penalty...and it all starts with loving your neighbors and consistently calling others to do the same.

Amen.

138.

February 12, 2014

We Can End This: Remarks to the Fort Worth Texas Coalition to Abolish the Death Penalty Prayer Breakfast

I believe in God…but most of all I believe in love. If we believe the writer of 1 John, God and love are synonymous terms. The question of the death penalty is a question of love. How far will our love and forgiveness extend? Will our love span the entire cycle of violence from the crime victims all the way to those who sit on death row to everything in between and beyond? Can you love someone and execute them? Can you love victims of violent crimes by creating more victims? Can you love your neighbor as your self and execute their dad or brother? I think we all know the answer to these questions. Will we live into the answers? Will we live into love?

The death penalty in the past has ripped and continues to rip apart the moral fabric of Texas. We teach people not to kill by killing. The system and cycle is as ludicrous as that statement sounds. We can end this. It is time that we lead the way in reigniting the moral imagination of our society. It is time that we challenge our fellow citizens with the questions of love. This is our prophetic responsibility. We are living in an age desperately in need of prophets. We can end this…but will we have to have the courage to push.

I invite you to join the Texas Coalition to Abolish the Death Penalty to stop the heinous barbaric practice of the death penalty. Now is the time for the abolishment of the death penalty. Now is the time for love. We can end this.

Amen.

139.

February 15, 2014

Turning Shitheads into Prayer Partners

I woke up one morning last week and this message was posted on the wall of one of our church Facebook pages, "This church is the sickest of sick. The evilest of evil. The vilest of vile." I deleted the comment like I do to all other queerphobic comments that are sent to us. Later in the morning, I had a conversation with someone I had not spoken with in some time and she quickly became enraged when she found out that I was leading what is in her words an "anti-Christ" church that was inclusive and celebrating of all people including again in her words "queers and faggots." Most of the time I am able to put all of these disturbing and hateful queerphobic comments behind me and concentrate on the ministry God has called me to...but this day was different. The queerphobia was up under my skin. I felt like these two people were shitheads and I kept calling them exactly that. Whether I knew it or not, I was growing angrier as every minute passed.

Later on in the day...while I was driving back from Dallas...someone cut me off in traffic and in a moment of full on rage...I thrust my middle finger as far as I could out the window and repeatedly screamed shithead at the driver. When I returned to the inside of the car, I didn't like what was happening to me. I pulled over and began to think about my day. It did not take long to realize how much I had been affected not just by the queerphobia I had experienced earlier...but by all the queerphobia our churches and I have experienced. I began to weep...as it had been somewhat of an emotional day. I realized I hadn't prayed in a while and I closed my eyes.

I prayed for love. I prayed for God to bring all those I called shithead alongside me. I prayed for God to forgive me for failing to love. I prayed for God to forgive me for the times that I have been a shithead. I prayed for a renewed love for my enemies and my neighbors alike. I prayed for a renewed commitment to dialogue and conversation with those whose hearts are filled with queerphobia and hate. I prayed for further clarity or revelation of what I had experienced...and in that moment I realized that those I called shithead had brought me to a deeper understanding of both God and love... and now they were no longer shitheads but prayer partners...and even more than that...they were the responsible party for my heart growing wider with love.

Amen.

140.

February 16, 2014

The Withered Hand, The Undivided Heart and The Undistracted Church

There was a man with a withered hand. Jesus approached the man with the withered hand and asked him to extend it. In an instance...the withered hand was healed.

Fortunately or unfortunately depending on your purview, I think Jesus is a secondary character in this episode. The main character is the man with the withered hand. It is interesting that Jesus asked the man to extend his withered hand. I believe the gentleman probably kept the hand stuffed securely behind a cloak or something so that no one would see it...yet if he wanted to be healed then he had to extend it.

We all have our withered hands...those parts of us that we hide. Indeed, we hide behind cloaks of our own construction in hopes that no one will find out about the withered hand. We get so used to hiding and lying that we can't remember what is truth about our self. Real healing can't take place in hiding however...we must make ourselves vulnerable and extend the withered hand. Vulnerability is not safe...but it is the only action that leads to healing. Extend the withered hand.

Not too much later, Jesus talks about the divided house. I think there are many of us who live our lives in divided houses...we run from closet to closet to keep up the lie that we are somehow whole. We hide our withered hands in hopes that no one will notice. Unfortunately, when we live in divided houses things begin to break down and we forget who we told what to and where we even are. There is no healing in the divided house or the divided heart. There can only be healing if we have the courage to come out of the closets and extend the withered hand...the courage to be vulnerable and experience the healing of love in honest community.

Toward the end of Mark 3, there is a story about Jesus' family calling to him and Jesus declaring that his disciples were actually his family. This story reminds me of when I find myself in the midst of important work and hear the phone ringing. I don't answer because I don't want to be distracted from my work. The proverbial phone was ringing and Jesus did not want to be distracted. Our churches are very distracted. It seems that most of what churches do these days is stay on the phone. There seems to be a need to hide the withered hand behind institutional layer upon institutional layer so that real community is something talked about but never accomplished. Institutional life is a distraction at times...and we must ask ourselves whether or not we or anyone else in our spaces have or are extending the withered hand. If we hide in closets and refuse to make ourselves vulnerable...we will find our selves decaying from the inside out...but if we choose to be honest...we will get to have the healing experience of honest community. Without the withered hands...a true experience of church or life is not possible. I pray that ours will always be a church exposed.

So on this day...I invite you to go expose that withered hand and be healed of all that might hold you back from living honestly in our world.

Amen.

141.

February 17, 2014

Leading with the Withered Hand

Rarely do I preach a similar sermon in the same day...but today is an exception. This morning at Prism Denton we discussed the man with the withered hand found in Mark 3. Jesus approached the man with the withered hand and asked him to extend it. In an instance...the withered hand was healed. Truth be told, I have been stuck on that withered hand all day.

The extension of the withered hand was a very vulnerable act of exposure that should not be minimized. I can imagine the man pulling that hand out from behind a cloak and everyone gasping. The man came out as having a withered hand. The healing that came next is thought of as a physical one...the scripture says the hand was restored...but I wonder what it would look like if we thought about it as Jesus healing everyone's judgment of the man with the withered hand. If we want to have true community and acceptance then we have to reveal our withered hands or those things that we hide. The closet is a similar analogy. The longer we run from closet to closet the more we forget who or where we are. The more we hide and closet those things about our selves that we don't want anyone else to know about the more we wither or decay. Healing is found in the freedom of extension.

The withered hand was probably decaying and if the man had kept it hidden I wonder if the decay would have spread. In our lives, when we hide our withered hands and remain closeted about pieces of our selves we begin to lose track of who we really are and begin to decay from day to day. The longer we live as someone other than who we really are the more we begin to rot spiritually...for we can't be honest with our self and if we can't be honest with our self we can't be honest with God. The vulnerability of being you is the beginning of the acceptance of being who you are and the beginning of the healing of honest and open community.

I think is time that we all lead with our withered hands and then they might not look so withered any more...they might just look like hands.

Amen.

142.

February 19, 2014

The Reason I Will Walk Prayerfully from Dallas to Fort Worth: Dallas County DA Craig Watkins, Tarrant County DA Joe Shannon, Jr. & the State of Texas' Death Penalty

On February 21, 2014, I will walk prayerfully from Dallas to Fort Worth with my colleagues from the Texas Coalition to Abolish the Death Penalty Rev. Wes Magruder of the North Texas Annual Conference of the United Methodist Church and Lynn Walters of Hope for Peace and Justice. Our Faithful Pilgrimage to Abolish the Death Penalty will begin with a press conference in Dallas and end with a rally and press conference in Fort Worth. We intend to speak directly to the death sentences pursued and secured by Dallas County District Attorney Craig Watkins and Tarrant County District Attorney Joe Shannon, Jr. I will walk prayerfully the approximately 35-mile journey with my colleagues because I know that it is time for death sentences to stop and the death penalty to be abolished.

In a 2012 interview with D Magazine, Dallas County District Attorney Craig Watkins repeated his often-stated line that he is morally opposed to the death penalty yet his job requires him to pursue death sentences (http://www.dmagazine.com/publications/d-magazine/2012/april/dallas-da-craig-watkins-on-witnessing-his-first-execution?single=1)...and pursue Watkins has...from 2007 to 2013 Dallas County led the state in persons sentenced to death (http://www.dallasnews.com/news/local-news/20131229-dallas-county-da-craig-watkins-leads-state-in-death-penalty-convictions.ece). It is not enough to be morally opposed to the death penalty. Texas is leading the nation in executions and there is a need for persons with tremendous moral courage to shutdown an immoral system that costs too much (almost three times as much as imprisoning someone for the rest of our lives); disproportionately executes the poor and minorities; deprives persons of the ability to love their neighbor as their self and continues the cycle of violence by perpetuating the ludicrous notion that you can teach people not to kill by killing. I am thankful that Craig Watkins has helped exonerate so many people...but it is not enough when you are consistently taking the lives of others. You would think that someone whose great-grandfather was executed by the State of Texas (Richard Johnson / August 10, 1932 / http://www.dmagazine.com/publications/d-magazine/2012/april/dallas-da-craig-watkins-on-witnessing-his-first-execution?single=1) would understand the toll that the continuation of such a system has on the moral fabric of families and a society. I need some time to pray that Craig Watkins will put his morals where his mouth is and so I walk prayerfully.

Tarrant County District Attorney Joe Shannon, Jr. proudly displays on his website the photographs and names of persons he has sent to death row (http://www.tarrantda.com/?page_id=153). Shannon is proud yet fails to realize that his actions perpetuate violence against more families and creates more victims...thanks to his efforts and the efforts of other District Attorneys around the State of Texas the cycle of violence continues. Having decided not to seek reelection, Joe Shannon, Jr. will soon no longer be the District Attorney in Tarrant County (http://www.wfaa.com/news/local/tarrant/Tarrant-County-DA-announces-he-will-not-seek-re-election-226023891.html). I need some time to pray that his successor will have an epiphany of what it means to love your enemies and pray for those who persecute you and so I walk prayerfully.

I walk prayerfully because I am a follower of Jesus that firmly believes we are called to love all of our neighbors as our self...even our enemies. I walk prayerfully because I believe murder is wrong no matter who thrusts the needle or pulls the trigger. I walk prayerfully because I know that more pain, perpetrators and victims are created with every execution. I walk prayerfully because I know that Jesus called us to sacrifice our life not the life of someone else. I walk prayerfully because I believe in the power of prayer to heal the hearts of the victims and turn even the hardest of hearts of perpetrators to love.

I know I will not just be walking and praying with my colleagues...I know I will also be walking with Jesus who has always stood for those that no one else will.

Amen.

143.

February 20, 2014

A Letter to Dallas DA Watkins

Dallas County District Attorney Craig Watkins,

Good morning. We bring you greetings on behalf of the hundreds of faith leaders who have joined the Texas Coalition to Abolish the Death Penalty. We must begin with commendations. We commend you for your pursuit of exonerations. We commend you for your honest assessment of the many race-based biases and injustices within our justice system. We even commend you for your often-declared moral opposition to the death penalty. Unfortunately, this is where our commendations must end.

Richard Johnson was executed by electrocution on August 10, 1932. I am sure the date of your great-grandfather's execution sticks with you in the same way present day dates of executions stick with the families who endure the similar trials and tribulations that your family endured. You often talk about your moral opposition to the death penalty but your need to enforce the law. We believe this is a smoke screen. There are many counties in Texas that have never pursued the death penalty in any modern case. No one is forcing you to pursue death sentences yet you do. In the past five years, Dallas County has sent more people to death row than any other county in the State of Texas. Your talk of moral opposition is not enough. Ten of the eleven men sentenced to death in Dallas County in the past five years are persons of color. We are ready for you to put your morals where your mouth is.

We are tremendously frustrated. We believe that you are participating in and perpetuating a cycle of violence that will only continue if you continue to follow the ludicrous notion that you can teach people not to kill by killing. We believe it is immoral for you to spend the amount of money that you spend pursuing these death sentences when you can pursue life in prison without parole and use that same money to accomplish the reforms that you have so often said that you want to see in our judicial system. We believe it is possible to achieve justice for the families of murder victims through a sentence of life without creating more victims. These are but a few of the many reasons to be opposed to continuing to waste moral and financial energy on death sentences.

We are persons of faith and know you to be a person of faith as well, so we write to remind you of that most basic of moral and religious principles "love your neighbor as your self." Do you think it is possible for you to love your neighbor as your self and execute them? How much more money will have to be spent, how many morals will have to be compromised and how many more people must die before you figure out the answer to that question?

Rev. Jeff Hood
Board Member, Texas Coalition to Abolish the Death Penalty

Rev. Wes Magruder
Chairman of the Board of Church and Society, North Texas Conference of the United Methodist Church

Lynn Walters
Executive Director, Hope for Peace and Justice

144.

February 21, 2014

The Start: A Faithful Pilgrimage to Abolish the Death Penalty

This morning we are gathered here in Dallas as a faith community to express our frustration at Dallas County District Attorney Craig Watkins. We have grown tired of hearing about his moral opposition to the death penalty. When people are being sentenced to death and executed...moral opposition to the death penalty is not enough. We do not want to see one more death sentence come from Dallas County or anywhere else in Texas for that matter. The Texas Coalition to Abolish the Death Penalty is united with hundreds of faith leaders and thousands of Texans in the pursuit of this goal. Wes, Lynn and I began this walk today to Fort Worth to draw attention to that timeless message of loving your neighbor as your self and knowing that there are so many people around the state and nation who walk with us in spirit. We invite all people of goodwill to join us in this cause and loudly proclaim that you cannot love your neighbor as your self or claim to stand for life while pursuing and carrying out sentences of death. We pray that Dallas County District Attorney Craig Watkins will stop the killing that begins in his office...but make no mistake we are going to keep walking and working for abolishment until he and everyone else who is a part of the execution machine does.

145.

February 21, 2014

The End: A Faithful Pilgrimage to Abolish the Death Penalty

We have garnered much attention around throughout Dallas and Fort Worth and around the Metroplex for the cause of abolishment. We are very tired...but though our journey has ended...we will not stop walking and struggling for justice. Tarrant County District Attorney Joe Shannon, Jr. has consistently pursued the death penalty and we have not forgotten that fact. Every step we took today brought us one step closer to the day when there will never be another sentence of death handed down in Tarrant County or anywhere else. We thank you for joining us this evening. Never give up. God is with us.

146.

February 23, 2014

love.

love created the universe
love created us
love came and died
love could not be killed
love lives
love awakens
love is an eternal love
love is love
and
love loves you

147.

February 24, 2014

Get in the Way / Bring them Close / Tell the Stories that Obstruct

In Matthew 25, Jesus talks about some sheep and goats...but this is more than a barnyard story. Jesus ultimately declares, "...what you have done to the least of these you have done to me." In this passage, Jesus places Jesus' self at the very center of injustice and oppression...and as such takes on such injustice and oppression. Jesus obstructs those who would want to continue committing injustice and oppressing people or would want to simply ignore such acts. Jesus gets in the way.

I heard a story a few weeks back that really moved my soul. For those who are convinced that the Spirit of God or Jesus only shows up in the Christian tradition, this story might not be for you. I met a Buddhist monk named Tashi Nyima...who is the director of the New Jonang Community in Dallas. Tashi Nyima told a story of walking downtown with a fellow monk when they stumbled on a group of men beating up on another man. The monk that Tashi was with walked up to the group and asked, "Wouldn't it be more fun to beat up on a couple of Buddhist monks as opposed to all of you beating up on that guy?" Tashi was unsure of what was going to happen next...surprisingly the group of men were so stunned that they simply walked away. Tashi told us as a group that it is the responsibility of the seeker of the divine to get in the way of injustice and oppression. I believe that this is a beautiful description of what it means to follow the way of love...the path that we call the way of Jesus.

One of the ways that we can all get in the way is to tell stories like the one that Tashi told that run counter to the prevailing narratives of violence, vengeance, oppression and injustice. As Sister Helen Prejean shared in the short interview we watched earlier, stories bring people close (http://www.youtube.com/watch?v=AzgTIbOFhNY). I told a group yesterday that we are not going to abolish the death penalty here in Texas until we are able to put people in the death chamber and let them feel the horror of what happens there. Stories bring people close. If we want something different for our then we must continue and perhaps begin to tell stories that challenge and disrupt. We must refuse to adapt our lives to the prevailing narratives and tell stories that run counter to such narratives. We must tell the truth. We must offer narratives or stories that get in the way of the great opiums of selfishness, injustice and oppression and bring people close to the destruction that such opiates cause. We need to be storytellers like Tashi, Sister Helen Prejean and Jesus are.

Stories change the world.
Get in the way.
Bring them close.
Tell the stories that obstruct.
Amen.

148.

February 24, 2014

Coconspirators in Uganda's Recent Homophobic Bill: Mainline Christians

Ugandan President Yoweri Museveni signed a bill today that gives a penalty of life in prison for many homosexual sexual acts. Despite the homophobic policies in their own denominations, the reaction from the mainline Christian world has been swift. Some of the mainline folks I have read have consistently spoken very nasty of President Musevini and sometimes bordered on the same hate that he is perpetuating in Uganda. I have also been surprised by the many questions about where this type of hate comes from? The easiest response is to blame the evangelical Christian leaders who are exporting hate in a world anti-gay movement. While there is blame to go around, I feel like those mainline Christians who cry the loudest fail to realize their own complicity in President Museveni's bill.

I spoke with a United Methodist Ugandan friend recently about the homophobia in Uganda. My brother taught me that it was United Methodist, Presbyterian and Baptist missionaries that used the Bible to instruct his village of origin in how to be homophobic. Could it be that some of our missionaries whose pictures hang in glory on some of the walls of our churches could be responsible for this homophobic bill that was just signed in Uganda? Could it be that the missionaries we have named our missions offerings for were also skilled purveyors of hate and homophobia? The mainline Christian world at the very least is partly responsible for what is happening. There is no question the actions of President Museveni and some of these evangelical Christian homophobes are very evil...but before you go to othering and talking about what they have done and what you would never do...it would be wise to look into the history of your church and talk about what you already have done to cause all of this.

We will only be able to call people back from the moral disaster that is their homophobia when we repent of our own.

Amen.

149.

February 25, 2014

Love Dangerously Dallas

Everybody wants to talk about love these days...but no one wants to talk about sacrifice. Everybody wants to talk about the love of Jesus...but nobody wants to talk about how embracing the love of Jesus leads to death. Everyone wants to talk about falling in love...but no one wants to talk about the need to jump off the cliff and sacrifice your self in order to experience it. Love is dangerous. You do not know whether you are going to get hurt. You do not know whether someone is going to break your heart. You do not know anything...but still we love. Why friends? Why take the risk?

There are times in which we mimic the divine. Love is one such time. God loved us without knowing whether we would break God's heart. Jesus died for us without knowing whether anyone would ever embrace the love of Jesus. When we love we take an enormous risk...but love is always worth the risk. For love is the only thing that is eternal. Love is the only thing that pulls us out of our selves and takes us to the eternal place where God dwells. 1 John 4:8 declares that God is love. So go and make some God my friends...go and make some love. Live dangerously...believe in all love...take the risk of sacrifice...Love dangerously Dallas.

Amen.

delivered at The Concrete Sanctuary

150.

February 26, 2014

The Judgment: Christians and the Ruling in Texas

This afternoon U.S. Federal Judge Orlando Garcia ruled that Texas' prohibition of gay marriage is unconstitutional. That is the judgment...but there are many Christians who will be talking about a different type of judgment in the coming days. I can already hear them in pulpits around the state talking about the coming hell and damnation for homosexuals or perhaps more problematic staying neutral. I have a word from God for all of you. There is a judgment and it is far different than what you have envisioned.

In Matthew 25, Jesus talks about separating the sheep and the goats. The sheep are aligned with the marginalized and the oppressed. The goats are aligned with the marginalizers and the oppressors either by their action or inaction. Jesus declares firmly, "What you have done to or failed to do for the least of these you have done or failed to do to me." Those who are judged by God are the ones who turn their backs on the marginalized and the oppressed. On this day you can either stand with the incarnated Christ that stands with our queer neighbors or the forces of marginalization and oppression...but you cannot do both.

The time is long overdue for Christians to live out what it truly means to love our neighbors as our self. The world is changing and we can either choose to love our neighbors or hate them. We can either stand with God or against God. The judgment is upon us. Where do you stand?

151.

February 26, 2014

Delivered Tonight: A Question for Dallas County District Attorney Craig Watkins

"My question is for District Attorney Watkins. My name is Jeff Hood. I am a Baptist minister and I also serve on the Board of Directors of the Texas Coalition to Abolish the Death Penalty. I am particularly troubled by the case of our panelist Christopher Scott who was wrongfully convicted of capital murder and served twelve years for a crime he did not commit before he was exonerated. What if Dallas County had pursued the death penalty in Scott's case? I also think about the cases of Cameron Todd Willingham and Carlos DeLuna who have been proven to the satisfaction of most to have been wrongfully executed. You have spoken much about doubt and race tonight...yet your office not only leads the state in death sentences...but also a large majority of those persons sentenced to death were minorities. With so much doubt...why does your office still pursue sentences of death?"

152.

February 28, 2014

The Week: Close to Death

Over the past few weeks, my mind has never been far from death. Last Friday, I delivered a letter from local clergy condemning Dallas County District Attorney Craig Watkins' consistent pursuit of death sentences and then walked from Dallas to Fort Worth in protest and prayer. Last Saturday, I stood before the hundreds of persons gathered in Fort Worth for the annual conference of the Texas Coalition to Abolish the Death Penalty to remark in part, "the politicians all start coming to church around election time...well I think it is time to take the church to the politicians." Last Wednesday, I did just that. I confronted Dallas DA Craig Watkins with a question at an Innocence Project event and pushed for clarification on his consistent pursuit of the death penalty. Yesterday, as I got in my car to head to Livingston to visit Will Speer on Texas' Death Row, I begin to wonder why I continue to expend so much energy and push so hard against the death penalty? This morning as I talked to Will and we commiserated about the status of his appeals, I was reminded that the death penalty creates the most hopeless of hopeless of situations and that is exactly where Jesus will always be.

153.

March 2, 2014
My First Job in Ministry, Forgiveness & the Imperfect Pursuit of Perfection

Forgiveness is not something I am good at...but I know it is something that I need to do. This is a short talk based around an experience...the experience was and is mine...but the discussion topic of forgiveness is for all of us. I began my ministry in a very small town in Alabama. I served as a youth minister for both the First United Methodist Church and the First Baptist Church. In small towns they can create such ecumenical arrangements. Nevertheless, my youth group was really growing and we began to have parties for all the kids at the First Baptist Church. I used the sound system to play music for the kids. Little did I know that there was someone who was very protective of the sound system in the First Baptist Church...actually the gentleman was so protective that on multiple occasions he physically assaulted me and threatened my life...again over my use of a sound system. The pastors of both churches did little to help and one even threatened that they would have to fire me for insubordination if I pressed charges against the gentleman (Alabama is an at will state I was reminded). There was so much injustice in the situation. I was angry then and every time I think about it now I get angry. I get tired of carrying the burden of the stupidity of a dumbass psycho control freak and the pastors who protected him in a small Alabama town. Are the words I use too strong? Forgiveness is not something I am good at...but I know it is something I need to do.

Jesus speaks to such a situation in the Gospel of Matthew 5:44, "Love your enemies and pray for those who persecute you..." The first step toward loving your enemies is forgiving them and the first step toward forgiving them is wanting to. I have wanted to forgive the situation that happened in Alabama for many years and yet I still struggle with letting go of the violation/inaction that occurred. Maybe letting go is not the point. Maybe the point is to hold tight to a desire for justice...but not let the hate for your enemy hold you back. Maybe the want to is often manifested in that act of volition known as a prayer.

I am not an expert at loving my enemies...but I know forgiveness plays a big part in the process. I don't know of any better place to look for an example of forgiveness in action than to the Truth and Reconciliation Commission that gathered to investigate the crimes that took place during the Apartheid Era in South Africa. Archbishop Desmond Tutu led the panel and often declared that forgiveness is an act of God. When I hear such words, I am reminded that I am not God...but that doesn't mean I should stop trying to forgive. May we never stop trying to develop the want to and desire to forgive even our worst enemies...and when our efforts seem imperfect...may we pray to be closer and closer to God. For one day as 1 John 3:2 says, "We shall be made like God..." I guess we all just need to keep trying to pray and forgive until we get there.
Amen.

154.

March 2, 2014

The Guys with the Guns on the Denton Square

The ice pellets hit my head as I negotiated the icy sidewalk. I heard a bunch of rustling to my right and looked up. Ten men walked past me carrying large guns. The flags and signs the men carried read, "Come and take it" or "Don't tread on me." I wondered who these folks thought were oppressing or treading on them...I mean they are the ones walking around with the guns. Right?

I found the spectacle to be rather amusing. I am not the most educated person on gun laws in Texas...but I can assure you that they are not oppressive enough of guns for my tastes. Nevertheless, I thought about what Jesus would say to these folks parading around these guns on the Denton Square...and then I remembered a scene from the Gospel of Matthew.

In a monumental injustice, Jesus is about to be taken away and executed by the state. If there was ever a moment to wave a "Don't tread on me" flag...this was it. Peter (identified in the Gospel of John) pulls out his sword to defend Jesus against the arrest. Jesus sharply rebukes Peter and declares in Matthew 26:52, "Those who live by the sword will die by the sword." A modern translation might read, "Those who live by the gun will die by the gun."

The problem is that the message of Jesus doesn't frighten too many people these days when it comes to gun ownership. It would not be too hard to convince me that there are more gun owners in the church than anywhere else. The United States has an addiction to guns and the more guns the more death.

There are more guns in the United States at 270 million than in any other country in the world. There are about 9 guns for every 10 people in the United States (http://www.washingtonpost.com/blogs/worldviews/wp/2012/12/15/what-makes-americas-gun-culture-totally-unique-in-the-world-as-demonstrated-in-four-charts/). The United States had more gun deaths last year than any other developed nation on earth (http://abcnews.go.com/blogs/health/2013/09/19/u-s-has-more-guns-and-gun-deaths-than-any-other-country-study-finds/).

It seems that what Jesus forgot to tell us "the nation that lives by the gun will die by the gun"...I think the statistics can help us go ahead and infer it though.

We are a culture addicted to living our lives staring down the barrel of a gun.

I think it is time for us as a people to go to rehab...that rehab that only comes from learning to love our neighbors as our self.

I think a good place to start is by not waving your guns in their face.

Amen.

155.

March 3, 2014

Cathedral of Hope Devotional for March 28

"But as for the towns of these peoples that the Lord your God is giving you as an inheritance, you must not let anything that breathes remain alive. You shall annihilate them—the Hittites and the Amorites, the Canaanites and the Perizzites, the Hivites and the Jebusites—just as the Lord your God has commanded, so that they may not teach you to do all the abhorrent things that they do for their gods, and you thus sin against the Lord your God." -Deuteronomy 20:16-18

If you love God then you should commit genocide? Do these sound like the words of God to you? They don't to me either...yet when I bring these passages up in most fundamentalist contexts most fundamentalists I know have said that God really does command genocide. The scriptures do seem to give the fundamentalists and anyone else who is interested in laboring the point much evidence that we serve a genocidal God. So what are we who have met the love of Jesus to do when confronted with such a genocidal God in scripture? I think the only thing we can do is declare in unison, "Whoever that bullshit God is...it certainly is not the same God that I have met in Jesus." I am tired of having these discussions where I am forced to talk about scripture as if I believe it all to be true. I don't. I think that Jesus is the only thing in scripture that is true. I follow the words of Jesus not words that people thought they heard from God.

In many contemporary discussions people want to point to scripture to prove their point. I think progressive folk need to admit that the scripture condemns homosexuality, promotes sexism, grants instructions for human slavery and speaks favorably to a whole host of evils that we know to not be righteous. Stop arguing. The scriptures are plain and we can say with certainty the writers of scripture believed and did evil things...but these are not the words of God. How can we be sure? If it is not love then it is not God for God is love and love is God. This is revealed in the person of Jesus that I and countless others have met. We must deploy the hermeneutic of love that Jesus has given us. If it is love then it is the word of God. I refuse to participate in these silly games around defending words that we know that Jesus could not have uttered. Don't waist your time anymore. Follow Jesus, love your neighbor as your self and love your enemies. The God that is more real than all the words contained in scripture...will meet you there.

Amen.

156.

March 3, 2014

A Sermon Entitled "Jesus for President" or The Reason I Will Never Endorse a Political Candidate

The church of my youth had a bad habit of mixing political candidates with spirituality. I am a child of the culture wars. I remember one Sunday morning our pastor gave a sermon entitled, "Jesus for President." The pastor told us that he would not tell us who to vote for and then proceeded to explain how the Republican candidate was more like Jesus than the Democratic candidate. I remember leaving the church and hearing a family say they would never come back. "One should never have to travel through a political candidate to get to the table of Jesus," the mother replied loudly to her child's questioning of her frustration. I didn't totally agree with her then. I do now.

A few people have asked me about my thoughts on certain candidates competing in the Texas Primary tomorrow. These are my thoughts. I believe Jesus transcends political candidates and political candidates should never create a barrier to Jesus. If I endorse a political candidate then what are the people who support the other candidate going to think about my ministry? I believe that supporting political candidates inhibits my ability to minister to people from all walks of life. I intend to minister to all people regardless of their thoughts on political candidates. There is no question that I am a socially active minister driven by strong beliefs about love and justice...but make no mistake...I do not believe that we have met or will ever meet a candidate that encompasses the totality of love and justice and so I refuse to publicly bind myself to that which is partial...which is why I simply stick with the peace, love, justice and hope that is Jesus.

I encourage all to pray for our future and participate in our democracy...but don't expect any endorsements out of me.

Amen.

157.

March 4, 2014

apoem: the why of ashe wednesday

ashes to ashes
dust to dust
the beginning of when
ashes to ashes
dust to dust
the incarnation of what
ashes to ashes
dust to dust
the end of where
ashes to ashes
dust to dust
the repeat of who
ashes to ashes
dust to dust
the beginning of when-the incarnation of what-the end of where- the repeat of who
the repeat of who-the end of where-the incarnation of what-the beginning of when
the why is the magic, the mystery and the meaning of all that is queer forever and ever
amen

158.

March 5, 2014

The Push of the Ashes: A Manifesto of Defiance for Clergy Colleagues

The words of ash and dust on this day are intended to usher us into a space of mourning and repentance toward God...but who is placing the ashes on our churches? The churches that dot our landscapes have become consistently consistent at discarding the least of these for a false sense of unity. The words on everyone's lips are "let's stay together" and yet nobody realizes that there are thick black crosses on our foreheads calling us to mourning and repentance. You cannot love your neighbor as your self by appeasing their oppressor. You cannot love your neighbor as your self by following oppressive guidelines and laws that take away their dignity and worth. How much longer are we going to ask people to wait their turn for justice and inclusion? Enough is enough. Look to the ashes, mourn and repent.

It is not enough to talk about where you are personally anymore nor was it ever. It is not enough to talk about your nostalgia for your church homes nor was it ever. It is not enough to speak as if division is to high a price to pay for justice nor was it ever. The time for justice and inclusion was yesterday. Jesus has placed a thick black cross on our foreheads this day and is calling for us to use it as a motivation to love our neighbors as our self. I call on all of my fellow clergy to stop playing games and follow Jesus. False unity is not worth sacrificing justice anymore nor was it ever. Inclusion in the church and the love of Jesus is not something that anyone should have to line up for.

There are many who are afraid that defying their churches will lead them to a place of losing their orders and credentials. To them I say...if your orders and credentials do not allow you to love and include all people then they were not from Jesus in the first place. The institutions and the buildings should never be enough to keep us from following Jesus and loving our neighbors.

The ashes should not only push to mourning and repentance...but also to defiance.

On this Wednesday of Ashes, I recommit the entirety of my being to standing with Jesus in defiance of injustice, bigotry and oppression no matter what form it takes and what it costs. I pray that you will join me.

Amen.

159.

March 7, 2014

The Danger of Missions in a World Desperate for Salvation

The religious world of my youth was filled with stories of so-called courageous missionaries who gave their lives so that so-called savages would come to know Jesus Christ. The more extreme the stories got the more folks seemed to find their way down the center aisle of the gathering to give their lives to going on missions. The idea of missions as something that happens elsewhere permeated much of my upbringing and still permeates much of the church.

I recently talked to some native Africans about the numerous pieces of bigoted homophobic legislation that have swept the continent in recent months and years. The response is consistent...the legislation is a product of the Christian missions and missionaries who taught our people to hate queer folk by teaching interpretations of the Bible that encouraged and justified violence and oppression. In the estimation of my African friends, the entire church is guilty of these hermeneutical crimes. I think the queer folk in these nations might have been better off if we had just stayed at home.

The danger of missions is the danger of exporting your hate for your self and your neighbor to somewhere else.

The world is desperate for the salvation of love...but our missions seem to have sown much hate. I want to spread the love of Jesus everywhere...but I am concerned that most of our churches here are fresh out of love and have none to export. One solution might be to spend time figuring out what love is and what it should look like so that we don't go exporting something called love that will only be revealed to be hate.

The mission begins within.

Amen.

160.

March 10, 2014

A Girl Named Peter and the Path to God

Welcome to Lent. This is not a time of celebration for the fuzz that sometimes inhabits your pockets. Rather this is a time of reflection for seeking and being. We gather this morning on a dark mysterious dot in the middle of the cosmos traveling into time and space as a community of people. This is a time of the year that reminds us to not turn around or sit down on our journey. We are to keep pushing boundaries and borders. We are to keep pushing into the creation and into the creator. In the pushing...in the seeking...in each step we find salvation or being granted from the God from whom we all flow. We are not the first to be brought into this time of reflection for the benefit of our being. Jesus ushers Peter into a similar space.

Jesus alludes to his impending demise and Peter makes a firm declaration that he will never allow anything to happen to Jesus. In a quick turnaround, Jesus declares that Peter will not only betray him but will do so three times before a rooster crows. I have known both Peters and roosters in my life. Have you ever had anybody tell you they would love you forever? Have you ever had anybody tell you that somebody you love was failing to love you?

Many years ago...long before I met Emily...I was involved in a romantic relationship. It was a beautiful love affair. There was a tremendous amount of attraction and passion. As the relationship progressed, I realized I was sick and there was no doubt that I was difficult to be in a relationship with. When I would have doubts about whether she would stick with me through the illness...the response was always the same "I will never leave you. I will always love you." The relationship grew deeper and deeper...but I was still sick. As the newness gave way to the grind of a day-to-day relationship, I received a phone call. I got the same words that countless people have heard...I love you but I am breaking up with you. I guess that temporal forever kind of love sometimes comes with a "but."

Jesus describes to Peter what a love that does not fail looks like. The rest of our narrative today begins with an admonishment from Jesus to not let our hearts be troubled. These are words for the moments of struggle when things seem to fall apart and there is little hope. Jesus speaks into those dark moments and declares there to be a way of being that is beyond death...there is resurrection.

Jesus declares resurrection to be within his very person. "I am the way. I am the truth. I am the life. No one comes to God except through me." The fundamentalists use this passage to condemn everyone to hell who is not a fundamentalist Christian.

Jesus is much bigger than such constructs. The story of Jesus is one is which love is the ultimate victor. Jesus declares that a love that sacrifices for others is the only way to the creator. Jesus says that love is truth and invites others to follow the path of sacrificial love to higher being.

Jesus is the way because love is the way and Jesus lives that way perfectly. The promises of Peter to never betray or leave Jesus mean little until Peter is willing to give his life for others and Jesus invites us to do the same.

Lent is a time of year that invites us to deeper sacrifice and deeper understanding through walking into and through death toward new being. The path to higher being and God is love.

Amen.

161.

March 11, 2014

A Love Letter to Mark Driscoll

Mark,

I was 12. I couldn't figure out what was wrong with me. I prayed and prayed. I walked down the aisle multiple times. I felt no assurance that I was truly a follower of Jesus and I couldn't figure out why.

There was a tough youth leader that I really liked and respected. I decided to take my conundrum to him. I poured my heart out and asked, "Why won't God give me any assurance of salvation?" After a long thoughtful pause, the youth leader replied, "Because you are a pussy."

A number of years ago, I sat down with a friend who told me about attending one of your church planting conferences. The young man was really struggling to make a living and pastor his small church plant. When he asked you "Why can I not make a living if God has called me?" you replied, "Because you are a pussy."

Much like the youth leader I experienced as a young man, Mark your behavior is that of a misogynistic bully. I think it is because someone had one of these "you are being a pussy" type conversations with you and it pushed you to be who you are. Jesus is not a bully, Mark. I actually believe if you really met Jesus you would probably call him a pussy too.

The language of pussy is very problematic in and of itself...as it furthers patriarchy and makes the assumption that one sexual organ is better or worse than another.

Mark I am tired of all of this oppressive stuff that you keep putting out. It is wrong and it is not of a God who declares God's self to be love.

With this said, I am also tired of the manner that Christians are responding to you. There is nothing wrong with explaining to you that your words about Jesus are apostasy and harmful, but there is something wrong with using the same language that you use to dehumanize and degrade you. I refuse to participate in the dehumanization of anyone.

Mark please make no mistake, your writings and ministry are incredibly harmful to a large number of people. Your work furthers misogynistic, homophobic, patriarchal, bigoted and other oppressive themes and as such is not of God. Mark, in many ways you are my enemy...but Jesus tells me to love my enemies.

So I just wanted to send you this love letter.

Love.

Jeff

162.

March 13, 2014

apoems from a plane to dallas-fort worth

bart

bart screamed out
and everyone told him not to shout
the one they called crazy blind man
screamed out and go to see again
we will not open the eyes of the blind
until we scream out about the oppression we find

the sign

everyone demands a sign from god
but perhaps the sign we need comes from us
sit down
love
hug
eat
go to the movies
laugh
cry
live
with those people you hate the most
be the sign both you and the world need

so before you ask for a sign tonight remember you are the one who is called to be light

the plane

tube flying
jeff sleeping
ground passing
light heating
engines pushing
stewardess checking
radio playing
phone buzzing
man sneezing
windows closing

aisle guiding
the pain of this moment is not the pain of tomorrow
i am in a microcommunity that seems always to be on the cusp of mutiny

there are demons round here

there are demons round here
i don't think they are a construct of yesteryear
i met one last night
all he talked about was his church's institutional might
the ones in mark slobbered and spit
the demons i know just talk a bunch of bullshit
money is always the word of the hour
they have no idea that in the poor is the power
jesus put the demons into pigs and they ran off a cliff
now they talk about the need to stay away from any rift
the demons had courage because they know it will expose
the institutional ruses they have going of which nobody seems to know
the houses for the demons have names like first
while the people who are desperate continue to thirst
the mandate was to love the least
but now when controversy rears its head
the demons pretend as if the the least are better off dead
apeasement is the flavor the demons like
but jesus called us to be light
the ones who dwell in darkness the most
are the ones who seem to think they are God's host
and get to decide who is in and who is out
and consistently want to talk about their clout
the demons go by names both conservative and liberal
but once the showdown hits and the least need allies
all of the talk of justice becomes dribble
the demons seem to weekly be cast out into the seats
and then the people go out to defend supposed feats
if you want to go to the institutional church
i only ask that you be careful for there are demons round here

the cleaning of the temple

the temple got a good cleaning
the church needs a good cleaning
jesus tossed out the money changers
the church needs to toss out the money changers
the religious leaders devised a plan to kill jesus
the church continues to devise a plan to kill jesus
jesus left

163.

March 15, 2014

The Trouble with Bishop Spong and Embracing the Mystery of Faith

I often prayed a familiar prayer when I was a child and remember one line very well, "If I die before I wake, I pray the Lord my soul to take." That line scared the shit out of me when I was a kid, but now there is some comfort in laying down my head and embracing the mystery of God's abiding love. Belief is not something that comes naturally for me. I struggle to believe in an afterlife. Most days I struggle to even believe in God at all...due primarily to God's absence in the midst of injustice and tragedy. On my best days though, I am able to embrace the mystery of God and simply exist in the questions. I think this is where faith is found.

I had lunch with a fellow minister a few months back. We had barely sat down to the table before he proclaimed loudly, "You know I don't believe in the literal resurrection of Jesus anymore." I responded quickly, "Your certainty and lack of wonder disturbs me."

One week ago, I had the chance to hear the infamous Bishop John Shelby Spong. I have always been skeptical of Bishop Spong. I find his denials of the mystical and magical in the Christian faith to be unimaginative and uninteresting. I went anyway. Bishop Spong does not disappoint. In both his books and in person, Bishop Spong is very skilled at taking veiled and some not so veiled shots at the resurrection, the virgin birth and other miraculous occurrences described in the New Testament. Unfortunately, Bishop Spong claims to know more than is even possible for him to know. Was Bishop Spong at the tomb of Jesus and able to see what did or didn't happen there? Did Bishop Spong perform a vaginal inspection on Mary to know if she had sex before getting pregnant with Jesus? Was Bishop Spong able to travel back in time and be present to see if and how all the other miracles in the New Testament happened too? These questions are ludicrous and so too is claiming to know whether or not the miraculous happened or not. I gave to Bishop Spong the words that I previously gave my minister friend, "Your certainty and lack of wonder disturbs me."

The church desperately needs less answers not more. I am a proponent of leaving behind conservative and liberal fundamentalisms to venture to a place where we don't have to even claim to know...we just embrace the mystery of faith. The beauty of the incarnation then and now is that it is too wonderous to be so easily defined.

Amen.

164.

March 16, 2014

Prayers for a Child of God

Fred Phelps Sr. founded the infamous Westboro Baptist Church in Topeka, Kansas. The only mantra of Phelps or the church appears to be "God Hates Fags." This afternoon word came out that Phelps is dying at Midland Care Hospice in Topeka. Our church is unanimously made up of people that Phelps would call fags.

In a very emotional moment for our congregation this evening, we prayed.

"God of all comfort. Join us at this hour. We come to you with broken hearts at the many things that Fred Phelps Sr. has said and done to the detriment of countless people. We come to you in our brokenness with a belief that you heal the broken places with your love. You have called us to love even the vilest of people. So tonight we pray for your child and our brother Fred Phelps Sr.. We ask that you take all the pain out of his body. We ask that you be present with Fred and that he know your love. We pray that even at this moment may Fred also know our love for him and all the others who have abused and treated us like shit. We love our brother Fred and we pray for his wellness in this life and in the next. Amen."

When we completed our time of prayer, there were a few tears in the room. It was as if God had reconciled many of us to someone we thought we would be reconciled to. There was also a sense that Phelps represents so many of those who have spiritually abused us in the past. I don't know if Fred Phelps Sr. will die tonight...but I do know that whenever he does he will be taking the love of our people with him.

Amen.

165.

March 19, 2014

Double Homicide Tonight: Racism Reigns in Texas

The State of Texas killed Ray Jasper tonight. Before his execution, Jasper wrote a letter describing what it was like to be a black man in the United States. The statistics are startling. Although black people make up 12.6% and white people make up 72.4% of the U.S. population according to the 2010 U.S. Census (http://www.census.gov/prod/cen2010/briefs/c2010br-02.pdf), black people currently make up 41.71% of the death row population according to the death penalty information center (http://www.deathpenaltyinfo.org/race-death-row-inmates-executed-1976#deathrowpop). Large questions of fairness with regard to race litter the justice system and specifically death sentencing processes. I do not think Jesus would have executed anyone...and much less sent them through a system to be executed that is biased against them due to their race.

Most of our government officials responsible for what happened tonight claim to be Christians. With regard to the death penalty, I will be in prayer that Jesus spiritually storms their temples and wakes them up out of the injustice that they keep perpetuating. You cannot love your neighbor and kill them.

Ray Jasper was not the only homicide that took place tonight.

I participated in a vigil for Crystal Jackson and Britney Cosby. The black lesbian couple was murdered between Galveston and Bolivar Peninsula, Texas sometime between March 6 and 7. Britney Cosby's mother claims that Britney's father James Cosby murdered the couple because he did not like that Britney was gay (http://www.nydailynews.com/news/crime/dad-killed-daughter-lesbian-lover-gay-mom-article-1.1722103). Regardless of the circumstance of the death, this was a tragedy of unimaginable proportions. The response from most LGBT non-profits and activist organizations has been timid at best. GetEQUAL Texas organized the vigil I participated in tonight and a few others throughout the state. These vigils have been one of the few organized reactions to the death of Crystal and Britney.

There were four people at the vigil I participated in. One of the participants declared that a second homicide had taken place. The many other state and local LGBT organizations in the state had killed her faith in them. "They only care about murders and beatings when white bodies are involved, " the participant declared. Someone else questioned, "When are people going to understand that you can't trade one oppression in for another?" There was undoubtedly a sense of betrayal in the air tonight...because we all knew there would have been hundreds of people present if a white gay couple had been murdered.

I have known for a long time and was deeply reminded tonight that racism reigns in Texas from the left to the right.

I pray that Jesus storms all of our temples, ends the reign of all of this racist shit and turns all of our hearts to love.

Amen.

166.

March 20, 2014

Jesus the God of Rage: Tossing the Moneychangers Out of Our Government, Our Churches and Our Self

For many of us, our lives are filled with the mundane and monotonous. It is as if we live for those moments when we might become something different...when we might become all that we were created to be...when we might have the opportunity to touch greatness or even the very face of God. This evening we are going to talk about one of those moments in the life of Jesus, where Jesus is undeniably God in action. The scene unfolded at the temple.

People or moneychangers set up tables selling access to worship throughout the temple. There were obstacles of class and status that people had to over come in order to participate in the life of the temple. Jesus became enraged at the injustice of it all and made a whip to drive out those who were doing the selling and creating obstacles to the worship of God. Jesus sealed his death by standing up for others in the narrative. For Jesus the time to stand with the oppressed was always *now*.

What temples must we storm? Who are the moneychangers? Where are our whips?

Our immigration policies create a society of obstacles for our brothers and sisters who we live and work with everyday.

Our economic policies oppress people all over the world...creating situations where billions of people have little access to the economic resources they need to survive.

The policies of our justice system consistently create a world in which we would rather imprison the poor than educate them.

There are innumerable systematic oppressions and injustices that we give assent to by remaining silent everyday.

If we are to be followers of the way of Jesus...then where are our whips?

It would be nice if I could point you to our churches to help you in your task of driving out the moneychangers. But, the truth is that the moneychangers and the obstacle creators far too often are operating out of these spaces.

I can think of no greater challenge facing the church in the United States than the rise of the prosperity gospel. Jesus did not call you to get rich and healthy. Jesus called you to come and die. I pray that we will drive out the moneychangers who are keeping us from talking about injustice and oppression by filling our pulpits with bullshit about accumulating health and wealth.

People in the church ask us to go slow on issues of justice. To them I declare here and now...we are not going fast enough. How many more young people will have to die before we wake up to the second-class status church policies and teachings are thrusting upon the queer community? How many more people are going to have to suffer spiritual abuse from our pastors before we wake up to the knowledge that God loves everyone? It is not enough to do this love-the-sinner shit. It is not enough to paternalistically affirm someone. We will either love all of God's children now or we will cease to be the church.

Where are our whips? What are we waiting on?

The most treacherous temple to storm is our own. We fail to realize the effects of growing up in a culture permeated with oppression and injustice at every step. I have come to terms with the fact that I will always be a recovering racist, homophobe, sexist, classist and a whole host of other ists. I have to storm my temple daily to get all the shit out. If we are willing to be honest with our selves, we all have to. We all have to root out daily the oppressive and evil attitudes and injustices that take root in our lives. Though we will never be perfect, we need to get more people in recovery.

Where are our whips? Why are we not down on our knees?

Are we willing to step into those moments where we are called to be something tremendously greater than what we are? Are we willing to fashion the whips and drive out the moneychangers that inhabit our lives and the world around us?

It is not enough to hide and live our lives quietly. We must give our lives for other others. The greatest response to a world gone mad is to refuse to stop storming the temple.

For Jesus the time to stand with the oppressed is always *now*.

Our time is *now*.

Amen.

167.

March 21, 2014

Why We Can't Wait: A Sunday Letter from a Baptist Pastor to my Methodist Colleagues Here in North Texas

There in the darkness a courageous Baptist Pastor sat furiously transcribing a letter. The words the Baptist Pastor wrote were a response to a letter from a Methodist Bishop and other clergy asking the minister to be patient in the face of injustice. The words the Baptist Pastor wrote still ring loudly in my ears, "But the judgment of God is on the church as never before. If today's church does not recapture the sacrificial spirit of the early church, it will lose its authenticity, forfeit the loyalty of millions, and be dismissed as an irrelevant social club with no meaning for our time." The minister was Dr. Martin Luther King, Jr. and his office was a jail cell in Birmingham. Baptists have always had a unique ecclesiastical place from which flows the freedom to speak and write prophetically about issues of social justice. It is from a unique place of being a progressive Baptist Pastor that I write to my Methodist colleagues this morning.

I believe that the judgment of God and the world is upon us. We have the opportunity to do right by all people of diverse sexual orientations and genders. Unfortunately, most are afraid to act for fear that they will lose their credentials or standing in their churches. Such fear is not unfounded. Everyday all over the country clergy are being prosecuted for acts of defiance. There was a time when acts of defiance were what made us followers of Jesus. Now, it seems that our standing before God is often equal to the comfort that the church has with us. Dr. King spoke of a coming irrelevant social club and most of us realize we are already there. The church has largely chosen to remain silent on many of the most pressing social issues of our time and we have forfeited our voice to the upkeep of institutions. Occasionally though, someone stands up and ignites the imagination of us all.

Three weeks ago, I witnessed Rev. Bill McElvaney courageously presiding over the wedding of Jack Evans and George Harris in direct violation of the United Methodist Church's Book of Discipline. I spent time earlier this week with Rev. McElvaney and I have met no kinder or more generous of a pastor. In both instances, I felt the presence of God in a mighty way. Now, I am told that a sympathetic fellow minister filed a complaint against Rev. McElvaney to manipulate the institution and soften the penalty he might face. I find it particularly troubling that any institution of the living God is pushing someone to violate conscience in order to achieve a desired outcome.

We can't wait any longer for you to defy and force reformation in these troubled institutions. Continued delays affect all of us. The soul of the church is being forfeited in nuance and negotiations. The church is better known now for delaying and denying justice than it is for fighting for it.

How long will we sit silent behind the doors of institutions while working through our processes as people bang loudly for justice?

The church has already grown increasingly irrelevant in our society. Our only hope of recapturing any semblance of relevancy is to conjure up the prophetic sacrificial spirit of the early church.

We can't wait.

The time is now.

Shall we stand together?

Amen.

168.

March 26, 2014

Power in the Blood: Oscar Romero, Bullshit Churches Teach and the Seed of Liberty

Growing up our church was a rather stoic place. On Sundays we sang stoic songs. There were only a few foot-tapping songs in the hymnal and only on rare occasions did we ever get close to any hand clapping. There was however one song that seemed to get the feet tapping, bodies swaying and hands colliding every time..."There is Power in the Blood." I will never forget the lyrics..."Would you be free from the burden of sin? There's power in the blood, power in the blood; Would you o'er evil a victory win? There's wonderful power in the blood. There is power, power, wonder working power In the blood of the Lamb; There is power, power, wonder working power In the precious blood of the Lamb." I loved that song...and if I am honest with myself I probably still do when my ears run across it. The earliest understandings I had of the death and atonement of Jesus flowed out of songs like this. I believed that the blood of Jesus was required to satisfy the wrath of God against a sinful planet. This understanding of the death of Jesus is called substitutionary atonement. The problem with this violent understanding of the atonement is that it is predicated on a wrathful God that is unworthy of our love and an idea that blood is required as atonement in the economy of God...you know the eye for an eye, tooth for a tooth type stuff. It seems like crazy bullshit to me now...but I believed it then. Oscar Romero changed my mind.

In the streets of San Salvador, El Salvador amongst the poor, one can feel the presence of Oscar Romero. When I first heard Romero talking about his blood being a seed of liberty, I knew that the idea of blood and seeds was stirring up new thoughts about the atonement in me. What if we were to look at the life of Jesus in the same way that we look at the life of Oscar Romero? Romero was the Archbishop of El Salvador who bound his life to the oppressed and ultimately gave his life in service to them. The sacrifice of one's life is at the center of the gospel. Jesus and Romero reveal to us that the blood is not a substitution...but rather an invitation to come and give your life for the marginalized so that you might find the salvation that comes from giving your life for others.

It is not enough to look back and assume that the gospel of Jesus requires nothing of you in the present because you believe an atonement has already happened...on the contrary it requires that you give everything. There is still power in the blood and that blood is yours. I pray that in discovering the inner seed of liberty that we all have to give...we will also discover the power of blood within and without.

Amen.

169.

March 27, 2014

Would We Execute Moses?: The Case of Anthony Doyle

One day, a man became overcome with evil, grabbed an object and repeatedly struck the body of another until that person was dead. After committing the murder, the man took the body, hid it and fled.

This series of events sounds eerily similar to what Texas Death Row Inmate Anthony Doyle was convicted of doing in 2003 to Hyun Cho. However, the initial story is not about Anthony Doyle...it is found in Exodus 2 and describes Moses' murder of the Egyptian. Most people of faith would not equate Anthony Doyle with Moses...due primarily to the fact that we think we can justify taking a life by creating a monster out of our neighbor. We fail to realize that the killer in the monsters we create is the same killer that was in Moses...and that also resides in us...evil.

Tonight, Texas will execute Anthony Doyle if no court stops them. We have been taught our whole lives that we are to love our neighbors as our self. Somehow it seems that we do not see Anthony Doyle as our neighbor. This doesn't change the fact that Moses would have been and so is Anthony. When Texas executes Anthony Doyle...Texas will execute part of all of us...the part that failed to love our neighbor as our self enough to stop it.

Amen.

170.

March 30, 2014

doubt the poem

tears flow
you found me
fist lands
you found me
screams condemn
you found me
people leave
you found me
hate takes over
you found me
in the dark chaos
you found me
but where were you to begin with

171.

March 31, 2014

The End of Gay Marriage

The end is near. The writing is on the wall. The courts are ruling in favor of marriage equality one after the other all over our county. So what happens when marriage is just marriage? I think there is something to be found both in the struggle and at the end of the road when the rights have been secured and the victory won...a mandate for all of us to champion love.

There is an older lady I have known who was married to another woman for a long time. One spouse died and the widow grieved. About a year later, the widow met a man and fell in love. The two married. I grew confused by the turn of events. I approached the woman and asked, "How do you identify?" I will never forget her reply, "Young man, when you get to be my age...you just identify with love."

There is a danger in forgetting that love is love. It takes us to a place where love must identify its kind and sort in order to have meaning or value. The struggle for marriage equality should be one that strengthens all loves and marriages. There should never be a time one love is elevated or lowered over or under any other love.

In October, I performed the wedding of two women. I will never forget how awkward it sounded when anyone at the wedding used the phrases same-sex wedding or gay marriage. For most gathered, the celebration was a beautiful wedding for two people who are madly in love and deeply committed. For the couple and their close friends that was enough...it should be for us too.

Let us prepare for this coming day where love is love by preparing our language for it now. Perhaps instead of gay and same-sex marriage we can use the language of marriage equality and equal marriage. This language seems to liberate us from a space of needing identity to qualify love...and gives language to describe where our hearts so often yearn to be...that queer and holy space where love is indeed love.

Amen.

172.

April 2, 2014

The Danger of Being Called Pastor

The sky has been dark all afternoon. Lately, it seems the sky is always dark. The drive down was longer than usual. Tonight, I sit in a hotel room. Tomorrow, I will be on Texas' Death Row visiting inmate Will Speer.

I had a tremendous amount of time to think on the way down. Sometimes such excesses of time are good and sometimes they are not. My mind wondered to my ministry over the last year. I have experienced tremendous highs and staggering lows. I have been called both a demon and a saint...sometimes by the same person in the same day. I guess such is the danger of being called pastor.

Tomorrow, I will sit on death row and love my friend Will Speer. We will share tremendous words and enjoy many laughs, but there will be one thing hanging over the entirety of the visit...the State of Texas is determined to kill my friend and I often feel like there is little I can do about it. Loving in those spaces where there is nothing you can do except love and having to face the consequences of life is the danger of being called pastor.

There will be those throughout my life who ask me to be there for them in their lowest moments...and then when I need them I will stand alone. This is the danger of being called pastor.

Tonight, I will lay my head down knowing that the way of Jesus leads to a lonely death and that I am called to follow. This is the danger of being called pastor.

173.

April 5, 2014

The Danger of Calls to The Wilderness: A Lenten Response to Rachel Held Evans and Other Progressive Evangelicals

The Southern Baptist Theological Seminary is a chief producer and promulgator of spiritual abuse. The guilt and judgment sucked the oxygen out of my body and soul and literally almost killed me on more than one occasion. I left with a degree and a broken faith in humanity and God. During this emotionally exhaustive period of time, I met a minister who invited me to a place called "the wilderness" for conversation and healing. I felt like I had found the place I needed to heal. After some time, I discovered that this minister's wilderness was a place to keep me talking and talking and talking and talking. The talking never led to love or justice...just headaches and more confusion. It actually felt like I got ambushed in the minister's wilderness.

The last few years, I have grown into a real wilderness space of theological activism...a space where I feel called to stand and speak prophetically of love and justice to all who have ears to hear. You don't make much money standing in this space. You actually get shit on much more than you receive praise. You often wonder if you are making a difference. You grow frustrated at the rest of the church when you look around and see very few people standing with you. You sacrifice metaphorically and physically your body for the benefit of all of God's children. You begin to see truth in a myriad of spaces. You demand love for all of those who have been left out. You do not need further conversation about justice for different groups of people and individuals for you know that justice is something to be accomplished not endlessly conversed about. You stand and when there is nothing else to do...you stand. I most fully found the person that I have spent my entire life seeking in this true wilderness space...Jesus.

This last week, Rachel Held Evans wrote on her blog, "Instead of fighting for a seat at the evangelical table, I want to prepare tables in the wilderness, where everyone is welcome and where we can go on discussing (and debating!) the Bible, science, sexuality, gender, racial reconciliation, justice, church, and faith, but without labels, without wars" (http://rachelheldevans.com/blog/what-now-world-vision). Over the years, I have also heard progressive evangelical leaders from Jim Wallis to Shane Claiborne to Tony Campolo among others call for us all to come to these so called wilderness places for conversation. The problem is that too often on controversial issues I have heard the conversation continue and continue and continue and continue in so called wilderness spaces until everyone has to leave because in a similar fashion to The Southern Baptist Theological Seminary there is so much hot air that no one can breathe. I invite my progressive evangelical colleagues to a real place of wilderness...a place where God has already decided how much God loves all of God's children and a place where we are called to sacrifice our bodies and empires for the sake of love and justice. It is not enough to keep calling for conversation...we must sacrifice.

I have grown so tired of people protecting empires with calls for conversation at the expense of love and justice.

The world does not need more tables.

The world does not need more conversation facilitators.

We have many of those.

The world needs more courageous prophets who are willing to walk the way of Jesus...which in this season of lent we are always reminded leads to death.

No more tables and endless conversations...calls for such have always been and will always be suspect when lives are on the line.

God's call for love and justice for all of God's children is now.

Amen.

174.

April 8, 2014

Actions Talk and Bullshit Walks: The Story of A Real Christian: Major Kathy Cox of the Salvation Army: Witness to 60+ Executions in Texas

I was scared the first time I visited Texas' Death Row. I knew no one and had no one to talk to. The rules about interaction are very strict...do not interact with anyone except the guards and the person you are visiting. I was sitting there in my visitation booth and I heard a whisper. Looking up, I discovered an older lady who introduced her self as Major Kathy Cox with the Salvation Army and quietly encouraged my work and ministry. I have seen Cox every time I have been down to Texas' Death Row since.

I hear all of the Christian prognosticators talking about the end of their denominations and the battles they are fighting for the future of their respective churches. In the midst of such battles, sacrifice and true courage seems to be increasingly rare. It is as if most prognosticators feel the need to run outside in the middle of a thunderstorm and tell everyone that it is raining and lightening. In a revised usage of an old adage...actions talk and bullshit walks. The sacrifices we make to live like Jesus speak much louder than the words we write and speak in the comfort of the sympathetic. Everyone wants to know what one is supposed to do in the midst of such perilous and trying times, I offer Kathy Cox as Exhibit A.

Major Cox exists in a denomination that is generally more conservative than she is. In her career, Cox has been present to witness over 60 executions. Through a Bible curriculum Cox developed, tens of thousands of people in Texas prisons have learned the basics of our faith. Each week, Cox leaves her home in Dallas and spends multiple days on Death Row visiting the some of the over 40 inmates she visits each month. I have met no more amazing of a Christian than I have in this woman.

Did I mention that Kathy is 90 years old?

Amen.

175.

April 9, 2014

Hand Washing: The Case of Ramiro Hernandez-Llanas

When injustices take place, there are always hand washers. To absolve his self of the responsibility of the execution of Jesus, Pilate washed his hands. The judges that sit on the numerous courts that have turned down the appeals of Ramiro Hernandez-Llanas have washed their hands of the burden of his execution. The governor of the State of Texas has become a professional at washing his hands of the burdens of execution after execution using words like monster and subhuman. The prison guards who force Hernandez-Llanas to the execution chamber this evening will wash their hands of responsibility. The doctors and nurses that administer the lethal agents will cleanse their hands or any burden when they are through. The citizens of Texas will wash their hands and either state they wanted it to happen or there was nothing that could have been done to stop the injustice of execution. Regardless, there will be much hand washing tonight to relieve the guilt of a murder we are collectively responsible for.

Ramiro Hernandez-Llanas was found guilty of murdering Glen Lich...and there will be much evidence to convict all of us in the murder of Ramiro Hernandez-Llanas.

The hand washing does not remove the guilt.

We will not stop murders in Texas until we stop committing them.

Amen.

176.

April 9, 2014

Finding Inspiration on Immigration in Strange Places // When Jeb Bush Sounded Like Jesus

I believe that there are rare moments when a person speaks to a political issue yet transcends political discussion to capture the clarity of one of the deepest pieces of all of our humanity...namely an ability to see love and speak of it for what it is. I doubt I will ever vote for Jeb Bush...in fact I am very close to giving up voting altogether for a variety of spiritual and moral reasons dealing with what happens when we compromise parts of our morals and integrity for the lesser of multiple evils...but that conversation is for another blog. Earlier this week, former Florida Governor and potential 2016 Republican Presidential Candidate Jeb Bush made the following remarks when asked about undocumented immigration, "*what they did is not a felony. It's an act of love. It's an act of commitment to your family*" (http://politicalticker.blogs.cnn.com/2014/04/06/jeb-bush-immigration-is-not-a-felony-but-an-act-of-love/). In one sentence, Jeb Bush spoke louder and clearer than most of our churches are willing to speak on immigration. This is not a blog about Jeb Bush...as I am sure that he has said many other things that are very problematic...this is a blog about what and who Bush spoke to...love.

Sitting in a class on immigration last spring, I invited my classmates to dream of a time when there is not a need for borders or boundaries...a time when all people are able to share resources and live as one. The responses ranged from being totally appalled to total shock that I would even suggest such a thing. My God...a world without borders? Where could I have even thought of such a construct? The answer is found in the life and ministry of the incarnation of a God called love...Jesus.

In Matthew 25, Jesus states very clearly that love or the presence of Jesus will be found with "the least of these." The borders that we create...by their very existence...are created to leave out the least of these. As we protect and create boundaries, there are always Jesuses at our borders. If we continue to have views on immigration that exclude rather than include, we will be sacrificing the very God of love that we all claim to serve...who sits on our borders.

Amen.

177.

April 14, 2014

Traveling into the Darkness

The children walk down the aisles of our churches waving palms all around. Together, we reenact the celebration of Jesus' entry into Jerusalem. Palm Sundays are always festive times. Everyone knows that the next time they gather it will be Resurrection Sunday and Jesus will have won a great victory over death. The problem is that no one wants to walk through where one has to go to experience a resurrection...the darkness. I won't say that resurrection celebration without darkness is not real...but I will say that resurrections do not happen without darkness...resurrections do not happen without death.

The story of Holy Week is that we have to travel into the darkness in order to arrive at a place of resurrection. Many of you only want resurrections...but you forget that darkness and death have to come first. The world is brought into being out of darkness. Life and light flows out of darkness.

Jesus becomes most fully God when Jesus decides to love and continues to travel deeper into the darkness. We all want sunny days...but God is found in the dark nights. Jesus becomes God in the Garden of Gethsemane. Jesus becomes God when there is the temptation to stay in the light but the knowledge that light is most fully realized in the darkness. Jesus pushes deeper still into the darkness so that Jesus might be the light of love in such a space.

If they got all the light they need and you strike match then they are going to complain about the smell...but if they are in darkness and you strike a match then there will be light for all to see a little bit better by.

Jesus pushes into the darkness and becomes the light of the world. You can too. Go to the dark spaces and bring some matches. For it is time that we all set the world on fire.

Amen.

178.

April 14, 2014

The Enemies Cometh and in them Lay Our Salvation

I have my fair share of enemies these days. I have found that the longer I work as both an activist and a pastor the more enemies I have. I hear lies. I experience violence. I interact with evil. In these experiences, I have discovered something surprising...my salvation.

The scriptures tell us to love our enemies...if you think about your enemies as your neighbors then we are to go a step further and love our enemies as our self. I believe we learn to love our self through loving our enemies. If we can learn to love our enemies as our self then we are set free to love the God within in us who calls our self made in that God's image. In loving our enemies lies our God realization and actualization.

Jesus learns to love the whole world through the pain of learning to love Jesus' enemies. Jesus learns to love the God that abandons Jesus on the cross through learning to love the enemies standing in front of Jesus. The enemies become the path to the liberation that is salvation.

God is in our enemies because in our enemies is God.

Our salvation comes through loving our enemies so that we might love God.

Yes our enemies cometh...but thank God in them lay our salvation.

Amen.

179.

April, 16, 2014

The Passion of Jesus Comes Early: Standing on the Via Dolorsa at the Execution of Jose Luis Villegas Jr.

When Jesus declares I was in prison and you did not visit me...and goes on to declare what you have done to the least of these you have done to me...Jesus directly binds his passion with the passion of those in prison. It is important to notice that Jesus does not say I was not guilty and in prison and you did not visit me...rather Jesus binds his self to all who are in prison.

In the midst of this Holy Week, Jose Luis Villegas Jr. is scheduled to be executed by the State of Texas at 6pm tonight. There is much evidence that Villegas murdered Alma Perez, Erida Perez Salazar and her son 3-year-old Jacob...but for the follower of Jesus evidence is not the point. Love is. Jesus' words in Matthew 25 remind us that we will be judged by how we treat the least of these amongst us...whether there is guilt or not...and further reveal that Jesus is incarnated into the lives of those we execute.

The Via Dolorosa or "Way of Sorrows" is the path in Jerusalem that Jesus carried his cross to his execution. In the economy of God, Jesus will be incarnated in Jose Luis Villegas Jr. and I have chosen to travel to Huntsville, Texas to stand along the Via Dolorosa in protest of an execution that will do nothing but further destroy consciousnesses and lives through the perpetuation of violence and hate. In Texas, the way of the cross ends in Huntsville.

Where will you stand? Will you be amongst those shouting crucify him? Or will you get in the way?

Amen.

180.

April 18, 2014

Jesus Didn't Die for Your Sins. Jesus Died to Show You the Way...the Way to the Cross.

Lately, I have had a lot of time to think about borders and boundaries. I am a doctoral student at Brite Divinity School and I was sitting in class last spring...and in this class on immigration we began to talk about the end game. What is the end goal? I raised my hand and said, "Can we imagine a world where there are no nationalities...where there are no borders...where there is simply us?" From their response, you would have thought that I was talking about Mars.

This morning I think it is important that we realize that the borders and boundaries we create in our lives cause violence...they separate...they divide...they keep us from being in relationship with each other. As we stand next to the Federal Building...so often when we think about what it means to be here in the United States...we don't spend a lot of time thinking about the 70,000 people who have been murdered in the drug war in Northern Mexico. Less than a couple hours drive from where we stand right now. That is because we have erected borders and boundaries in our lives that allow us to other people.

Just this past week, I was in Huntsville, Texas. I told people this week that, 'Here in Texas, the way of the cross ends in Huntsville.' We live in a state that is executing more people than most nations on earth...and somehow we seem to be able to pass concern by saying that those people are monsters. Those people are something less than human. We look outside of our national boundaries and we are often able to not care because somehow those people are different...somehow those people are other.

It is Good Friday and there is Good News.

If we want to talk about gun violence, gun control...ending the need for all of these things....then we need to talk about the borders and boundaries that we put between each other. That lead us to protect things. What would be the big deal if the border between the United States and Mexico was taken down this afternoon? ...and people came and got all your stuff...and we were pushed in a direction where stuff don't matter...a direction of Jesus. Where we share. Where we learn to love each other.

You see I don't believe that Jesus died to save us from our sins. I believe that Jesus died to show us the way. And the question is... 'Are we willing to go the way of the cross?' Are we willing to put down our power...our violence...our hate...and learn to love our neighbors as our selves?

As we were walking over here, this guy said something to me that made me so angry. I wanted to turn around and punch that guy in the face. He said, "I wish I could protest with y'all but I'm working." I wanted to get right up in his face and I told myself, "Jeff you are about to talk to people about loving their neighbor as their self and it might not look nice to get in a tussle with this guy on the sidewalk before you get there." But I think...names like Adam Lanza, Fred Phelps, Corporate Executives...all of these people that we have othered. Now wait a second...you didn't expect me to say those names. You see in our activism...what will be the measure of whether we follow the way of Jesus will be how much love we show to those that we have othered. It is not just the people on death row. We exist in a time of increasing polarities...increasing division...and I want to know something...do we as Christians have the courage to get up on that cross and say, "Father forgive them for they know not what they do"...? and when we travel to that space...that is the space where we can say that we are following the way of Jesus. When we go to that space that is not just about justice but it is about reconciliation. That is when we can talk about following the way of Jesus.

Will we push toward the cross today? It means loving our neighbors as our self even if they are killing us. Today, whether we are American or Mexican, black or white, gay or straight...whatever dichotomy, boundary, border or identity that we can come up with...Jesus is calling us to a cross where such things die and we are asked to love our neighbor as our self no matter what.

Will we put down our guns...whether they be our mouths or physical guns...and begin to love our neighbors as our selves?

This is the hour of the crucifixion. This is the time of forgiveness. This is the place where reconciliation happens.

So I invite you all to climb up on that cross and hang there for a little while until love is all that is left.

Amen.

181.

April 22, 2014

Jesus Sells Drugs: An Easter Message

I have known many Easters.

I remember one Easter morning as a child realizing Jesus quite literally loved us to death. I was overwhelmed by the enormity of such love. Later that same day, I looked up at a depiction of Noah's Ark and thought that this Jesus of love sounded much better than the God that destroyed the world with the great flood. The conclusion was simple for me. I loved Jesus and Jesus loved me.

The more Easters I experienced the more complex Jesus became for me. The preacher kept talking about a God who saved us from our sins. I couldn't figure out if I was saved or not. The truth of the matter was that I got saved hundreds if not thousands of times. I was terrified and desperate to know Jesus.

As the high school Easters turned to college Easters, I decided the only way to deal with my doubt was to become certain. I subscribed to a theology that blessed my desire to be wealthy and not care too much about the needs of others...a fundamentalist brand of Calvinism. I believed that if someone was not blessed or saved then God obviously didn't choose them for blessings or salvation. Similar theologies allowed the racist keepers of apartheid in South Africa to describe themselves as Christians. I decided to go to the Southern Baptist Theological Seminary to learn how to teach others such a theology. Throughout this time, I had my doubts.

The event that changed my life was my mentor coming out to me on his death bed. That was the moment I met Jesus in someone who truly represented the least of these and realized I could return to the Jesus of my childhood...that Jesus that loved me and taught me how to love others. It was a resurrection moment. Since that time, I have opened my mind and heart to a wide diversity of people and places...and the resurrections haven't stopped.

The wideness and vastness of God's love is where resurrection magically and mysteriously happens. I am not afraid of resurrection. I don't have to explain it. I just simply push into it. I believe that love never dies...I believe that love can conquers death...I believe that love changes hearts...and I believe that love can set us free. We must experience a revolution of the mind and heart that allows us to push into love past our borders and boundaries...past our stones.

In the resurrection, we find a love that saves us from death. If we want to talk about salvation...then let's talk about a God that dies so that all might learn to live and teaches us to do the same. Everybody wants to talk about eternal life...but no one wants to talk about the call to give our lives so that others might live. I don't give a shit if you can pray the right prayers, recite the clearest doctrines or stay within the boundaries of the most precise dogmas...I care whether you are connected to the love a resurrected God who declares what you have done to the least of these you have done to me. It seems like many people are sitting outside the tomb of Jesus...which is often our churches...and wondering where the resurrected God is. Unfortunately, most have forgotten where to look.

We race to church past Jesus sleeping under the overpasses in the dirt.
We read books and miss the lesbian Jesus knocking on the doors with a desire to get married in our churches.
We pray for a word from God when Jesus is standing there with a word that says "Will Work For Food" every morning.
We fight over doctrine and dogma as Jesus dies of aids down the street.
We sing our songs as Jesus sells drugs to make a living a few abandoned buildings down.
We keep programming and Jesus is down at the bar getting drunk to forget his problems.
We recite verses and and miss the Jesus having sex for some money to eat.
We have so many quiet times that they have caused us to remain quiet about the injustices that Jesus faces all over the world.

If you believe in a God that allows you to ignore the oppressed incarnated God down the street then I respond with the words of Mary: You have taken my Lord and I don't know where you have laid him.

You cannot preach about a sweet by and by and ignore the resurrected Jesus in your midst. This is the message of Easter. This is the message of love.

Do we believe in resurrection or not?

Jesus is all around us calling us to the resurrection in the least...and if we will stop worrying and fretting about our life and souls long enough...we just might get a chance to meet her.

Amen.

182.

April 25, 2014

Bent: Why I Decided to Act.

There is danger in forgetting. There is also danger in remembering incorrectly. The tragic systematic genocide of six million persons of Jewish descent has filled most of our thoughts and history books concerning the Holocaust. The arrest and systematic murder of tens of thousands of homosexuals has not. The German government did not acknowledge and apologize for a systemic murder of homosexuals during the Holocaust until 2002. There is danger in forgetting. There is also danger in remembering incorrectly.

This weekend at the Cathedral of Hope in Dallas, I will have a minor role in a play called Bent that highlights the plight of homosexuals during the Holocaust. The acts and scenes depict the struggle to survive and remain human during despicable times. I play a criminal who gets in an argument with a homosexual over soup in a concentration camp. I act to play a small part in helping to tell a story that is not often told...that of courageous people who were systemically condemned and murdered for how and who they loved during the Holocaust.

The Gospel of Jesus is quite simple...we are tasked to keep telling stories that need to be told. Bent is an action of fidelity to the message of Jesus for me. The play also inspires me to tell other stories as well.

Let us not forget that state sponsored killing is what led to the Holocaust. Texas leads the nation in executions.

May we remember that the dehumanization of homosexuals began with denials of certain rights that led to the denial of more. One is not allowed to marry someone of the same gender and anyone can still be fired from their job for being gay here in Texas. Many churches still deny homosexuals the right to be ordained clergy or to be married.

Just a few weeks ago, F. Glenn Miller killed William Lewis Corporon, Reat Griffin Underwood and Terri LaManno while on a rampage against Jewish targets in Kansas.

Make no mistake...the hate that can cause a Holocaust still exists.

The stories of evil are strong...but we must keep telling stories of love that are stronger.

This is why I decided to act.

Amen.

183.

April 25, 2014

A Child of God and the Violent Hate that Killed Her

Maren Sanchez was stabbed to death today a few days after turning down a fellow student's invitation to the prom at Jonathan Law High School in Milford, Connecticut. The incident happened less than 25 miles from the site of another school massacre...Sandy Hook Elementary School in Newtown. The killers in both instances had a primary motivation...hate.

Unresolved anger pushes us to hate which often pushes us to violence. In Matthew 5, Jesus treats murder and anger as equal crimes. The wisdom of this moment is that Jesus knows what unresolved anger will push people to do. Like a cancer that overtakes the heart and mind, anger develops into hate and takes over our lives as we begin to destroy the lives of others. Jesus pushes us to dispel the anger and hate in our lives with love.

The only way that there will be no more victims like Maren Sanchez or Adam Lanza or Olivia Engel or Ana Marquez-Greene is if we begin to invest in love as the only substance that can dispel anger and hate in our lives and in the lives of others.

May each incident in which hate wins a temporary victory only strengthen our resolve to love harder and stronger.

May we honor the memory of Maren Sanchez by boldly loving the entire world in her stead.

Amen.

184.

April 26, 2014

Glen Stassen 1936-2014 / A Tribute from a Southern Baptist

Baptist Christian Ethicist Glen Stassen died today after a battle with cancer. We only spoke once. The conversation occurred after I sent him the following email on September 5, 2009:

Dr. Stassen,

My name is Jeff Hood and I am a ThM student at The Candler School of Theology at Emory University studying Christian interaction with social movements. I am currently enrolled in a doctoral seminar entitled 20th Century Christian Social Ethic with Dr. Elizabeth Bounds. I am contacting you based on her advice. I am a recent graduate (Dec. 2008) of The Southern Baptist Theological Seminary in Louisville, KY. I had a very difficult time at the school and have had tremendous faith issues ever since. I have been through a number of personal tragedies and have struggled with the question of suffering in the face of a loving God. I became a pariah at Southern due to my questions and my disagreements. I have yet to find a faith home since leaving Southern. I am very confused and could use some advice on how to proceed forward processing my experiences. I was told a little about your background and have always respected Fuller so I decided to take Dr. Bounds advice to contact you. She seems to have much respect for you and your scholarship. I would be very grateful for the chance to speak with you on the phone about your experiences and how you moved forward following life at Southern. Thank you for your time and I look forward to hearing from you.   -Jeff Hood

Dr. Stassen graciously replied with his home phone number and talked to me on the phone for over an hour. When told of my interest in social ethics and activism, Dr. Stassen encouraged me to see myself as part of a long lineage of progressive Southern Baptist ethicists and activists. I remember this being the first time I ever heard the names of Henlee Barnette or David Gushee. Whether he intended to or not, Dr. Stassen bequeathed me a legacy and one of the reasons I still call myself a Southern Baptist to this day is because of him. A few months ago, I accepted the PFLAG Equality Award for LGBT Activism as a Southern Baptist minister and activist. Thank you Dr. Stassen.

Amen.

185.

April 27, 2014

Donald Sterling, Churches and Race

I grew up on the Southside of Atlanta. Our county transitioned from a majority white context to a majority black context in my youth. In first grade, I was a student under Ms. Ellington...the first black teacher at Lake Harbin Elementary School in Morrow, Georgia. I will be forever grateful to Ms. Ellington for teaching me about Dr. Martin Luther King, Jr. In January of that year, Ms. Ellington chose me to recite Dr. King's speech at the March on Washington. I will never forget the excitement in the room as I loudly proclaimed, "I have a dream." Later that month, Ms. Ellington chose me as the Dr. Martin Luther King, Jr. Student of the Month. I was so very proud. Then came the rude awakening. There were white folks in my life at the time...who for racist reasons...encouraged me not to accept such an honor. I also became aware of grumblings from black parents that a white student should not be given such an honor. Ms. Ellington proudly stood beside me and helped me at a very early age to understand that I was a part of Dr. King's dream. By the time I graduated from high school, our community was mostly black and I had been very influenced by black culture. When I talk to people who are not from Atlanta, they have difficulty understanding the racial integration I experienced. I think this is primarily due to the fact that everywhere I have experienced since Atlanta is so largely segregated and people simply refuse to talk about race.

I have lived in both Alabama and Mississippi, but I have never experienced a more segregated and closed space than North Texas. What is worse and what I suspect to be the case in many parts of our country and world...is that not only are our churches not having conversations about race...but in their silence they are even further exacerbating the problem.

Donald Sterling is the owner of the National Basketball Association's Los Angeles Clippers. Last week, a recording was released of Sterling allegedly making repugnant and shameful racist remarks. When I heard his comments, I wondered what the National Basketball Association would do...but even more than that I wondered what most of our churches would do in a similar situation. There is too much comfort in our churches with people who make remarks and act like Sterling did. They are allowed to tell repugnant jokes, make sideways comments and act in ways that further segregation with little response. I am not a proponent of excluding anyone...but I do think we are failing in the ministry of Jesus if we don't respond to the blatant prejudices right in front of us.

We are called to afflict the comfortable and there seems to be many comfortable segregationists in our midst.

We speak often of wanting to affect change in our society...perhaps it starts by afflicting our self.

Amen.

·

186.

April 28, 2014

Stand Up! : Remarks at Pastors for Texas Children-Dallas

I have spent a few days thinking about Pastors for Texas Children generally and this meeting in particular. My thoughts and spirit has consistently been transported to this vision of standing up. What does it look like to stand up? What does it look like to have courage? We have many churches represented and many denominations represented here today...but I think that there is one thing that all of the gathered can agree on. I think we can all agree that the gospel mandate of Matthew 25 to stand with the least of these amongst us takes courage. I am thankful that we have a number of people who are showing tremendous courage on this issue of public education. The gospel mandate takes us to places where we know we have to be concerned with the welfare and well being of the entire spectrum of children...from the most to the least. So as we think about Pastors for Texas Children...as we think about being present on this important issue let us think about standing up...let us think about having courage. So I invite you to stand up. Literally...stand up! Visually as we stand together and as we listen to Luis Malfaro...may we stand with him in achieving his mission of a quality education for all of God's children in Texas. Amen.

187.

April 29, 2014

Botched Executions: A Visit, Jesus in Oklahoma and Us

This morning I visited a young man in the Tarrant County Correctional Facility in Fort Worth, Texas. When I arrived at the appointed booth, I felt the urge to ask the young man about his crime. Then I remembered the words of Jesus in Matthew 25. "I was in prison and you came to me." Jesus does not say anything about guilt or innocence in this declaration of incarnation with those who are in prison. I mentally botched the execution of love. So, I decided to pull my question and just sit with the young man for a while. In these moments, the jail became my church and I felt the presence of the living God. It was a moment of intense spirituality and love. I realized that the image of God in front of me was helping me to know the image of God within.

In Oklahoma today, Jesus was in prison and nobody gave a shit. Jesus was brought into the Oklahoma death chamber as numerous witnesses looked on and nobody gave a shit. Jesus was given the opportunity to say any final words and nobody gave a shit. Jesus was sedated then given the second and third drugs and nobody gave a shit. After some time, the physician observed that Jesus' vein was blown and that he was not receiving the lethal drugs and still nobody gave a shit. The execution was botched...Jesus later suffered a heart attack and died and nobody gave a shit.

When will somebody start giving a shit about the executed Jesus that declares..."I was in prison and you did not come to me"?

Courtney Lockett is no saint...but neither are we.

Stephanie Nieman was Lockett's victim. Now Lockett is ours.

When will we love?

The very incarnation of Jesus is calling out to us to love our neighbor as our self...to see the image of God in all of God's children...and end the death penalty.

I demand that the people of God put down the syringes and open up your hearts.

Stop botching the execution of love!

Amen.

188.

May 3, 2014

Courage Not Comfort: A Word to the Rich Young Rulers of Our Churches

I got a phone call from a friend the other day. "I have decided to perform a same-sex wedding in defiance of the denomination," she said. I congratulated her for her courage and encouraged her to come out publicly with her decision. "I can't do that. I will end up with no job, no insurance and no pension. I want you to write about this to encourage others…just please don't use my name or denomination," she replied.

I need to first say that I am proud of my friend. She is performing a ceremony that most ministers I know in similar situations would not. I am also disappointed in my friend for not standing publicly with the couple she is marrying.

I believe it is a half step to stand with a couple privately and refuse to do so publicly. There is no doubt that a job, insurance and a pension is nice…but such things are incomparable to the beauty of courageously following Jesus.

The situation that many modern religious people find their selves in echoes of a former time that has so much relevance for today. Jesus encountered a ruler with means…the text calls the ruler rich…but I guess I will let you be the judge of that. Jesus asks the ruler to abandon everything and follow him. The ruler is unable to follow Jesus because he has so much. Our modern religious structures have made it very difficult to follow Jesus…not because we are declining…but because we still have so much.

The infrastructures, buildings, jobs, insurance policies, pensions and on and on have confused us. You see we have arrived at a place where we think that this is why we have been called to this work. We forget that Jesus has called us to follow him and give our lives in courageous acts of service to others. Just like the rich young ruler…our comfort has taken away our ability to actually see.

The call of Jesus is to courage not comfort.

The question for the rich young rulers who lead our churches is stark.

Will you stand with comfort or courage?

Future generations will not hold back judgment for those who do not take courageous stands at this moment in time.

Jesus may forgive you but history will not.

Amen.

189.

May 6, 2014

Lives Less Valued: Why Black Girls Matter

The classrooms were filled with learning and dreaming. Students were playing on the playground and eating in the cafeteria. The gates of the rural academy flew open and gunmen demanded everyone go to the courtyard. Someone was able to make a quick phone call to authorities but it was too late. The students were already loaded into trucks and driven off...kidnapped from their refuge of learning. Now imagine the students were white girls.

The lack of outrage from most people in our country concerning the kidnapping of over 200 girls in Nigeria is troubling. This is a trend. Girls of color seem to matter less. My mind wonders back to the abduction of Natalie Holloway in Aruba a few years ago. Here in the United States there were reports of black girl after black girl being abducted...but the media spotlight and our collective conscience stayed on Aruba. Anyone who has lived in the urban areas of our nation know that the news is filled with abductions and murders of black girls...but it is breaking news and a top story when something happens to a white girl. I want to make something abundantly clear...black girls matter...black girls matter because they are beautifully and wonderfully created in the image of a loving God.

Until we arrive at a place where our hearts break and our collective outrage burns at violence perpetuated against all women in every corner of our cosmos...we do not know the God who dares call God's self...love.

Amen.

190.

May 10, 2014

The Ethics of Our Table: Jesus and Meat

Outside during the visit, everyone enjoys playing fetch with the family dog. When the host of the house whistles for the dog to come around back, no one pays attention. A few hours later, everyone gathers at the dinner table and prepares for a great feast. After a prayer asking God's blessing on the meal and the hands that prepared it, the hosts bring out all sorts of breads and vegetables. Then...as the gathered lean in expectantly for the main course...the host brings out a platter...on top is the family dog roasted with an apple in it's mouth.

For a long time, I wondered why this scene bothered me so much...and yet I had no problem eating all sorts of creatures. I lived in this juxtaposition for many years and finally decided to test my convictions and dare travel to a slaughterhouse. The images I encountered of filthy animals being systematically and painfully tortured are forever ingrained in my psyche. The visit left no question for me that a slaughterhouse is a violent place and eating what is produced there only encourages violence. I stopped eating meat.

Though I had firm convictions after the visit, I sensed that there were wider issues of justice associated with eating meat. There are. It takes unbelievable amounts of water and grain to raise animals. Can you imagine if we stopped eating animals and started feeding humans what it took to raise the animals? Global hunger would be a phenomenon of the past. The meat industry is one of the biggest causes of climate change. The meat industry releases huge amounts of carbon dioxide, methane and nitrous oxide into the air. Estimates range as high as 51% of global warming being caused by the meat industry. Not eating meat is also healthier for you. A diet without the cholesterol and saturated fats in meat gives you more energy and can help prevent a wide range of illnesses. The previous reasons deal with the effect of eating meat on humans...but it is also important to realize the animals that we kill can feel and experience the torture of their deaths. How interested are we in continuing the torture of both humans and animals in order to keep eating meat?

So would Jesus eat meat now? The answer lies in Jesus' declaration to be incarnated in the least of these. Jesus would not eat meat at the expense of feeding the world. Jesus would not support an industry causing such a huge portion of climate change. Jesus would disapprove of an industry that is making us sick. Jesus does not approve of the systematic torture of any living thing. I have no doubt that Jesus would not participate in the meat industrial complex and nor should we.

Amen.

191.

May 11, 2014

apoem: beloved & the next day

depression is setting in
is it a result of my sin
i am growing in rage
perhaps due to my age
you call
then hang up
just call me
i will pick up
why such a difficult cup to drink
the world is awful i think
speak now
is it you
but how
you are the beloved
is what you say
now i can live
another day

192.

May 12, 2014

The Cross and The Needle: Deep in the Heart of Texas

Numerous officials hurried into a back room. The meeting was called to order by the top official. The conversation began with the official clearing his throat and declaring, "The press is getting bad out there. Stand your ground and do not release any details about what is going to happen. This process must remain secret." The officials left the room with no comment for the press.

The murmurs of execution were a long time in the making. Then the day came. The tools of execution were brought in and the executioners went to work. In the final moments...the prisoner cried out to God in agony and no one listened. Most thought they were doing the right thing and strangely everyone felt worse when it was over. There was no freedom...only death.

Whose execution was this? Was this an execution by cross or needle?

The gospels are full of secret murmurings and conversations about the desire to execute Jesus. Officials in the State of Texas have been secretly murmuring and conversing about how to keep the execution process of Robert James Campbell secret for some time. Jesus cried out in agony on the cross. The needle that Texas will use to execute Campbell will be agonizingly full of an experimental dose of pentobarbital. Will Campbell cry out like Oklahoman Michael Lee Wilson did at his execution last January 9, "I feel my whole body burning"? Or will Campbell experience the botched execution of Clayton Lockett and experience tremendous pain on the way to a poorly executed death? Jesus suffered tremendously on the cross...and I think there is little question that so too will Campbell. If Robert James Campbell is executed...there will be those who say God allows execution and perhaps even blesses them. People said the same thing about the execution of Jesus. Most participants will think they are doing the right thing...yet after the execution there will be questions in their hearts. The same was true at the execution of Jesus.

When we talk about these executions whom exactly are we talking about?

The words of Jesus help us to answer such a question, "I was in prison and you visited me." The words of Matthew 25 do not reveal guilt or innocence...just incarnational presence. If Robert James Campbell is not successful in his appeal based on the secrecy of the State of Texas' execution process, I have no doubt that Jesus will be up on the gurney with him. I also have no doubt that Jesus will experience the needle going in and whatever agony comes next. Jesus will be in that chamber and Jesus will be executed...just like Jesus died with victim Alejandra Rendon...because this is what an incarnated God does.

Is there need for more killing? Is there need for more blood? Shall the cycle of execution continue raging from the streets of our cities all the way to Huntsville and back again?

Will we be the ones deep in the heart of Texas shouting crucify him or will we be the ones who try to save his life?

I call on President Barack Obama, Governor Rick Perry, the Courts, prison officials and anyone else in authority with courage to not wash your hands of another execution.

Put down the cross. Put down the needle.

Amen.

193.

May 16, 2014

Progressive Christians Often Seem to Not Give Two Shits About the Persecution, Imprisonment and Martyrdom of Fellow Christians and I Think I Know Why: A Retrospective

I was scanning the news a few nights ago and ran across the name of Meriam Yehya Ibrahim. I doubt many people in our churches know the name of Ibrahim or the fact that she was sentenced to death in Sudan last week for being a Christian. There are without a doubt components of patriarchy and misogyny in Ibrahim's case...but what about Kenneth Bae? Imprisoned for proselytizing, Bae is in declining health in a North Korean prison. Saeed Abedini sits in a tough Iranian prison for practicing his Christian faith...while his wife and two kids beg for his release from their home in Idaho. In 2013, estimates run as high as 8,000 Christians being martyred for their faith. In North Korea alone, the government is believed to have imprisoned somewhere between 50,000 and 70,000 Christians. Over 100 million Christians worldwide are believed to experience regular persecution due to their faith.* So why don't progressive Christians get outraged about the persecution, imprisonment and martyrdom of fellow Christians? I think the answer lies in an evangelical youth camp I attended when I was about 16.

The music was thumping, hands were in the air, everyone was jumping up and down and shouting the name of Jesus over and over again. For most this sounds like a cult, for me it was the evangelical world of my youth. I remember a man running out on stage and describing his experience being imprisoned in a foreign country for his faith. The man recalled how he had set up an underground church and faced the consequences when the authorities showed up. I was enthralled and on the edge of my seat as I listened to his story. I got emotional and turned to my friend sitting next to me. I will never forget his reply to my emotion, "Why are you crying? Why did his dumbass openly live out his faith over there in the first place?"

The response of many of my fellow progressives is the same as the earlier response of my skeptical evangelical friend. Why live your faith openly in the first place? Why go? Why care? It is interesting that we encourage our LGBTQ friends to come out of the closet and we expect both our self and Christians overseas to keep faith closeted. We come out and live out our faith openly and sometimes travel to do that in foreign countries for one simple reason...to spread the love of God that we have found in the life and message of Jesus. I think it is time that we start respecting all people who choose to give their lives so that others might have life. Maybe the true dumbass Christians are the ones who fail to understand that the call of Jesus is to come out and in the loving words of Mark 16 "go into all the world." I think the moment for outrage at the religious persecution that is being faced by fellow

Christians was yesterday. When will progressive Christians wake up and see that our destiny is inextricably united with those Christians we have so often called other? Let's take a break from deconstructing shit and love these folks. Please?

Amen.

* http://www.huffingtonpost.com/2014/01/09/christian-persecution_n_4568286.html

194.

May 19, 2014

To the Muslim Student at Southwestern Baptist Theological Seminary: A Satire

Congratulations. You are to be commended for starting your journey toward a doctorate in archeology at Southwestern Baptist Theological Seminary. I was surprised when I read of your matriculation and even more surprised that Southwestern's President Paige Patterson is supportive. Dr. Patterson is a fair man. Just ask all the professors he fired at Southeastern. Not far down the road from Southwestern is Broadway Baptist Church...a church that he helped usher out of the Southern Baptist Convention. I heard that you signed a moral conduct statement. I want you to know that all of those stipulations are negotiable and forgivable except for the women in ministry, the having sex with men and the mental illness parts. I experienced all of these stipulations while a student at an almost identical institution...Southern Baptist Theological Seminary.

I remember one of my classes at Southern berating a woman who opened up about her desire to pastor a church. Everyone called this woman a "strong woman of God" until she expressed a desire to pastor. The calls of "heretic," "backslider," being "biblically illiterate" and the worst "egalitarian" were not far behind. I found the woman crying down the hallway a little while after the class concluded, but I was too scared to go up and apologize for the way the class acted. I recommend you stay afraid, follow your fear and you should do well in your doctoral program. From all the reports I have read, you are at the very least able to pass as a man. I recommend you keep the perceived masculinity up and stay away from the home economics courses that Southwestern offers. Dr. Patterson would not approve of any slips of masculinity.

One of my classmates at Southern told me he was gay while I was a student there. I found out after a Southern Baptist pastor on the Board of Trustees hit on him in the gym. It was an awkward moment for my friend and he didn't know what to do...so he told me. I recommend you keep any attraction you have to guys under wraps. Your penis is often your worst enemy at a Southern Baptist school. Don't masturbate either...because you never know when a naked dude is going to pop into your head. Dr. Patterson would not approve of any thoughts or masturbating associated with dudes.

I recommend that if you get depressed, struggle with bipolar disorder or any type of mental illness...don't tell anybody if you want to stay in school. I almost killed my self on multiple occasions while a student at Southern and I was told to read my Bible and pray about it. When you feel like you are losing your mind, just read the Bible and pray so that eventually you will be so psychotic that you will not realize all of the unbelievably harmful things going on all around you. This technique worked for me at Southern. Dr. Patterson would not be happy with any medicated and managed mental illness on campus.

Quick recap...stay perceived as masculine, stay away from dudes real or perceived and don't medicate or manage any mental illnesses and you will be fine.

Just remember that you are at an institution that makes Brunei look like a utopian paradise.

Rev. Jeff Hood
Southern Baptist Theological Seminary, 2009

195.

May 21, 2014

A Few Thoughts on the Occasion of the Second Birthday of My Sons Jeff and Phillip

You are young now. You can only say a few words. There will come a time when you will know more words and will be called upon to speak. I want to write a few words to you before that time comes.

We are the inheritors of a tremendous faith tradition of love and justice based on the life and teachings of Jesus. I have known no greater love than that which Jesus has spoken into my life. No matter what you decide to call it, the love of Jesus will be the greatest ally you will have in this life.

I follow the example of Jesus in consistently seeking to place my body in that place that Jesus calls "the least of these." Jesus is constantly incarnated into such a space and will give you the courage to speak if you dare incarnate your self there. I commit to you that we will give you all the tools you need to courageously stand on the side of love. Jesus will always meet you there.

There will come a time were people will try to other or marginalize you for things that are beyond your control. Never listen to them. You are perfectly made in the image of a loving God and nothing will ever take that away from you. Theories and philosophies will come and go but the image of God that is within you is eternal and if you cultivate it...you will be free.

Love your enemies. There is no surer path to the heart of God than to love those who persecute you. We are a family committed to peace and we pray daily that you will be too. Jesus gave up her life rather than commit violence. Place your body between those who seek to commit violence against others and their potential victims. This is the call of Jesus. God is there.

Pray often. The cultivation of the soul lies in the courage to speak into it as a means of discovering the God who made you. Never be afraid to call out to the one who loves you more than I will ever be able.

Theology is important. Some theological musings for later... God is love. All constructions of a God that is not love are evil. There is no hell. Hell was created to scare you and there is no fear in love. Everyone is going to heaven. I would never send you to hell or annihilate you and this is how I know that God won't either. Jesus is God. Jesus is the incarnation of love perfected. The Spirit is still speaking. Quiet your self and listen for her voice. The chaos is what Jesus is always incarnated into and that is where you will find God. Buddha and other manifestations of love have much to teach you about what it means to love and follow Jesus. The greatest theologies are...love God, love your neighbor and love your enemy. If you follow these and discover their power, you will leave the world better than you found it and the life you save will be your own.

I will love and stand with you along this journey as long as I have breath.

Dad

196.

May 23, 2014

Jesus is Calling...Please Pick Up: An Open Letter to Brother Bill Haslam, Governor of Tennessee

Brother Bill.

I bring you greetings in the name of our savior...Jesus the Christ. We both graduated from Emory University...a university that I know gave us both a strong social conscience. I write because I am deeply pained in my spirit by your decision to use the electric chair for executions in Tennessee. I feel like your decision is an outward manifestation of a much deeper struggle going on within you...and all the rest of us who profess faith in the risen Christ...the struggle to follow Jesus when there is so much pressure not to. With regards to your actions on the death penalty, I would like to offer you a quick story that might help you follow Jesus.

Before his own execution, Jesus visited the potential site of an execution one time. I ask your grace in allowing me the liberty to set the circumstances in modern times to better purvey what happened and how it relates to us. The politicians, judges, district attorneys, warden, doctors, nurses and other attendants threw a woman on the chair. Accused of horrible crimes, the woman wept and knew that she had broken the laws of the society. There were witnesses who looked through the windows. The chaplain asked God to have mercy on the soul of the woman. As the switch was about to be flipped, a strange man stood up and used his finger to write in the fog that had gathered on the window. The names on the windows were those who had been affected by the failure of those in power to alleviate the needs of the marginalized, oppressed and suffering. Many had perished because those who had the means didn't help. When confronted with the hypocrisy of the entire situation, those who were called to carry out the execution picked up the phone in the chamber and asked for the governor. The folks in the chamber read out what was written on the window. The governor stopped the execution...because he knew Jesus was calling and had already spoken. This story reminds us of the convicting message of Jesus...we have all sinned and fallen short of the glory of God. There is life when we turn from the death of sin and dedicate our lives to following Jesus in the path of existing to give life to others.

Gov. Haslam...Jesus calls us to be better than this. Jesus calls us to be better than killing people. Jesus calls us to be better than electrocuting those who commit even the heinous of crimes. Jesus calls us to be better.

Jesus is calling from the chamber my brother.

Please pick up.

Rev. Jeff Hood
Southern Baptist Minister and Public Theologian
Texas

197.

May 25, 2014

The United States Flag at the Front of the Church is Blasphemous

A United States soldier processed the flag of the United States of America in to our sanctuary as we stood at attention singing "God Bless America." The veterans in our midst were honored as we sang the "Star Spangled Banner." The "Battle Hymn of the Republic" proceeded the pastor's fiery sermon on the coming destruction of our beloved nation if we "...did not turn from our wicked ways." Somehow gays, abortion and popular culture always made it into these services...but that is another story. The service concluded with an invitation to salvation as the congregation sang "God of Our Fathers." To say that the services of my Baptist youth were precariously wrapped in nationalism is an understatement...we believed that God's military was the United States military. Despite the fact that we did so much else that was problematic, my mind remains focused on the United States flag on that gold stand up on the altar.

In many Memorial Day services throughout our nation, some of those who have fallen victim to our ravenous thirst for violence and power will be honored and celebrated. We will remember the soldiers and attempt to reconcile their sacrifice with our faith. Unfortunately, there will be little conversation about peace and preventing the deaths of any one else. There will be no conversation of the millions and millions of people who have died as a result of our failed foreign policies and military interventions. The words of Jesus will be forgotten amidst the words of patriotism and nationalism.

No one will recite Jesus' words in Matthew 26:52, "...those who live by the sword will die by the sword." Matthew 5:44 and Jesus' reminder to "love our enemies and pray for those who persecute us" will not make an appearance. Least of all will we remember the millions and millions of people who have died in places with names like Hiroshima, Hanoi, Waziristan, Nagasaki, Kabul and Baghdad in the infernos created by our bombs...those "least of these" dead because we failed to see Jesus in their midst. No these words won't be remembered... and I know most congregations won't be talking beyond the soldiers who have died and will miss the opportunity to have a conversation about the wider call of Jesus to peace and justice.

My mind wonders back to that flag though. To put the United States flag on the altar of a church is to insinuate that somehow the United States has a claim to the grace of God that other nations and peoples do not. To put the United States flag at the front blurs that glorious declaration "For God so loved the world..." Can you imagine what someone from another country thinks when they see that United States flag up front? There is no barrier to the altar of God. Jesus does not love the United States more than any other nation...to put a flag at the front and bless the violence committed by an incredibly powerful people in the name of Jesus is blasphemous.

A real conversation about the non-violent love of Jesus and our purpose as followers can only happen when we take down the United States flags in our sanctuaries that stand in the way.

So let's toss out all the flags and have a real Memorial Day next year...one that memorializes and celebrates a time when we began to emulate Jesus' love for all people and put to death the nationalism that fooled us into thinking that violence can bring about peace.

Amen.

198.

May 29, 2014

The Danger of Dr. Maya Angelou

I turned the corner after hearing her speak and there she was. I shouted out, "Dr. Angelou...It's me...Jeff." Dr. Maya Angelou didn't know who I was and I have no idea why I thought it would be a good idea to call out to her like we were old friends. Regardless of my buffoonery, Dr. Angelou turned around and clasped my hand. We locked eyes for a few seconds as we talked about our faith. I will never forget those moments. I felt the incarnation of love, liberation and reconciliation embodied in every bit of her presence. This was a dangerous encounter. I knew I had to be something when I left.

Many times in many spaces Dr Angelou uttered these beautiful words, "People will forget what you said, people will forget what you did, but people will never forget how you made them feel."

I will never forget how she made me feel...like a human with tremendous potential to love and be loved.

Dr. Angelou speaks to all of us right now in these moments of unimaginable injustice. The success of our pursuits of justice will not be judged on what we say or what we do...they will be judged on how we are able to love and be loved. Dr. Angelou had every reason to spit in my white male face and walk away. From the rape of her seven-year-old body to the racism that she experienced throughout her life, there was no reason for her to be so generous to any white male...but she was and it changed me. We can continue to pursue activism in ways that create division and make people feel like shit or we can follow the path of Dr. Angelou and engage people in love.

Remember...

People will forget all the bullshit you say.
People will forget all the bullshit you do.
But people will never forget how you make them feel.

How do you make people feel in our efforts toward justice?

The danger of Dr. Angelou is that the totality of her life makes great demands of all us that she leaves behind.

Amen.

199.

May 30, 2014

Cathedral of Hope Devotion

"...you were dead in your transgressions and sins, in which you used to live when you followed the ways of this world... But because of her great love for us, God, who is rich in mercy, made us alive with Christ even when we were dead in transgressions—it is by grace you have been saved." -Ephesians 2:1-2, 4-5

There is something mystical to be found at the junction of life and death. I have stood at the bedside of many dying people and listened to the last words their minds and mouths would ever conjure up. Repeatedly I have heard, "I wish I had been myself." The yearning for the self is the response to a normalizing world that consistently asks of us, "How do you identify?" Too often we follow the paths that others have laid out for us and respond with a litany of identities that we claim or that claim us. We refuse to stand alone and our very self is stolen from us in the process. How shall we live in the midst of such a world? The beauty of Jesus is that she constantly draws us deeper into God...deeper into that queer space called, "I am." That space where we are raised from death to life by being who and what God has created us all to be...queer.

There is little safe about this space...but Jesus is there. We are reminded in the passage that in Jesus is resurrection. If you want to stay dead and aimlessly follow the expectations of others then ours is not the God for you. This is the God who calls all of us to life. Shall we rise?

We can be the formerly dead. We can stand boldly and declare in the words of our God, "I am."

The greatest transgression is to deny the God that has created us and most of us do that every day by denying the God within in whose image we are made. I invite you to leave behind the foolish thinking of forced identity behind and be. There is resurrection and it will come when you have the courage to be...queer...just like Jesus.

Amen.

200.

May 31, 2014

Jesus' Rampage or a Quick Lesson on Jesus and Guns

Judas gave Jesus a kiss. Peter knew what was going on and tossed Jesus an assault rifle. Jesus proceeded to mow down all of those who persecuted him. The rampage lasted through the night and Jesus hung all of his victims on crosses for the entire world to see. When the sun arose, there were all the enemies of Jesus hanging there together. Jesus stood proudly next to his victims and held his beloved assault rifle high above his head in triumph.

There is nothing remotely Christian about this story and there is nothing remotely Christian about parading an assault rifle around.

If you want to live as Jesus did then stop parading guns in the face of those that Jesus loves.

Open your eyes...Jesus...the one who told us to 'love our neighbor as our self'...is standing at the end of your barrel...begging you to put down the gun.

Amen.

201.

June 12, 2013

On the Eve of Pilgrimage: Contemplating Walking 200 miles from Livingston to Austin in Opposition to Execution

Community leaders of the day stood with their stones ready. The law said that the woman caught in adultery was to be killed. Everyone looked up to see what Jesus would do. Joining the woman in the dirt, Jesus used his body to save her. Without the body of Jesus, the woman would have perished.

I seek to emulate Jesus. Community leaders of our day here in Texas and around the country stand with their stones ready for another execution. I am ready too.

Over the next few days, I will give my body to the struggle for abolishment of the death penalty. I will pilgrimage from Livingston to Austin to help my neighbors understand that you cannot love your neighbor as your self and execute them. With every step I take, I will pray for an end to the violent crimes committed by both individuals and through state sponsored executions. I know the God that was a victim of a violent execution is with me.

I am seeking to love my neighbors as I never have before and I pray that the world will follow suit.

Amen.

202.

June 12-19, 2014

The Complete Pilgrimage Journal: A Short Story of a Long 200 mile Journey

June 12 and 13

Roads comfort me. I often find myself on bright days and dark nights between strips of white and yellow paint. When I meet him, I often wonder who he is and what he has done with my self. The confusion lets me know that I am still alive and perhaps growing in my humanity. There is something comforting about being reminded that we are still alive. This is a story about roads and life.

My heart was full. My heart is always full when I travel to Livingston. From rainy drives to sunny drives, I always feel the same on the way down...full. I had my first visit of the trip right when I pulled into town. There were tears and love in that place. Regardless of the crime, I knew I had just encountered a child of God. I didn't want to leave. I never want to leave. It always hurts to feel like you are leaving someone in such desperate need of love.

I pulled up to the hotel and took a few pieces of clothing out of the car. I nearly forgot my medicine, but I knew that my physiology can't handle the fullness of the next few days without the right amount of medicine in my system. I get up to the room and start to pray. "God make me an instrument of your peace...and if I die...let it be for you." I was scared. I had never walked this far in my life and there were so many unknown variables. Prayerfully, I pressed on to morning.

The door slammed behind me. The Polunsky Unit is good at making everyone who enters feel like a monster. I sat down across from a man I have been visiting for some time. We chatted about love and courage. I never grow tired of these topics...especially in a place so devoid of hope. I told him that I was about to do a 200 mile walk and he told me to walk for him...and I did.

The door slammed behind me. I jumped out of the car in my robe and stole to begin my walk. I said a brief prayer and turned the corner to start walking away from the Polunsky Unit. I made it five minutes before one of the guards from the residence of the warden drove up in a van and rolled down the window with his hand on a shotgun. "What are you doing out here?" "Walking." "Where are you going?" "To Austin." "That is a long walk. Why are you walking?" "I love Jesus and oppose the death penalty." "You need to hurry up and get out of here." I walked faster.

There was a beautiful shade tree that invited me to stop next to the road. It was hot and I paused to briefly collect myself. There was sweat dripping off both my glasses and face. There was a truck that slung into the driveway next to the tree and an angry young man jumped out to scream at me. "This is private property!" "Where does the right of way begin and I will move." "Right there where that ditch is and if I see you so much as take a step over that line...you will regret it." I held the line.

The gas stations and restaurants were unique experiences. Everyone stared and many commented. "What in the fuck are you wearing?" "Are you gay?" "That is an amazing costume." A blue minivan swerved to the side of the road. "Do you need a ride?" "No, I am on a pilgrimage to abolish the death penalty." "I am for the death penalty. Why are you against it?" "Because I am a Christian." "I am a Christian too and I am still for the death penalty. Why do you think being a Christian has anything to do with opposing the death penalty?" "Because I don't believe you can love your neighbor as your self and execute them." "Damn that makes sense. I am going to have to think about that some more." She said goodbye and drove away.

The sun was going down as I crossed the bridge over Lake Livingston and the Trinity River. I wept at the beauty of the moment or I wept out of exhaustion...I am still not sure which. I journeyed over to the side of the road to prepare a place to go to sleep. As I nodded off, I couldn't believe that this was only just the first day and I prayed that God would somehow give me the strength to finish.

June 14

Sleeping is not easy when you are not on a bed. We take our rest for granted. Homelessness is a pervasive problem in our world. We do violence everyday when we don't consider the sleepless nights of others. I spent the first few waking hours of my second day on pilgrimage walking against the death penalty and thinking about homelessness.

To say that it was hot on my pilgrimage is like saying that Antarctica is cold. My body consistently produced more sweat than I could have ever imagined possible. The robe I was wearing felt like being wrapped in a wet sheet. Regardless, I kept on walking to my next stop...the home of the Texas Execution Chamber.

Huntsville is a typical small town. Most people work for the local company...the Texas Department of Criminal Justice. Wesley Memorial United Methodist Church is a bastion of hope in a space often darkened by a refusal of the people to engage in serious conversation around topics of social justice.

I walked into the church and the people greeted me with open arms. I spent the first 20 minutes telling my story and then I heard from the gathered their stories. We came to a conclusion that Jesus loves us all more than we will ever know and that is the most important thing to carry with us. It was a beautiful evening. When I thought I couldn't be moved further by their hospitality, a woman appeared with a basin full of water to wash my feet. Jesus lives in Huntsville. I met her.

Upon pilgrimaging to the Huntsville Unit or the site of the Texas Execution Chamber, I placed my hands on the brick wall. "May the cross that is on top of this place...be the cross that leads the State of Texas to stop perpetuating the cycle of violence by killing people. Make me an instrument of such peace." I departed into the cold dark night.

The porch of the abandoned trailer was very lonely. I didn't know if I was going to be safe or not. My phone died and I didn't know if the folks I was counting on knew where I was. When the car pulled up, I was gushing. I would sleep in a bed tonight and arise to walk another day.

I had worried about violence and anger when I walked into Huntsville. As I laid my head down on a soft pillow, I worried about violence and anger as I thought about walking into Brazos County the next day. I prayed for God to keep me from fear. God didn't...but I decided to walk anyway.

June 15

I was not too far over the Brazos County line when a Sheriff's Deputy rolled up. Jumping out of the car, the Deputy started a line of call and response with me, "Where are you going?" "To Austin" "Walking?" "Yes, I am walking from Livingston to Austin in protest of the death penalty." "Ok..." Then another officer pulled up and jumped out of the car. "Can we take a look at your license? We just want to make sure that dispatch has your name and knows that you are going to be walking." "Sure." The officer proceeded to check for prior arrests and warrants. I was thoroughly investigated for walking down the road. The entire situation made me think about the numerous persons who are put through a similar situation without the benefit of being able to speak English...often for the same reason that I was...walking.

I got my sweat on after the incident until I was stopped by a photographer/videographer for the local newspaper to do some interviews and pose for some pictures. When you can barely walk, you feel weird participating in such rituals...but you do it in order to get the message out. I kept on moving after the media interaction was over. I felt like I walked all day needing to take a shit. There are very few bathrooms on the way in to Bryan or College Station. Then I saw it...the closest thing to paradise I had seen in some time...a hole in the wall honky tonk called "The Beer Joint."

Pushing the doors open with force, I walked in and spoke past the five guys sitting on bar stools to the woman working behind the counter. "Can I please use your restroom?" "Of course." Before I could get to the restroom though, a man at the bar turned to ask, "What in the hell are you doing?" I guess they had never had someone come in with clergy vestments on before. "I am walking from Livingston to Austin in protest of the death penalty." "Why in the hell would you do that?" "Because I am a Christian." "That sounds pretty silly to me." "I promise I will come back out and tell you why it is not silly after I get done using the bathroom." "Go right ahead. I ain't trying to hold you up." I took one of the most impactful and freeing shits of my life before I came back out to have a long conversation about the death penalty and faith with the guys at the bar and the woman working behind the counter. Before I left, most of the folks present told me they admired what I was doing whether they agreed with me or not. I left and started walking once more.

Sweating profusely and in a good deal of pain, I made it until about four miles from the Brazos County Courthouse. I called the reporter who was to interview me that evening over dinner and asked her to come pick me up. I was exhausted. The reporter drove me by the Brazos County Courthouse where I prayed for District Attorney Jarvis Parsons to stop pursuing death sentences. I asked that Jesus would manifest in the life of this deeply religious man in a way that would not let him participate in the killing of anyone else. I got back in the car. Upon arriving at a real deal Mexican restaurant, I waxed poetic the rest of the night with the reporter about life, faith and the death penalty.

When I laid my head down, I was comforted to know that the next day I would not be walking alone.

June 16

I woke up. I woke up. I woke up. The transition from sleep to engagement with the world was difficult. I felt terrible. This was only to be my fourth day on my pilgrimage. How would I survive? I prayed and started to force my bones to move.

Still moving slowly, I met a group of people to walk down the middle of College Station and Bryan with me. We talked about the death penalty. The weather transformed the conversation quickly. There were not many steps before we transitioned to talking about how miserably hot we were. When we got to the church, I was soaked through my robe again. Traveling in a wet robe to a cold inside causes you feel like you are turning into a sea lion.

I climbed the pulpit. I was nervous. This was the first time I had ever preached in a Roman Catholic Church before. I thundered down about needing to place our bodies into the conversations concerning social injustice. I had spoken about such things previously, but now I was truly starting to embody and believe it in a new way. After about 15 minutes, I said "amen." There were awkward moments between the time of reflection and the time of departure. I didn't know who was supposed to dismiss the group. The awkward blossomed to beautiful when I stood up and the people came to the aisles to bless me on the way out. The love of God flowed through the many hands that were placed on my body as I walked by. I now had the strength to finish.

Walking through the dirt and grass, I yearned for what I knew was approaching. The sun hit my eyes in a majestic reflection of light when I stumbled forward. I stooped down to drop both my hand and soul into the Brazos River. All of my sins were redeemed. I felt cleansed. I knew that I had to continue...I had to continue sounding the alarm of what the death penalty is doing to our souls.

Night was rapidly approaching as I stumbled through Caldwell looking for something to eat. I found a Chinese restaurant still open. I gobbled up strawberries, fried rice and coconut shrimp and washed it down with a cold Sprite. CNN was running a show about the anniversary of O.J. Simpson and the white Bronco. For some reason, I felt like the struggle to abolish the death penalty was similar to the situation playing out before my eyes on television again...it is a tragedy from start to finish.

I got bed bugs overnight.

June 17

Storms were coming that looked fierce but never truly developed into anything but a short shower.

Red bumps filled the skin covering my right hip. Each step I took caused my robe to rub up against those bumps and made them itch more. I knew I was in for a hot itchy day.

The wet hot dusty asphalt and rocks of Highway 21 were the most miserable part of my entire journey. I had trouble balancing and stumbled around. I prayed for help at numerous junctures. On more than one occasion, I had to decide to force my back to straighten a bit and simply keep walking.

One of the major stories to come out about my walk went to press in the middle of the day. I was proud to have been interviewed by Shane Claiborne and his product was phenomenal. I was highly encouraged. I knew that this article would shed much light on the death penalty in Texas. I walked faster...I guess because I felt like we were making progress.

I made it all the way to Bastrop. I conquered physical infirmary and boredom to begin my final two days of descent into Austin.

The bed bugs kept me company.

June 18

Walking down a busy highway is different during rush hour. People were honking and yelling as I walked. I don't think anyone was honking and yelling because they liked the look of a man in a robe either. I was unnerved. I thought about stopping. I was tired. I wondered what it would be like to stop. I kept going.

The sidewalks disappeared and I trudged through the tall grass. I felt like I had bugs in every crevice of my body. I walked.

I arrived at a motel close to the big airport in Austin. Sleep came quickly. I knew that I was almost done.

June 19

There is nothing like waking up and knowing that you are going to finish. I knew that every step I had taken and was taking was a step toward abolishing the death penalty. I called and talked to many people throughout the day as I walked into Austin. I stopped for some lemonade. The sweetness of the taste almost made me forget the pain in my feet and legs. I pushed on with lemonade in hand.

Two fellow pilgrims greeted me on South Congress Avenue and walked with me the rest of the way holding signs opposing the death penalty. Their presence was comforting. Multiple blocks later, two of my dear friends met me along the way. One of my friends had on a LGBT Pride shirt. I didn't think anything of it...until someone drove by screaming out of a truck window "Fuck you faggot!" There is nothing like a little phobia and hate to try to ruin a moment of triumph. We didn't let it...we just kept on walking.

Excitement filled all of us as we crossed the street and planted our feet on the grounds of the Capitol of Texas. I felt electricity shooting out my toes. The gathered friends and supporters began to clap and cheer as we walked up. I gave a brief statement and we walked into the Capitol. I stopped for a brief second to pray in the rotunda before moving on toward our closing event at University Baptist Church.

During the program, I talked over and over about the need to give the body to the struggle for justice. After my walk, I believe the group understood what I meant. I can think of no more fitting a place to finish my journey than where it began...in a Baptist church.

I walked for life. I walked for love. I walked for us.

203.

June 25, 2014

My Struggle with Stonewall

There are names of places whose mere utterance evokes description of social movement. Stonewall is one such name. On the 28th of June 1969, police raided the gay bar at the Stonewall Inn and bar patrons fought back. Many historians and social observers argue that this was the singular moment that launched the queer rights movement. As the 45th anniversary of the Stonewall Riots approach later this week, I took a second to visit the establishment and ponder the meaning of Stonewall.

There is danger in judging events of the past. Oppressed people often do things when cornered that they would not do under normal circumstances. The violent harassment of the police ultimately became too much and the people violently rebelled. I sat there for a long time struggling with the violence of Stonewall. I still don't know what to do with it.

I believe Jesus teaches his followers to love their neighbor/enemies as their self and this is hard to do while you are rioting against them. Jesus also stormed the temple and caused quite the commotion. For the follower of Jesus, is there a moral action known as a nonviolent riot? I think that such a riot would have to be centered on the destruction of property and not people. There were too many injuries to both police and protestors for this event to fit that definition.

Sitting at Stonewall with Jesus, I could struggle with these things all afternoon. For now, I think it is best to spend our time figuring out how to love our neighbors as our self and realizing that love cannot be accomplished through oppression.

Amen.

204.

June 27, 2014

The Tragedy of Mark Mayfield and The Call of Love

For followers of God, politics and religion have always been very closely connected. We are a people determined to see the hand of God move in the land of the living. We start to go astray when we remake God into a Republican or Democrat. We forget that we were made for so much more...namely love.

This morning, I woke up to news that Mark Mayfield committed suicide in Mississippi. Most probably didn't or don't know anything about him, but Mayfield was an attorney and leader of the Mississippi Tea Party. I didn't know who Mark Mayfield was either until he was charged with conspiring to photograph Senator Thad Cochran's wife Rose in her nursing home last month. The incident happened when Mayfield's preferred candidate Chris McDaniel was running neck and neck with Senator Thad Cochran in the Mississippi Republican Primary. A little more than one month later, Chris McDaniel lost and Mark Mayfield took his own life a few days later.

The message of God calls us to love our neighbor as our self. Mark Mayfield confused the allure of politics with the calling of love. I think we do too. Throughout my ministry, I have said political things on social media and in person that were neither loving nor kind. Lately, I have become increasingly reconvicted that followers of God must live beyond the partisan nature of politics and into the life of love. With his wife and two kids, we mourn the loss of Mark Mayfield not because we agree with him politically...whether we do or not...but because we agree with God about love.

Tragedy strikes when we place party before people. I pray that we will commit ourselves anew to loving each other regardless of our political stances. Perhaps before that next partisan post or conversation confusing God and partisan politics maybe we should remember Mark Mayfield.

Amen.

205.

June 28, 2014

The Danger of Debating with Jesus: Hobby Lobby and the Incarnated Christ at LaGuardia

"If you want to be a slut then be a slut on your own dime not mine." These were the second to last concluding words of a conversation I just had with an older Christian woman at LaGuardia Airport in New York. Just to be clear, I don't just walk around talking to random people about the Hobby Lobby case. I was praying and I think the woman thought that I would be someone she could easily commiserate with about the recent Supreme Court ruling. From the moment we started talking, it was clear that we disagreed. The interesting piece of the conversation was that we both kept referring to Jesus as our voices rose and fell. We were debating with Jesus. Eventually, I got so frustrated with the woman for her failure to see the slippery slope this decision could take our nation down that I packed up my things and walked away. I didn't think it could get much worse after the slut comment and then the Christian woman offered, "…and I hope you find the real Jesus too."

I left the conversation convinced that I had just encountered the demonic. I was more than angry. I was embarrassed and felt that an injustice had taken place. I believed that this woman was slandering the very Jesus that I serve. I had deep hate in my heart. I knew without a doubt that this woman was my enemy…and then in a vision she came to me again saying…"love your enemies, bless them that curse you, do good to them that hate you, and pray for them that despitefully use you, and persecute you."

The danger of debating with Jesus is that he might actually show up. You see I had a vision of the incarnated Christ at LaGuardia and she was an older Christian woman with a hateful tongue. If I am to follow Jesus…I will need to love and bless her.

Amen.

206.

July 2, 2014

Don't You Dare Turn Your Head: The Self-Immolation of The Rev. Charles Moore

The fiery passion of 79-year-old retired United Methodist pastor The Rev. Charles Moore is raging in my soul right now. On June 23 around 5:30pm, Moore exited his vehicle in Grand Saline, Texas, doused his body with gasoline and set himself on fire. After rescue efforts by bystanders, Moore was taken by helicopter to Parkland Hospital in Dallas and eventually died late last night. Based on notes left behind, Moore chose to self-immolate based on his frustration with the United Methodist Church's position on human sexuality, opposition to the death penalty, disdain for racism (especially in his hometown of Grand Saline) and his deep anger at Southern Methodist University's decision to house the George W. Bush Presidential Center.

Rev. Moore knew how we would react. On June 22, the day before he self-immolated, Moore wrote, "I know that some will judge me insane." When I first shared Moore's story with a table full of people at a Dallas restaurant, everyone immediately declared him insane. I know different.

While a graduate student in history at the University of Alabama, I spent six months studying self-immolations that took place in both the United States and in Vietnam during the Vietnam War. With stark consistency, the persons who self-immolated that I studied were remarkably sane and unquestionably persons of deep conviction. The temptation of the hour will be to turn our heads and call The Rev. Charles Moore insane. If we do…we should also turn our heads from Jesus and call him insane too. For we must not forget, Jesus sat in the Garden of Gethsemane and made a conscious clear decision to step out into death…just like Moore.

Instead of judging Rev. Moore, maybe we should try to ignite the passion for justice that burned so brightly in his life in ours. When Texas tries to execute Manuel Vasquez on August 6, maybe we should do something more than simply turn our heads and protect our dignity. When our churches and societies ignore racial segregation and discrimination, maybe we should do something more than simply turn our heads and protect our pride. When we are asked to perform a same-sex wedding ceremony or ordain a same-gender loving person, maybe we should do something more than turn our heads and protect our salaries/pensions. When institutional injustices occur all around us, maybe we should do something more that turn our heads and bless them with our silence. I will go to bed this evening thankful for the public witness of The Rev. Charles Moore and pray that the church would garner even an ounce of his passion and courage.

On a personal note, I serve on the Board of Directors of the Texas Coalition to Abolish the Death Penalty. Rev. Moore helped found the organization. Because Moore lived, I am able to do the work that I do. My respect for Moore is unwavering and I am proud to follow in his footsteps. Jesus asks us to give our lives and Moore did.

Tonight my passion for Jesus burns as intensely as ever. When I look straight ahead into the dark, I see Moore's bespectacled image burning. I see Moore giving his life so that others might live. I refuse to turn my head. I know that Jesus is speaking to me from there. The courage of a passionate follower of Jesus can set the world afire with love. May the great martyrdom of The Rev. Charles Moore make it so.

Amen.

details from:
http://www.umc.org/news-and-media/retired-pastor-saw-destiny-in-self-immolation

207.

July 7, 2014

Jose Antonio Vargas at Cathedral of Hope

Once there was a couple with a young son who were forced to flee their homeland. Throughout the treacherous journey, the family wrestled mightily to finish the trip. Upon arrival, the family struggled to adapt to their new surroundings. The language and customs were so different from their home. People would often stare and make life uncomfortable. The couple couldn't understand why everyone was so afraid of them. While this could be the story of many people who presently immigrate to the United States, this is actually the story of Jesus the Christ and his family's flight to Egypt.

Jesus is an immigrant.

In this radical space of reimagining social engagement and spirituality, Jose Antonio Vargas arrives to meet us. Born in the Philippines and raised by his grandparents in San Francisco, Vargas is an openly gay immigrant and person of deep faith. In 2008, Vargas was awarded the Pulitzer Prize while a journalist at The Washington Post for his coverage of the Virginia Tech shootings. The public perceived Vargas as the ultimate success story of a documented immigrant. No one knew his secret. In a 2011 essay in The New York Times Magazine, Vargas outed himself as an undocumented immigrant. Since this courageous act, Vargas has written, spoken and traveled extensively advocating for our nation to live up to the invitation and promise contained therein so beautifully written on the Statue of Liberty, "Give me your tired, your poor, your huddled masses yearning to breathe free."

Jose Antonio Vargas has lived courageously.

Do you have the courage to open your heart and allow your self to be moved to action by what he says?

The millions of immigrants in Texas and around this nation are waiting for your response.

208.

July 13, 2014

Across the Borders and Into the Flames: Rev. Charles Moore, Dr. Robert Jeffress, Bishop Yvette Flunder and Us

Resurrection is not possible without death. Rev. Charles Moore knew about resurrection and his fullest revelation of death came about quite violently. The flickering flame at the front of his funeral reminded us of the immolation and alluded to the endless possibilities of resurrection. The world is on fire and Moore wanted us to follow him into the flames.

The death of Rev. Moore is a call to radical discipleship. The problem is that radical discipleship is not taught or even valued in our churches. We want borders and boundaries. We want identities and labels. We want an "us and them" kind of world. There is nothing radical about such normative and violent constructions. We have grown so comfortable with not being like the ones we have othered. The call of Jesus is not "other than them." The call of Jesus is to a love so radically beyond borders that your love engulfs friend and foe alike.

When Dr. Robert Jeffress of First Baptist Dallas claimed Jesus would construct a border fence, I watched person after person trip over each other on Facebook and Twitter to bash the man. Then what? Radical discipleship comes after the bashing (or perhaps after not participating in the bashing in the first place) and is found in the loving that is the doing. Why are we not working to take down all borders? Why do we believe there is anything righteous about living behind a border in the first place? For the follower of Jesus there should be no immigration debate...we are called to be a people that refuses to let any border come between us and loving someone else. Daring to try and live beyond borders is a radical step. Loving Dr. Jeffress is divine.

Bishop Yvette Flunder declared in worship today at the Cathedral of Hope, "We serve a both/and kind of God." I am ready for the church to be a both/and kind of church. Fling the doors wide open! Don't let any normative identities or borders get in our way. We must realize that "How do you identify?" or "Where are you from?" are not Gospel questions. God does not care how you identify or where you are from if you can't love your neighbor or your enemies. If you want to follow Jesus...then follow him across the borders and into the flames.

Amen.

209.

July 14, 2014

The Pilgrimage: Reflections on 200 miles

How far will you go? I didn't know until I tried. Maybe I still don't know. This is the story of a few steps I took.

The Polusnky Unit or the home of Texas' Death Row was colder than usual that morning. I thought I came prepared. My thin jacket was simply not enough. The inmate and I talked for a long time. Then came the question that changed everything for me, "When are you going to place your body into the struggle to save my life?" I was offended. Did I not just tell you all the stuff I have been doing in the struggle to abolish the death penalty in Texas? I felt like I was doing everything I could. I left without answering. Truth be known, I didn't know how to answer the question.

Multiple weeks went by and the question haunted me. How do I place my body into the struggle? Then a transformation happened. I was reminded of the story of Jesus and the almost execution of the adulterous woman. The deeply religious governing authorities were about to throw stones at the woman and Jesus placed Jesus' body in the way. Jesus declared, "Whoever is without sin can cast the first stone." The authorities walked away in shame. I now understand what it looks like for someone to place their body into the struggle.

I was exhausted before I ever started. There is something mentally debilitating about the build up to walking 200 miles. I visited two inmates on death row and then I started walking. I felt the wind of God at my back. I had never been so hot in my life.

The first time I thought about quitting was right before the bridge over Lake Livingston. I was in tremendous pain and just 15 miles in. How was I going to finish? I looked even worse than I felt.

A blue minivan swerved to the side of the road. With a puzzled look on her face, the driver engaged me in a back and forth. "Do you need a ride?" "No, I am on a pilgrimage to abolish the death penalty." "Well, I am for the death penalty. Why are you against it?" "Because I am a Christian." "I am a Christian too and I am still for the death penalty. Why do you think being a Christian has anything to do with it?" "Because I don't believe you can love your neighbor as your self and execute them." "Damn that makes sense."

I slept on the side of the road. There is nothing comfortable about sleeping on the side of the road. Dreams on a journey like this are haunted with the faces of the departed. I woke up startled and walked on.

The robe felt like a soaking wet bed sheet by the time I arrived at Wesley Memorial United Methodist Church in Huntsville for the evening event. There was nothing out of the ordinary until one of the church members walked a basin of water over to me and started washing my feet. I didn't know what to do. I was very taken aback. Why would anyone want to wash my disgusting feet? I realized in that moment that grace is so rare in our age that we don't know what to do when we encounter it yet it seems that grace is what makes us most human and the only thing that can give us a future.

There is something less than human about denying grace to those who sit on death row. When I stopped at the site of the execution chamber, grace was on my mind. I touched the outside brick wall and prayed that Texas might know the beauty of grace.

I walked as the sun arose the next day and did not stop until the afternoon. I pushed open the doors of a bar a few miles inside of Brazos County. I desperately needed to go to the bathroom. Besides the woman behind the counter, there were five guys sitting at the bar. "What are you supposed to be?" hollered one of the guys. "I am on a pilgrimage from Livingston to Austin in opposition to the death penalty," I replied. "That has got to be the dumbest shit I have ever heard," replied another guy. "Friends, the pilgrimage is not dumb as shit and I will tell you why once I go to the bathroom," I offered as I pushed away. By the time I left the bar over thirty minutes later, all the guys and the woman behind the counter said that I had made them think much deeper about the death penalty than they ever had. It felt as if something magical had happened and I started walking. Later, I arrived at the Brazos County Courthouse where so many have been sentenced to death. I knelt and prayed that District Attorney Jarvis Parsons would open his heart and mind to abolishment like the folks earlier.

Everyone in town recognized me the next day. I had done an interview with Bryan-College Station's The Eagle and landed on the front page. I walked with a group of fellow abolitionists on Texas Avenue to Santa Teresa Catholic Church and climbed into the pulpit upon arrival. I am not sure if they had ever had a Baptist preacher in their pulpit before. When I walked out, the gathered walked with me and wished me well. Later in the day, I dropped my hand into the Brazos River. The water reminded me of the baptism of love that I had experienced on my journey.

There is little to report for the last few days of the walk except that it was awful. I was in relatively unpopulated areas. I was scared and alone praying for the abolishment of the death penalty. I spent the night under a bridge one night and found softer spaces on other nights. Why am I doing this? I kept wondering about my sanity. I had to push myself harder than I ever have before. I had to conjure up a love and hope that was beyond vengeance and reason to finish. I did.

I can assure you that the gates of heaven will look no finer than the Austin skyline did to me the day I saw it after walking in from Livingston. I had arrived. There were only a few more miles to go.

When I placed my feet on the grounds of the Capitol of Texas, I could feel electricity shooting out my toes. The gathered clapped and cheered. I gave a brief statement, prayed in the rotunda and went to University Baptist Church for the concluding event.

During the program, I talked over and over about the need for us all to give our bodies to the struggle for justice. After my walk, I believe the group understood what I meant. I can think of no more fitting a place to finish my journey than where it began...in a Baptist church.

Someone at the program asked me, "How far do you think you will have to walk to abolish the death penalty for good?" I replied, "I don't know...I guess we'll both know when I stop."

Amen.

210.

July 15, 2014

God is Our Passive Enemy: Reacting Fairly and Honestly to a Day Like Today

Christians have a bad tendency to rush to offer excuses for God in the wake of tragedy. In the last 24 hours, John Middleton was executed in Missouri with a lingering legitimate claim of innocence, four cousins were killed while playing soccer on a beach outside of Gaza City, Malaysia Airlines Flight 17 was shot out of the sky by Ukrainian separatists with a contingent of the world's top HIV/AIDS researchers on board, a six year old girl was raped in India and Israel launched a ground invasion of Gaza. The last 24 hours have been bad enough without ever getting into the millions of people who have been raped, kidnapped, beaten, robbed, murdered, committed suicide, starved to death, died of a horrific illness, had their lives destroyed by natural disaster or fallen victim to any number of other tragedies. In the midst of such a world, I think we should stop rushing to give God a pass. We must reflect fairly and honestly. On this of all days, God should stand completely alone in the judgment seat.

The great judgment of Matthew 25 should apply to God too. I was hungry and you gave me nothing to eat. I was trying to take a flight and you didn't stop a missile from hitting my plane. I was trying to solve the HIV/AIDS crisis and you let a missile obliterated my body. I was on death row and you let them kill me. I was simply playing soccer with my cousins and you let the bomb kill all of us. I was cooking for my family and you let tanks into my neighborhood. I was going for a hike and you let me be kidnapped and tortured to death. I was walking down the street and you let people burn me alive. I was raped at my school and you did nothing to hold back my attackers. I shot myself and you didn't come to help me. I died of cancer and you didn't bring me a cure. I starved to death and you gave me nothing to eat. The tragedies that have taken place today are too numerous to list. What you have done to the least of these you have done to all of us. What do you have to say for your self? Silence...just like always.

In the absence of any defense, my judgment today is that God is our passive enemy.

Regardless, Jesus tells us to love our enemy and speaks as if our salvation is found there.

So, I love you.

In the future, I am going to serve all those who feel like you have failed them and I have a feeling that you will meet me there.

Amen.

211.

July 19, 2014

Eric Garner, the Silence of White Churches and Sins of Omission

The muffled screams of a dying 43-year-old husband, father and grandfather named Eric Garner..."I can't breathe! I can't breathe!"...are absolutely haunting. The coming silence from most white congregations in their worship services will be even more haunting. In the silence, we will discover one of the worst kept secrets in religious life...white churches do not care about the violence that is consistently perpetuated against black men in our society.

How many more black men will have to die before the white church takes their lives seriously? One does not have to watch the video more than once to realize that a New York Police Officer is directly responsible for the death of Garner. One shouldn't have to think too hard to realize by our omission so are we.

Jesus met the Samaritan woman at the well. A racial and ethnic divide separated Jews and Samaritans yet there was something about that well that fostered conversation. I am afraid that most white churches omit thinking about the well...let alone making a trip there.

If the name Eric Garner is not mentioned during your church services, then your church is complicit in the next brutal killing of an unarmed black man. For some this might sound harsh...if so...I would recommend that you think about the last time your church prayed for an end to the consistent brutality black men face in our society. In the light of the obvious reality of never mentioning brutality against black men for most churches, perhaps such a statement is not harsh enough.

The good news is that there is a well my friends...from it flows the living waters of justice and reconciliation. If you have the love and courage to go to that well with Jesus, Eric Garner will be standing there to offer you redemption for your sins of omission.

Amen.

212.

July 21, 2014

The Borderless God in a Time of Borders

When I was growing up, we/I believed everyone who disagreed with us/me about God was going to hell. I continued to cling to and organize my life around the border of saved and unsaved for a long time. Then I started doing some deeper reading about the limitless love of God and everything began to change.

I am not interested in your borders. I am not interested in your nationalities. I am not interested in the mistaken belief that we need to live behind borders. I am interested in the God who loves the world and that is all.

When you raise your guns to protect a mythical border...you are raising your guns at God. When you declare disdain for people in other countries...you are declaring your disdain for God. When you think that our country exists to offer light and sanctuary to the world...you are assuming that God only lives here. When you lift up borders as the answer...you are not lifting up God as the answer.

Jesus wouldn't close our borders. Jesus also wouldn't talk about the United States as the only place on earth worthy of inhabitance. Jesus wouldn't be a patriot one way or the other. Jesus inhabits every nation on earth...how could he be partial toward any?

Conversations about borders are not political. Conversations about borders are a deeply spiritual matter. Failing to understand the limitless love and presence of God is failing to understand God. We are not the light of the world...God is. The borders we keep talking about divide God's children. I work and pray for a day free where borders will be no more. This is the path of the borderless God.

Amen.

213.

July 24, 2014

The Last Testament of Joseph Wood: The Prophet of a Botched Execution

"Why have you forsaken me?" is a proper description of what many of us might feel if someone was standing over us about to intentionally inject deadly chemicals into our body. Joseph Wood spent time talking about his love for Jesus. How are we to respond when a man who has been convicted of heinous murders speaks of Jesus as his dearest friend? There is a temptation to dismiss such spiritual proclamations as jailhouse religion meant to assuage the guilt that Joseph Wood must have felt. To provide such an easy answer is to deny the faith that has sustained so many of us through even the most horrible of circumstances.

There is a murderer in scripture. The writings and testimony of the Apostle Paul make up most of the New Testament. If we had executed him then we wouldn't have them. We value the testaments of the Apostle Paul. What is the last testament of Joseph Wood?

"Love your neighbor as your self." Love seems simple to most...I think this is because most don't know what it means to practice it. Joseph Wood proclaimed a love for Jesus. This prophetic statement uttered by a convicted killer strapped to a gurney in Arizona asks a profound question of us...Joseph Wood's neighbors, "Will you love me as your self?" The answer we gave Joseph Wood last night is "no."

Throughout my upbringing as a Southern Baptist and evangelical Christian, I heard a question over and over again, "Are you saved?" In the light of Joseph Wood's final statement and the travesty of a two-hour delay that happened next, the question "Are you saved?" repeats over and over again in my mind. If being saved has anything to do with learning how to "love our neighbor as our self," then I can tell you that the answer to the question of "Are you saved?" is a resounding and unequivocal "no." We are all damned for the torturous evil that we participated in last night.

Imagine. Your anxiety is skyrocketing. You decline a final meal. You say goodbye to your family and friends. You pray that somehow peace and love will be with you throughout the process of your death. The guards open the door. You walk to the chamber. The door opens and there is the gurney of your death. You are strapped in. You speak your final words into the microphone. The chemicals start to pump through your veins. You think something is wrong. You panic and painfully struggle to breath for almost two hours. Just before you die...you hear the doctor assure others, "they are completely sedated and not feeling a thing." The evil you do unto others you do unto your self.

With each execution we are executing our own consciences. We are growing accustomed to doing evil against others and inflicting evil on our self. We need a revival of love and moral imagination. We must realize that when we kill we are perpetuating a cycle of violence that will eventually come to all of our doorsteps. The last testament of Joseph Wood is for us to love each other and stop the heinous practice of executing people. Wood's love for Jesus reminds of that most basic human calling to "love our neighbor as our self." One cannot love their neighbor while filling their body with deadly chemicals and watching them suffocate to death for two hours. In light of Arizona's botched execution last night...I think it is time that we all got saved from this moral cancer of execution that is eating at all of our souls. Love is the antidote.

Amen.

214.

July 27, 2014

God is in Hell

"You are going to hell!" I have always hated people damning me to hell. There was something about someone speaking you into a fiery torment for all of eternity that is the ultimate "fuck you." I am not there anymore. This morning after yet another incident of being damned, I realized I get told I am going to hell the most when I feel the closest to God. The epiphany changed everything.

From poverty to sickness to racism to violence to sexism, there are a whole host of variables that create a living hell for people throughout our world. I think that most of us have forgotten about or don't care about the hell that people are going through. Jesus cast his lot with the least of these who find their self in hell...meaning the least of these amongst us are the very incarnation of God. The living hell that people experience is where God is.

The conversation I had this morning surrounded the topic of human sexuality. Someone thinks I am going to hell for describing myself as a queer person. To top that, I was also told that I was marching my three sons to hell too. I was so angry until Jesus came to me. "I am in hell" came the measured words of my savior. The love of God never ceases to amaze me. I realized that I am called to go to hell too.

Now is the time for the church to go to hell. To locate our missions and visions in the very place where God said that God would be. Let's all go to hell and trust that there is no more loving or righteous place to be than in the flames with God.

Amen.

215.

July 29, 2014

Twins Again! : A Tale of Unexpected Love for the Hoods

We were planning our lives. We were adjusting to life after children (twins and a single) in less than two and a half years. We knew what we were doing. Then we came face to face with a black and white screen.

I sat next to Emily as they rubbed goo all over her belly and prepared the sonogram. The sonographer was a little too cheerful for the moment. I was simply uninterested in her musings about her life. Nervousness reigned. Emily maintained her poise and grace. The screen came into focus and it quickly became clear that life was going to change.

We can plan our lives all that we want to...but the truth is that love changes our plans and us. Emily laughed. I was speechless. Following some ungraceful moments of not knowing what to say, I reached out and grabbed Emily's arm. There was something comforting about touching my wife. I stared at the screen harder and refused to turn my head. I fell in love.

Our house is very busy right now. Emily and I are actively changing the world. Jeff and Phillip grow wilder by the day. Quinley Mandela demands his attention. We have no idea what life will be like when these twins come. We only know that we love them and that will be enough.

Amen.

216.

July 29, 2014

Let the Children Come to Me: Arriving for an Immigration Action in Washington D.C.

There is a child crying nearby and we ignore it. The louder the cries of the child become the more we cover our ears. The crying grows louder and louder until it reaches a desperate scream yet still we refuse to be moved. Then the cry goes silent. This is the story of our relationship with the cries of the children of Central America. We have ignored their cries demanding justice for so long that they have now arrived at our doorstep. Will we continue to ignore them?

No. I simply cannot. I arrived today in Washington, D.C. to participate in an action with clergy and immigration activists from all over the country to demand morality in our approach to the children of Central America. I will raise my cry to shake the consciences of all that I come in contact with. Our words should always be the words of Jesus, "Let the children come to me."

Amen.

217.

July 31, 2014

There Are Children to Love

The black-and-white beans danced around the screen. The heartbeats thundered through the speakers. My wife and I could not believe our eyes. We knew exactly what they were: twins.

My mind raced: *We are already the proud parents of twin toddlers and a single baby. We are not planning to have more kids. We are actively working against the possibility of another pregnancy. We do not feel like the timing was right. We do not have the resources in place. We are adapting well to the three kids we have.* Regardless of the thoughts on planning or preparation, we met a new reality on the screen.

Though they are strangers, I quickly fell in love with those beans on the screen. There was a deep, undeniable understanding that those two children belonged to me, and I to them. I have had my doubts that I could love any more children as much as I love the three children we already have... until I saw the screen.

Sometimes we are not ready or prepared, and yet love finds us anyway. The scenes of children crossing our borders and arriving to this country have touched me no less than the scene I experienced on the sonogram. Now we are a nation sitting next to a metaphorical sonogram machine and staring at the screen. The concerns that I had are no different from the concerns that many in this country have. We were not planning on more children immigrating. We were actively working against the possibility of any more children crossing the border. We don't feel like the timing is right. We feel as if we do not have the resources in place for more children. We were adapting well to the immigrants who were already here. Regardless of the thoughts on planning or preparation, there is a new reality that has met us on the screen. Though they are strangers, it is hard not to fall in love with the faces of all of our human future. These children are our children, and we belong to each other.

When we realized that we were expecting twins, my wife and I could have allowed our plans and preparations to cause us to get upset and angry. We could have blamed each other. We could have blamed the failed birth preventions. We decided not to waste time on such trivial matters; there are children to love. Our nation can be angry that our plans and preparations have been met with unexpected increases in immigration, or we can open our hearts at the realization that there are children to love.

There are often more questions than answers. There certainly are for us. God meets us in those places of questions and dangerously guides us past our borders to a place of love. There are children waiting there who need our help. Will we open our hearts and follow the love we felt when we first saw them on the screen?

Today I join religious leaders and immigration activists to give my body up for arrest in an act of civil disobedience at the White House. I commit myself to this act because I know that the God who loves all children regardless of their nation of origin will be standing with me. Will you stand with us wherever you are?

Amen.

218.

July 31, 2014

An Open Letter to the Cathedral of Hope

Friends.

Jesus fled after his brothers were shot to death. There was nowhere to go that was safe. Jesus pushed north. Traveling across nation after nation, Jesus was abused and almost killed numerous times. Months into the journey, Jesus started his trek through the desert. The dehydration worsened with each step. Collapsing to the sand, Jesus closed his eyes and did not expect to wake up again. The bright light caused him to open his eyes. Jesus found himself guarded by Border Patrol in a clinic. A few days later, Jesus was loaded onto a bus and driven to a new facility. People stood along the roadways holding signs that said, "Return to Sender." The people had no idea that the sender was God.

Jesus is present in those that have crossed our borders without documentation seeking a better life. Will we deny the ones that God has sent? I will not. I am prepared to give my body to the struggle for immigrant rights. Today, I will be joining with dozens of ministers from around the country to participate in an act of civil disobedience leading to arrest at the White House. I am a faith leader ready for serious immigration reform. I can no longer deny the Jesuses that have crossed our borders. I have chosen to act. Cathedral of Hope will you act with me?

You will have the chance this weekend. Renowned journalist and undocumented immigrant Jose Antonio Vargas will be joining us for multiple events (http://h4pj.org/activist/071514.php). This will be an opportunity for you to learn more about immigration and be inspired to further action. In this difficult hour, I pray that you will come to learn how we can stand strong together for the sake of all of God's children. We are an extraordinary church capable of doing extraordinary things. Now is the time for us to be extraordinary on immigration. See you this weekend.

Rev. Jeff Hood

219.

August 1, 2014

The Danger of the Immigration Debate is Forgetting God's Love for the World

We stood outside the White House chanting slogans about immigration. Leaders of the protest kept trying to put signs and other things into my hands. I kept rejecting whatever was handed to me. The truth is that I was most interested in holding a cross.

The rhetoric surrounding immigration often centers on ideas of United States exceptionalism. I am a pastor. I am interested in Jesus above the United States. My heart regularly breaks as other nations and peoples are condemned and tossed aside to make an argument for more generous immigration policies. Jesus cares about all peoples not just those who live in the United States.

The officers closed in on us. I closed my eyes and started to pray. Though we had been sufficiently prepared as to what the process would look like, I was still a bit nervous about being arrested. Over all of the chants and the flags, I rested my mind and heart on Jesus. I knew that the love of God was the only thing that could make silence and wholeness out of the perpetual noise.

"Borders keep us safe." "I believe that God respects our borders." "I believe in borders." These are a few of the comments that I heard when I shared my belief that borders are part of the problem and not the solution with other pastors and activists. There is a fundamental inability to dream of a world beyond the United States as the most powerful and wealthiest nation on earth. Why can't all people experience power and wealth?

The zip tie handcuffs tightened and I began to have some doubts. Why do I support immigration reform when the debate is so often centered on United States exceptionalism? I knew the answer and I kept reminding myself of it. I believe that migration is a human right. I also believe that immigration reform can bring us closer to a day when all people can love each other and be one without borders.

I processed out of the Park Police Detention Center and flew home. The sight of my children when I returned to Denton was overwhelming. I couldn't help but think about the families who have been separated for decades. I believe any border or system that separates families is evil.

Famed journalist Jose Anonio Vargas preached at the Cathedral of Hope this morning. I sat on the chancel and pondered Vargas' "Define American" campaign. As the music thundered, I had an epiphany of what is often missing from the immigration debate. I don't think you can define the word 'American' without defining the word 'human.'

Amen.

220.

August 9, 2014

The Cost Scandal of Theological Education

"God called me and now I'm broke!" My dear friend Sara was distraught. Unable to find a job, Sara wondered if she should have ever pursued a theological education. Sara is not alone. According to a study produced by the Center for the Study of Theological Education at Auburn Theological Seminary, "More than a quarter of students graduating in 2011 with a Master of Divinity degree had more than $40,000 in theological debt and 5 percent were more than $80,000 in the red." With dwindling denominational numbers, fewer jobs and often-discriminatory practices compounding the debt problem, many theological graduates are leaving the ministry to pay their bills.

Before many students start a theological education, the cost of theological education is also pricing out the diversity that so many of our denominations so desperately need. Theological education is now reserved to the privileged few that can afford it and to those lucky enough to get scholarships. With most denominations requiring a Master of Divinity for ordination, the pathway to ordained ministry is closed to many otherwise called and qualified individuals.

The grievances about cost could go on and on, but the main point is that we don't want people leaving ministry because their debt is too high and we won't theological education to be affordable enough that all who are called to ordained ministry can attend. I have a solution. The denominations and churches that send students to the theological schools should pay for their theological education. If denominations and churches can't afford to send students to theological schools, then obviously theological education is a luxury we cannot afford. The church has a responsibility to theology students and right now it is not meeting it.

http://www.pcusa.org/news/2014/4/8/moonlighting-pastors-and-postponed-health-care/

221.

August 11, 2014

The Night I Almost Took My Life

The year was 2008. The spring semester at Southern Baptist Theological Seminary was coming to a close. I sat alone in my room staring at my closet. The depression was overwhelming and I didn't know if I could take it anymore. I tried to get help. Professor after professor told me that my severe depression was a result of my sin and that I needed to truly give my life to Jesus. I tried over and over. One of my secular friends suggested that I get on medication. I just couldn't. I just knew that if I took drugs I would be letting my conservative family and friends down. The bottle of pills that I bought earlier in the night at the local drugstore stared back at me from the closet and invited me to end the suffering. I cried and cried. When the dawn broke, I knew I had made it through the night.

Following two further periods of sustained depression, I sought help against the wishes of many who love me. Pushing through the darkness, I was diagnosed with bipolar disorder and placed on medication. Even with the drugs, suicide has never been far from my mind. The thoughts of ending the suffering revisit me a couple of times per year. I have learned to talk with those thoughts as if they are old friends. The truth is that I have known such thoughts as long as I have known anyone in my life.

I am a pastor. I wish that I could have reached Robin Williams. I would tell him that God loves him and so do I. Alas, it was not to be.

The tragedy of Robin Williams' death has brought me face to face with the realities of my mental condition once more. I have a chronic mental illness that never leaves me totally well. There are many who would never write these words. The constant fears of employment retaliation and general shaming are never far from our minds. We live in a society that refuses to understand us.

The tears are flowing at this point. Our society must take mental illness seriously and not desperately reach for alternative explanations to our plight. We are an oppressed faceless minority. Suicide should not be what it takes for people to notice our presence or provide the resources so many of us so desperately need. Will you continue to ignore us? Will the mental health facilities continue to be overrun? Will you continue to stigmatize us? We need you.

I believe in the incarnation of God with the suffering.

God is with those who have mental illness.

God has bipolar disorder.

Amen.

222.

August 13, 2014

Emily: An Ode to Three Years

I don't know how much it cost me to set up an account on eHarmony. I just know I got my money's worth and then some.

"We got married in a fever, hotter than a pepper sprout..." I can think of no better words to describe the origin of our relationship than the opening lines of Johnny and June Carter Cash's "Jackson." We knew each other all of two months. From family to friends, everybody thought we were crazy. I guess we were. I guess we are.

Three years ago today, I will never forget holding your hand on the beach of Vieques, Puerto Rico. Words of love and dedication filled the air. The pictures illustrate how beautiful the landscape was for a wedding. I don't remember the hues. I only remember you.

The operating room felt like a science laboratory. We were scared. I prayed aloud. You pushed and screamed. Jeff came first. Phillip came thirteen minutes later. You held my hand. We held their hands.

We moved across the country to forge a new life in Texas. I never wanted to move here. I was convinced it was going to be far worse than Mississippi. You knew I was nervous. You held my hand.

The living room is an interesting place for a baby to be born. We jumped in the pool together. I held your hands as you pushed. Quinley came next. I will never forget the fierceness of your love in those moments. We held his little hand.

"There's two of them!" We were shocked. "Five under the age of three???" You reached for my hand. I didn't need anything else for joy to replace my fear.

I have long proclaimed a belief that God is love. I didn't know what that meant until I met you.

I conclude with the words of Fyodor Dostoevsky in *The Brothers Karamazov*, " Love is such a priceless treasure that you can redeem the whole world by it, and cleanse not only your own sins but the sins of others."

May God continue to make it true in us.

Amen.

223.

August 13, 2014

The Souls of White Folks

I have grown angrier and angrier following each post and video. White person after white person writes and talks as if they know what happened with Michael Brown and how to solve the racial crisis in our nation. The benefits of being white in this nation are immeasurable. One of the present benefits is that you get to define our collective racial crisis in your own terms. I have no question that most of the people speaking and writing do not have any idea what it means to be black in this nation. I know that I don't.

I am white. There is no getting around it. There are pieces of the black experience that I will never understand. This week has taught me that there are moments that I simply need to listen. This is not an indictment of me, but rather a statement of reality. I know what I need to do. I need to silence my mouth, listen and pray. I wish that many of my white friends would follow suit right now. You can't speak against injustice until you hear and learn what is going on. Listening does not give you the ability to speak, but it does help you have something worthwhile to say.

Ministering to the souls of white folks is a difficult task. It is hard to tell people they are sick and dying when they think they are well. Racism is our enemy. White people are not. Unfortunately, white people in this nation are racist whether they want to be or not. This is the nature of a system that offers benefits to one race over all others. So how are we to extract the racism from white souls? Loving our neighbors as our self is a good place to start.

Amen.

224.

August 17, 2014

Prayer for Racial Reconciliation and Justice at Cathedral of Hope

We are a church...we are a congregation forged out of oppression and marginalization. This is a church that is no stranger to violence. Many of you have experienced violence in your own lives...and against your own persons. The death of Michael Brown and the events that have followed in Ferguson, Missouri have reminded us that ours is a world on fire and I know that this is not a congregation that is willing to sit quietly as people and cities burn. In the midst of violence and oppression against black people and black bodies, I have asked these two young men...who are members of our church...to join me here on stage and to stand with me to remind us of what is at stake in this conversation. I ask you to raise your hands. In raising our hands, we are joining with churches throughout the world...to say not that we are a people of surrender...although there are people who have been shot raising their hands in the midst of surrendering...but rather to say that we are people that stands together united to resist racism in all of its forms. And as we stand with our hands raised, we raise our hands to God knowing that it is God who can take away the racism, bigotry and oppression out of our society and even out of our own hearts. Let us pray deeper.

God we invite you to convict our own hearts...to convict this church. God to fill us up...that we will be a people that stands for justice...that stands for reconciliation...and that truly becomes the change that we want to see in the world. Make it so. Hallelujah. Amen.

225.

August 19, 2014

The Call to Ferguson

The phone rang. I wasn't expecting a call so late. "Would you be willing to go to Ferguson on our behalf?" I was surprised by the question. For the last few days, I told numerous people that I would not be traveling to Ferguson. *I didn't have the money. I knew I would miss the kids. I worried about Emily and the pregnancy. I assumed that more people would only make the situation worse.* I told the caller, "I'll pray about it." I left the conversation very skeptical.

I took a moment to close my eyes. The thoughts flowed from a deep place. *God. I don't want to go. What about Emily and the kids? What could I possibly do to help? Where would I stay? God. I will go wherever you lead me.* The thoughts did not lead to an answer. Questions were more forthcoming.

Throughout the night, I kept watching the live footage coming out of Ferguson. The scenes of chaos rushed my senses over and over again. The arrests, screams, tear gas, shouts and guns spoke deeply to me. I saw the people of God being trampled upon. The call of God is to place our body into such spaces. I could no longer ignore the call.

I now sit at a gas station in Oklahoma. I don't know what is going to happen in the next few hours. I only know that I am responding to the call of God to carry my body to Ferguson to be a part of the racial reconciliation that I desperately want to see in the world.

Amen.

226.

August 21, 2014

The Death in Ferguson

"Love is going to fuck you up." The ominous words rang out from a woman standing on the street corner. Pointing at me, the woman declared, "You are going to have to die before you can love anybody here." I knew she was right. The Prophetess of Ferguson reminded me of all the times I have tried to pretend that I don't carry my own bigotries in life. I knew that love had brought to this city of death, but more was going to be required of me.

The brilliant array of flowers and colors does not mask the fact that Michael Brown died there in a flurry of bullets. The spot is tucked within an apartment complex where poor people live. Walking up, I didn't know if I should be there or not. I stopped and prayed over the spot. Stepping to the sidewalk, I sat on the curb next to a woman.

"I hate white people," she offered without any solicitation. Taken aback, I inquired, "Do you want me to leave?" "No, you are the only chance I've got at redemption," she softly spoke through tears. For a few moments, we sat silently. I didn't know what to say. Through the tension, the woman looked at me and asked, "Are you a bigot?" "Yes ma'am," I offered. "We are both bigots then. I guess we can be a salvation to each other," she replied. For the next little while, we talked about the effect that bigotry has on all of us whether we want it to or not. "If there has ever been a time to be honest about what is going on in our own hearts, it is now. I guess it starts with the honesty we offered to each other," she concluded. After concluding pleasantries, I walked back to the car and thought about what had just happened. Our joint sensibilities of self-protectionism had died and for a brief moment we had an honest vulnerable conversation about bigotry. I think we both left having experienced a moment of resurrection. Death and resurrection go together. I guess that ours was a resurrection in Michael Brown.

I don't believe the incarnation of God was a singular event. I believe that God joins us when we open our hearts to love. I walked to the epicenter of the Ferguson protests, W. Florissant Ave. The night was thick with tension, but I felt alive in love. I joined the chants, "Hands Up, Don't Shoot!" With every foot that hit the pavement, I felt like we were growing together in love and honesty. Someone next to me shouted out, "Where the fuck is God in all of this?" One of my dear brothers responded quickly, "Right here with us! Look around at all these colors of folks holding hands and standing together. God is right here with us." Our hearts were moved by each other. The power of God was right there in the people of God.

There truly is no such thing as death without resurrection. The death of Michael Brown continues to grant new life to all who are willing to open their hearts. May our own pursuit of racial justice and reconciliation begin with the death of the dishonesty in our own hearts and conclude in our own resurrection with the wild diversity of the people of God.

Amen.

227.

August 22, 2014

The Violence of Demanding Peaceful Protest: The Missteps of Clergy in Ferguson

"We don't want anyone getting arrested or lashing out in anger. It is your job to keep people calm." These are the words that a local clergyperson shared with me before I traveled to West Florissant Ave. to participate in demonstrations in Ferguson. Throughout the night, clergy consistently congratulated each other that everything seemed to be going according to plan. On multiple occasions, I heard clergy shout down a young person for getting too angry or confrontational. I grew increasingly uncomfortable with the clerical collar on my neck. I wanted to be with the people not above them. While not every clergy I encountered acted like this, I felt like many of the clergy I encountered functioned as appendages of the ruling class. I was not interested in being anybody's appendage except God.

"If we remain peaceful then we will get what we want!" I will never forget those words. The statement struck to the core of my pacifist ideals and caused me to question the very nature of why I was even in Ferguson. I was told that clergy were needed to help calm the crowds. I saw what clergy being a voice of calm in the crowds meant first hand...clergy controlling the crowds. When people have every right to be angry, there is nothing of God about squashing their ability to exercise their birthright to civil disobedience. Clergy in Ferguson consistently tried to control the protest and steer it away from any civil disobedience. This consistent attempt to exercise power over a vulnerable group of people was an injustice and made me very angry.

I am not sure that these clergy in Ferguson would have let Jesus demonstrate in the temple. The false promise that "peace will get what you want" is absurd. Sometimes you have to shut things down in order to bring about justice. The work that I do is to ensure that acts of civil disobedience remain nonviolent not that they remain nonexistent. We must not forget that civil disobedience is an unpeaceful act. Civil disobedience is not intended to create situations of calm. Civil disobedience escalates situations to a point where people have to pay attention to injustice. To try to squash civil disobedience in Ferguson is to try and squash a movement for racial justice in our nation that is long overdue. Anger must not be extinguished for the sake of maintaining calm. Anger should be utilized to create a racial revolution that brings all people in this nation and perhaps even around the world to the table for an honest conversation and a subsequent reformation.

I don't think you can have an honest conversation about race in our nation when you are always telling people to calm down. If peaceful protest is about controlling people's emotions, then I believe it to be violently taking away the agency of people who have every right to be angry and engaged in resistance. I am for nonviolence. I believe it is by far the most effective and moral way to confront injustice. I am not for the violence of clergy-controlled protests in a space where people have every right to exercise their anger. If we as clergy want to do something to change this nation, then we need to get up and capture the spirit of these angry demonstrators and nonviolently make life intolerable for those who want to keep perpetuating injustice.

Amen.

228.

September 7, 2014

"Becoming Queer and Growing Queerer"

When we think about God...we often go to this pace of thinking about Zeus or something in the sky hurling lightening bolts. This Greek or Roman God is way off and only interacts with us when HE is pissed. This God can only be negative or nasty and then we act like Jesus is the sweet God that comes along to redeem God. I believe we all yearn for the God that has been with us the whole time. I have often wondered about this phrase the "God with us"... the incarnation...this Emmanuel. What does such an expression of God mean for the long experience of people created in the image of God?

When we do theology that is queer...we are responding to a God that truly is ultimately indescribable...a God that is beyond our ability to describe...a God that is simply not normative. When we create an idea of God that uses our normativities...when we dare say God is ultimately like this...we are always going to come up short. When we say that God is love...how can one describe a love beyond love? When we say that God is joy...how can one describe a joy beyond joy? How can we explain a peace beyond peace? Ultimately the God that is God is in the words of Paul Tillich, "the God beyond God." When we arrive at such a space, we realize that God is quintessentially queer...quintessentially beyond our normativities...quintessentially beyond our wildest dreams.

Unfortunately, we have bound up God with our terms, dichotomies and normativities. I believe it is time to set God free in our minds and souls. We have to find the God beyond our terms and our descriptions. We have to find God. The God that is unique and truly queer created us in God's image. If we want to get to the truth of the matter, then I believe we have to go back to the beginning.

In that place of beginning, the Queer God created human beings in God's image. Why would we want to describe God or our self in any other way? Why would we want us or God to be anything else? When we start to head down the road of identity and normatizing...creating boundaries and borders...dichotomizing and trying to describe who and what we are...we have already lost. You see the courage to follow God the God who is God is again in the words of Tillich, "the courage to be"...the courage to find your self...the courage to locate your self within the God that declares God's self to be love...the God that declares God's self to be beyond. Will we dare locate such a God within? Ultimately, when we locate such a God within...we gain the courage to declare that we are created in the image of a God that is queer and we are queer. Such a declaration changes things.

When we look at the first sin...the trouble that went down back there in Eden...and we think about the first persons. I am not interested in dichotomizing them. God declared them to be both male and female. I think there was some gender-bending going on in Eden. Could it be that each person had a gender that was unique to the person? Wouldn't that be something??? Regardless, the story is quickly progressing toward the fall.

When the serpent approaches one of the first persons, the serpent seeks to persuade the person by telling the person if the person eats of the tree then the person will be made like God. Ultimately, the first sin is locating God somewhere apart from the self...believing that God is somewhere beside the image of God that is within you. The first sin is always a denial of self...a denial of the God in whose image you are made.

Jesus tells us in Mark to "love our neighbor as our self." I am going to have to revert to the great theologian Ru Paul on this one, "How the hell are you going to love somebody when you can't love your self? Can I get an amen?" Really...if you can't love your self, how are you going to love anybody else? This God that is queer and that created us to be queer wants us to place love in the self so that we might love somebody else.

In the life of Jesus, I see Jesus constantly living into this queer context. Jesus is not afraid to go into situations and demand a place. When is the last time you went into a situation and demanded a place? Why? Because of who you are...created in the image of the living God. When is the last time you stood your tallest and declared your self to be queer and said that's it? What if we all said..."If you want to talk about God then you need to talk to me"? People might reply, "How do you know God so well"? Because God is within us! God created me. We have to start championing the queerness of our self in order to start championing the queerness of all people.

For far too long we have tried to create conversation and community by pushing everyone to be the same. I think that this has been a fault for a long time of many of our LGBT spaces. When we create community based on sameness, we are stifling people's voices. I don't believe you can demand everyone be the same in a space and allow room for queerness at the same time. When we demand sameness, we are stifling queerness.

I do much activism and work around issues of social justice. I work because I believe that people matter...individuals matter...not because they can be made to be the same...and not because they can be made to fit into certain identities and groups that carry certain collective identities...but because people simply matter. Somebody asked me the other day "How do you identify?"...I responded, "Well I saw a cute guy walk by the other day. I am married to a beautiful woman. I sometimes have some female tendencies that well up inside of me. There are all sorts of things going on." Can anybody else relate? For so long we have only offered binaries for people to name their sexuality and gender. What happens we decide to stop having these conversations? What happens when such conversations end at queer? The conversation changes when we just decide to be who we are created by God to be and expect nothing more from anyone else.

The queer project asks people to come together based on differences not similarities. I believe the world can be changed if difference becomes what we hold up as sacred not sameness. When that happens, we will start valuing the image of God within each individual and begin to come together.

The story starts to progress toward the end. How does it shake down? How does it end? I believe that God is drawing us all to a place where the queerness of every individual will be made complete and celebrated. In that place, all will be loved, cherished and respected.

We often come out of the closet in terms of our sexuality and gender, but stay in the closet in terms of allowing our self the freedom to be who we are. I think that God wants to talk about much more than our sexuality, our gender or our race. I think that God wants to talk about the queer that is deep within us...and letting that queer run free and wild.

I believe the beginning of the Gospel of Mary Magdalene speaks directly to the finality and eternality of the queer experience. "...Will matter be destroyed or not?" The savior replied, "All natures, all formed things, all creatures exist in and with each other, and they will dissolve into their own root." If the root is queer and we are all going to dissolve into that root, then shouldn't we live for the day when we are all truly living as the queers that God created us to be in the first place? We need to go ahead and get that process started so that we can go and do and be who we were created to be at the root.

What does all this have to do with justice? What makes you think that we need national boundaries and borders anyways? Why do we need a United States of America? Why do we need Canada or any other country either? Why do we need nations? Do you think you will get to heaven and St. Peter will ask for a US passport? When we start to think about things queerly and allow our selves to be queered, then borders and boundaries start to be blurred and people start coming together. The reason we have an immigration crisis in our country is because we have resources that we believe are more valuable than human beings. When we think that resources are more valuable than human beings, we become the epitome of normativity. I think that a large part of the problem comes from bad theology. We come from a Christian tradition that has often talked about being chosen and blessed by God. When you believe your nation has been chosen or blessed by God to be rich, then you don't have much problem with everyone else being poor. Wouldn't it be great if we opened up the border and people came here and started eating your food, sleeping in your bed, driving your car and what not? We would all quickly get to see if we are truly Christians. The justice conversation has to move beyond identity. The queering of the conversation has to go all the way from national identities to racial identities to gender identities to sexual identities to intelligence identities to many other categories we have created.

I do much work on Texas' Death Row. Most of the people on death row are lacking in capital. Whether it is a lack of financial capital or intellectual capital or whatever, our state kills the least of these on a regular basis. I was down on Texas' Death Row about six months ago visiting a gentleman who has killed multiple people. People call him a monster, say he doesn't matter and other him in all kinds of ways. One of the reasons the gay rights movement, the LGBT rights movement or whatever you want to call it has been so instructive for the rest of the populace is that we have all been taught that people matter...we all matter...love matters. When we start talking like this, the conversation gets wider and wider to the point where we begin to go places we never expected to go. Would you have imagined that claiming your identity as a child of God would have allowed someone on death row to claim their identity as a child of God? The widening conversation gets wider and more beautiful by the hour. Queer talk and action keeps taking us to wider and wilder spaces.

In closing...when we have a queer God who creates us in God's image queerly. We are all able to locate our person in God. When we do that, God takes on interesting shapes and forms. One of the great theologians of our time is former Emory University professor Dr. Nancy Eisland. Chronically disabled, Dr. Eisland passed away a few years ago. Dr. Eisland wrote a book entitled, "The Disabled God." In the text, Dr. Eisland imagines the disabled God in a puff wheelchair rolling around heaven. The question for Dr. Eisland and for us is: How far are we willing to go to locate the image of God? If we can't locate God in folks from every walk of life and circumstance then how can we locate God in our self? If we are bold enough, we will say that God died last night trying to get across our southern border, we will say that a nine-year-old God was shot six times in Chicago a few nights ago and we will say that God is suffering and dying in our hospitals...among many other Gods. How far are we willing to expand our minds and our hearts? The queer project says there should be no end.

I believe that God is here with us. I don't believe that God is some kind of wind. I believe God is in you and you and you and you and all of us. The beautiful image of God is here. As you leave this place...remember if you want to make a difference in the world then you have to be different. Go and be the queer that God has created you to be.

Amen.

Marvin Meyer. *The Gnostic Gospels of Jesus*, 'The Gospel of Mary" (New York: HarperOne, 2005), 37.

229.

September 8, 2014

Claiming Justice and Killing Jesus: The Execution of Willie Trottie

"...I was in prison, and you visited me." Jesus doesn't say, "I was not guilty in prison, and you came to me." Jesus binds his flesh with the flesh of those who have no hope. Willie Trottie is left with little hope. Tonight, the State of Texas will kill Trottie by lethal injection. We love to say it like that. If we can name the State of Texas as the perpetrator, we can follow in the footsteps of Pilate and wash our hands of the crime. Who are we really killing? Whose blood is to be shed tonight? Do we have the guts to answer such questions? If you believe the words of Matthew 25:36, the person to be strapped to the gurney is none other than Jesus.

The unfathomable love and grace of God is what binds Willie Trottie to the person of Jesus. The murders of Barbara and Titus Canada cannot keep Trottie from such grace and love. Why is this so difficult to believe? I think we want vengeance. We want blood. "Hate your enemies and kill those who persecute you." Can you imagine if our wants were actually the message of Jesus? I actually can. I see the message of hate played out each time we demand the blood of another. I don't see much Jesus in killing and all of us here in Texas love to kill. When will we stop? I want us all to get saved from killing.

I feel like Jesus is calling for us all to choose love, but we refuse to pick up. To assuage our consciences, we will pretend like nothing is happening. We clutch our children and give no thought to the mother in Huntsville who just clutched the glass as she watched the life drain out of her child. We will kiss those we love and not consider those who just kissed someone they love goodbye. We will glance over the news with assurance that all will glance over the crime that we just committed. In all of these actions, we will forget that we were made for each other. When will we remember?

There will be much forgetting after tonight. People will go on about their lives as if nothing ever happened and many will go to church. Pastors will offer communion in the coming days. The problem is that the communion our churches offer will not be real. For, it is impossible to have real communion when no one knows if they will be the next one killed. The God that is celebrated will be a fraud. For, how can anyone claim to believe in a God that kills because of anger and vengeance? For people who claim to follow Jesus here in Texas, we are the great pretenders.

Amen.

230.

September 13, 2014

the weather

you are under my skin
what are you doing here?
we were so hot
now i'm so wet
why are you soaking in?
the clarity is gone
you are cold

231.

September 16, 2014

Remembering Queerly: Words from A Conversation on Queer Theology and Activism at Galileo Church

There are moments we never forget. These moments meet and transform us. I am the product of such a moment.

I was a young man with much assumed knowledge and even more conviction about who and what God was. I believed that the Bible spoke clearly and our task was to respond clearly. The Southern Baptist Theological Seminary was not a place for doubt. We were expected to be prophets of certainty and I was. The game ran out when my Southern Baptist mentor and pastor called to tell me that he was dying. I drove fast to see him. Through it all, I somehow believed that God would save him. When I arrived to his bedside, my cherished mentor and pastor pulled me close and told me, "I'm gay and I always have been." The words startled and dislodged me. I have been changing ever since. No matter how far I travel, there will always be a piece of me that stayed behind in that bedroom. I will never get over the change in God and me that I met in that moment. I will spend my life thinking back to that bedroom and pondering what it means to live into the fullness of the gift of salvation that was given to me there.

We are a people of memories. In hopes of finding and providing something better, we work to make meaning of memories. My dear Southern Baptist pastor and mentor lived in a closeted hell. Through his revelation, my friend and pastor brought me out of mine. I now base my work in theology and activism around the idea that people matter. I cling to such an idea based on a memory of mine from the beginning.

Eden is important for a variety of reasons, but perhaps not the ones that you think. I don't really care whether there was an actual physical place called the Garden of Eden. I am not concerned with whether or not Adam and Eve were real people. I am primarily interested in the idea of Eden, because I believe that there was a time when things were right.

The real God that we seek tonight is beyond the God our imaginations, descriptions and normative faculties can construct. God is queer. I often speak of God as the Queer. No matter how hard we try to normatize God, God will forever remain queer. We are created in the image of such a God. We were created to be queer. When we live into what we are created by God to be, we live into the queer that we were created by God to be. I believe all was queer in Eden. I remember.

The serpent tempted one of the first persons with a promise that eating of a tree would make someone like God. The problem with such thinking is that the person was tempted to believe that God is located outside of the person to begin with. The person took the bait and denied the Queer within. The first sin was making the mistake of locating God somewhere besides the Queer that is within. I don't believe that we should have any Gods before the God who is the Queer. When we left Eden, we left behind who we truly are and who God truly is within us. Theology is about finding a way back.

Jesus comes to show us the way. We are stuck in our closets of normativity. We have the door shut and the bolt latched. Jesus knocks. Will we move beyond our fear and dare to follow the one who can show us the way to our true self? Will we have the courage to live into the Queer? Behold, Jesus stands at the door and knocks...

I am an activist because anyone becomes an activist when they seek to live into the Queer that is within. You cannot be queer in this life and not work for love and justice. There are many people who come out with regards to their sexuality and gender, yet never leave the closet of conformity to the normativities of others. We have to be different in order to make a difference. Jesus shows us what difference looks like.

Jesus crosses strict boundaries and this makes him queer. Crossing the boundary of race and gender, Jesus finds the woman at the well. Crossing over boundaries of sickness and disability, Jesus meets the blind and lame. Crossing over the boundaries of class and privilege, Jesus meets Nicodemus, Matthew and others. Jesus was a boundary crosser. Queer activism is about daring to cross boundaries and blurring together the world we once knew.

Jesus crossed the boundary of death and created life. I tell people all the time, there is nothing queerer in this life than being alive when people think you are supposed to be dead. We are called from the depths of our queerness to raise the dead to life. People are dying under the weight of injustice. Women are being brutalized. Children are starving. Civil rights are being denied. Immigrants have nowhere to lay their heads. War rages around the world. The list goes on and on. What do we do about it? From nation to nation, we all stand up and declare in unison, "At least that ain't not us!" Queerness is embracing something more than just being happy to exist. Queerness is remembering that a world devoid of injustice was where we started. Do you remember?

Amen.

232.

September 16, 2014

A Lesbian is Murdered and Nobody Cares...

"Lesbian Murdered." What if that was all the news headlines said? I have a feeling that most of the progressive community would be up in arms and ready to fight. There would be petitions and rallies demanding action. We would invoke the name of God and whatever else we could get a hold of to demand justice. Many would sacrifice our time in front of our favorite television shows and movies to push for accountability. Tonight, a lesbian will be murdered and nobody cares.

The conversation about justice begins to change when the word "Black" is placed in front of "Lesbian Murdered." From domestic violence to demise at the hands of the police, black lesbians in this country have to worry about a frequent and large variety of murder possibilities. The progressive community cares very little about this situation. For whatever reason, we have a fundamental inability to acknowledge and deal with the racism in our own hearts. We believe that we are not like that. Let me assure you, we are like that and the road to true racial healing is paved with acknowledgement.

The conversation changes even further when "Convicted Killer" is placed between "Black Lesbian" and "Murdered." All bets are off when you talk about killing convicted killers. We assume that blood is required of those that kill. I think we get this from flawed atonement theories that hold that Jesus died on the cross as a substitutionary atonement for our sins. We often assume that God requires blood for sin. I think God is more interested in love and we fail to show it every time we execute someone.

Lisa Coleman is the black lesbian who will be murdered and we are the ones who do not care. We point to the murder of 9-year-old Davontae Williams and say that Coleman deserves to die. We might be right. The death of young Williams was particularly heinous. But the bigger question is: Who deserves to kill her? The convicting words of Jesus in John 8:7 come to mind, "Let the one who is without sin cast the first stone..."

One week ago, a young woman approached me outside the Polunsky Unit. Each month, I visit death row inmate Will Speer. The woman quietly asked, "Will you stop by the window where Willie Trottie is meeting with family and offer him a blessing before he is executed?" I told her I would. After my visit with Will, I stopped by the window and made the sign of the cross on Trottie. I also offered a fist of resistance. With a deep confident smile, Trottie thanked me and assured me that he was ok. I knew that was going to be the last time I saw him. I will never forget interacting with a child of God that I knew was going to be murdered. Less than seven hours later, Trottie was dead.

In Texas, a similar scene will play out again today. We will murder Lisa Coleman. We will kill her because she is black and we are racist. We will kill her because we perceive her to be a woman and we are sexist. We will kill her because she is transgender and we are transphobic. We will kill her because she is poor and we are classist. We will kill her because she is a lesbian and we are homophobic. We will kill her because we think we have the right to murder a child of God once again. We will be wrong.

Amen.

233.

September 18, 2014

LOVE: Wrestling with the Wrestlings of Paul and the Root of Our Self

*Delivered at Cathedral of Hope United Church of Christ in Dallas, Texas on 9/18/2014

We are in the midst of a series entitled "Wrestling with Romans." I think if we are going to be honest with our self and study the book of Romans then we have to talk about the wrestlings of a Roman in the life of the Apostle Paul. For me, when I look to the life of Paul...I see someone who is constantly wrestling and struggling with one truth...God loves me. It seems that in our day-to-day lives and the worlds that we inhabit we wrestle with a similar question. The question of Paul is not all that different from our own question that arises in our own experiences. Does God love me? How can it possibly be?

Tonight, I am going to wrestle about with the question of love. What does it look like for God to be love and love being for us? If love is for us then what can be against us. Before we arrive to such a truth, we must first get to the point where we believe that love is truly for us. If we are able to reach that liberation and that place...then we truly become free. Paul talks about being unchained and unbound. Hopefully tonight, we will proceed a little bit along that journey together.

To proceed, we start with one basic affirmation...God is love. 1 John 4:8 states, "Whoever does not love does not know God, for God is love." It is a simple three words, yet still so profound. That sentence forms the basis of all of scripture...God is love. Ultimately, does love and God become synonymous? If love and God become synonymous, then what does that mean for our worship and what does that mean for our lives? What does that mean for how we read scripture?

The scripture states, "Whoever does not know love does not know God..." We live in an age where people like to hold up signs that stating that God hates this and God hates that. Perhaps even in our own lives we slip up and say God hates them or that. How can love and hate coexist? If God is love then God has no quarter with hate. If God is love then that is the totality of who God is. God is love.

I am someone who is profoundly attached to beginnings. I think beginnings are so important. Part of it is that I am trained as a historian and have always loved history. But you know I think if you want to understand someone then you have to talk about and learn about where they come from. When we wrestle with Romans and think about the wrestlings of Paul throughout the New Testament, we must not remember to think about where he came from...killing Christians...a part of the upper echelons of society...it is not hard to see why Paul might need to do a little bit of wrestling. When we take the time to think about and look at where we come from, it is not hard to understand why wrestle either. I am going to take us back to the beginning to a place called Eden.

The scriptures say that humans were created in the image of God. We already said that God is love. So if God is love...then we are created in the image of love. There is tremendous profundity there. Love. We are created in the image of love. What is the image of love? You are. You are. Paul is. Paul was. What does that mean?

When we think about being made in the image of love and we think about all people everywhere being made in the image of love, it is difficult to believe when we watch the news. When people are killing and destroying each other, it doesn't seem like all people are made in the image of love. People surely aren't acting like it. Maybe sometimes we're not acting like it. But I think there was a time when things were right. I think there was a time when people functioned in the image of God...they functioned in the image of love...perfectly. But ya'll all know the story. We talk often about apples and snakes and what not, but for me the fact of the matter is that something incredibly tragic happened in those moments. When the temptation is given and the temptation is taken. One of the first persons comes to this moment and believes that God is a part-time lover. Don't nobody want a part-time lover. But somehow in that moment, the first person is led to believe that God is a part-time lover...that somehow you have to go around God to get what you want...and that somehow God is not all that you need, all that you want and all that you will ever need. There was a fundamental inability to believe that God is love and that we are created perfectly in love's image.

Well, the gates flew open or whatever flew open and the folks ran out. But the good news is that we all kinda made off like bandits and I think that is how this whole thing works out. In making off like bandits, we ran out carrying the image of love...the image of God...with us. If there is to be redemption for us...if there was or is to be redemption for Paul...it came from that piece that was left. That piece of God...that piece of love...that image of God...that image of love. For hundreds of thousands if not millions of years we have struggled to grab hold of that image of God...that image of love that is within us.

Well, then we have this Jesus pop up on the scene. I believe that Jesus comes to show us what love is. Even further, I believe that Jesus is the very incarnation of love. Jesus is the perfection of this image of love...this image of God. You see I think we call God...Jesus and Jesus...God because in Jesus we see love perfected.

Well, if we go to believing that Jesus is the incarnation of love and God is love and love is God then the way that we read scripture changes a little bit. In John 1:1 can you imagine if we have the courage to declare, "In the beginning was love, love was with God and love was God." The word was love and love was the word and the word that was up was the word love. When we begin to go back, things change.

Beginnings are important. Jesus lives into the fullness of Eden. Jesus lives into the fullness of the image of God...the image of love. Then what happens? The love is attacked. Love is challenged. When we start living into the core of who we are...when we start living into that core of love that is within us...there will be an attack...there will be skepticism. If I looked at you right now and said, "I love you"...most of us would say no you don't and you might even call me crazy. So let's not be too hard on those folks who experienced Jesus walking around telling everyone that he loved them.

Ultimately, Jesus lives this way of love out. If we are going to follow Jesus then we have to follow the way of love. John 3:16, "For love so loved the world that love gave love's only begotten love that whosoever believes in love shall not perish but have everlasting love." When the story becomes about love, then it is all about love. When God is love and we believe that truth...when we live into that truth...our perception of the story begins to shift...we become less concerned about what is going to happen to me? and what's going to become of me?...what can I do?...what do I need to be?...and ultimately we arrive at a space where we realize that we were created to be love. Now, if you are love then you are obviously going to be loving...but the first step is to be love...to be the image that you were created to be in the first place. That is the story of Paul. That is the wrestling of Paul...to be the image of love that he was created to be in the first place.

I do believe that love is the way, love is the truth and love is the light. So often we get to preaching and we want people to believe it exactly like this...bam bam bam...we talk about doctrine and dogma...my friends the message is simple...God is love and love is God and love can liberate all of us...if we will live into the way, live into the truth and live into the light.

When we talk about the incarnation of love and say that Jesus is the incarnation of love, we must not run past these basic truths. We must stay there and tarry for a little while. Folks talk often about following the way of Jesus...most folks don't add that the way of Jesus is death. Jesus died and maybe that is the difficult part for all of us...because we realize that if we live into love and live into the image of God...then some things that we hold onto tightly here are going to have to die. The good news is that I don't believe in death without resurrection...but sometimes we have to make a stop and figure out what is going on and figure out what needs to be put aside.

Everybody wants to talk about getting saved. I grew up as an evangelical and everybody always asks, "Are you saved?" The responding question should always be, "Saved from what?" If you want to be saved and truly saved, then embrace love...embrace the truth that is love. You see, I believe that this image of God this image of love that we all carry...that festers in us on occasion...I believe that image can carry all of us. Not only do you carry it, but I believe it will carry you. I think Paul had suspicions of that too.

When we get to Romans 8:38-39, I think you will hear the wondering of Paul. Can it be true? Can it possibly be real? God not only loves me, but the love of God is inside me. I think that when Paul uttered the words I am about to utter he is making a promissory note. Sometimes you have to think futuristically and declare a belief in something that doesn't quite seem real yet. I am going to put my hand on it and grab it. Maybe I can't totally believe it and maybe I'm not totally there yet, but that is where I want to go and that is what I want to believe. I think that is what Paul is saying when he says, "For I am convinced that neither death, nor life, nor angels, nor rulers, nor things present, nor things to come, nor powers, nor height, nor depth, nor anything else in all creation, will be able to separate us from the love of God in Christ Jesus our Lord" (NRSV). You know you might move, but I don't think you can shake it. You might sit down, but I think love will still be standing with you. I don't think you can outrun love and if you can't outrun love then you can't outrun God because God is love. You might hide and think that you are hiding, but love is there. You might be laid up in the hospital bed and think that there is no hope, but love is there. There might be war raging all round you, but love is there.

This past week, I was with Willie Trottie on Texas' Death Row. Who was executed about 7 hours after I got to spend a short amount of time with him. You talk about the most hopeless of hopeless of situations. Somehow though and I can't explain it. I don't even know how to describe what it felt like...but love was there. I knew that God was there. I thought about these verses. I was reminded that nothing can separate us from the love of God...and I hope that all of you here tonight knows what that means.

Whatever is going on in your life and wherever you are at, nothing can separate you from the love of God. I hope you know...and I based this on a really good indication and feeling that I have about how all of this plays out...that love will be revealed and perfected in you. 1 Corinthians 13:13 says in the end or there abides faith, hope and love, but the greatest of these is love. You see in that image of God and that image of love...that hope that you have within you...is like a cheat sheet on your heart that reminds you that somehow or someway everything is going to turn out ok.

When I think about the fate of all of humanity...when I think about Paul...when I think about Paul's wrestlings and his desire to believe that nothing can separate us from the love of God...I feel like a baseball announcer during the World Series in the Bottom of the 9th inning and I want to cry out and scream out Love Wins! Love Wins! Love Wins! Hallelujah! Love Wins!

Amen.

234.

September 18, 2014

Book Review: I AM TROY DAVIS

On the evening of September 21, 2011, I stood outside of the Georgia Diagnostic and Classification Prison. In front of me, row after row of police officers stood dressed in riot gear, slapping their batons against their shields and daring anyone to make a move. The protest cries of "I AM TROY DAVIS!" filled the air. Shortly after 11:08 p.m., word reached us that Troy Davis had been executed by the State of Georgia. "They executed an innocent man!" shrieked out a fellow protestor.

During the extended campaign to stop this execution, innocence was the major word on activists' lips. Jen Marlowe and Martina Davis-Correia's book picks up this theme, using private recollections and exhaustive collected evidence to make the case that Troy Davis was innocent and wrongfully executed. Davis did not own a gun. Davis was not involved in the incident. Davis did not fire the gun that killed Officer Mark Allen MacPhail. Most witnesses who placed him at the crime were coerced by the police and have since recanted. Racial tension in South Georgia necessitated a quick charging of Davis.

The evidence casts enormous doubt on the conviction of Troy Davis, but the bigger story seems to be the inhumanity of the death penalty. My current state of Texas and many others dehumanize their populations to try to satisfy some carnal sense of vengeance and misguided justice.

The God that many of the pious persons carrying out these executions and I claim to serve demands we love our neighbor as our self. It is hard to love your neighbors as your self when you force them into a legal process that is unjust, racist, classist, and a whole world of -ists and -isms, strap them to a gurney, murder them, create victims of all parties involved, and brutalize individuals and families that are left to ponder who are the victims and who are the perpetrators in such a process.

The beauty of *I Am Troy Davis* rests not in its authors' claims of innocence, but in their ability to illustrate the human cost of the death penalty. We are drawn in to witness the unbelievable stress and dehumanization forced upon the Davis family. We are brought close as the family experiences the heartbreak of legal defeat after defeat, repeatedly attempts to address the MacPhail family, seeks more legal support, and ultimately are forced to sit outside the Georgia Diagnostic and Classification Prison as their beloved uncle, brother, and friend is executed. Apart from the attention, this story is not too different from many tales of execution.

I would not be so invested in fighting the death penalty if not for Troy Davis. Throughout his case, I kept thinking: Surely, someone will do the right thing. Yet at each step, the injustice continued.

Never was I more heartbroken by a body of people than by the Georgia Board of Pardons and Parole. Growing up in Clayton County, I knew a member, our former District Attorney Bob Keller. He was a regular attendee of First United Methodist Church in Jonesboro, Georgia. When the board issued its decision, relief from execution was denied. I couldn't understand it. I knew that Bob and all of the board members claimed to be Christians. Did anyone remember Jesus' demand that we love our neighbors as our self?

I Am Troy Davis begs us to be more human and humane. As we read this text, may we never be able to shake its painful images of injustice and execution, may we be emboldened to declare that murder is murder no matter who pulls the trigger, and may we learn to live out a love that dictates that life always has value regardless of the circumstance.

Amen.

235.

September 19, 2014

I AM the Light of the World: Connecting Queerly with the Gospel of John at Living Faith Covenant Church

Queer Theology goes beyond identity. Queer Theology seeks to affirm people for who God has created them to be. So often we give categories and identities to provide description for who we are. We forget that we were created in the image of God and that the core of us is that dear image. We have eternal value beyond the categories and identities, beyond whatever we can do and beyond whatever we can claim to be. When I start thinking about who God is, I head back to the beginning.

People created in the image of God come on the scene at the hand of God in a place called Eden. These people were created to be both male and female. This church did not invent gender bending...God did. The first people were genderless or genderfull. We too are a genderless and genderfull people made in the image of God to be so much more than the categories we struggle to claim. When I talk about a Queer God, I am talking about a God that is beyond our normative constructions. Who can describe a God that is love beyond love? Who can describe a God that is hope beyond hope? Who can describe a God that is justice beyond justice? Grace beyond grace? Mercy beyond mercy? When we start talking about and seeking God then we have to be prepared to experience the God that is beyond the God that we can conjure up...for that is the true God...the God that made us...the God that is queer.

There are these queers that are running around in Eden. Perhaps they were bumping into each other, they didn't have any clothes on and we really don't know what was going on. We know that a serpent slithered up and changed the narrative. We know that the serpent says in Genesis 3:5, "If you eat of the tree, you will be made like God." The temptation was given and taken. Too often we simply brush off the first sin as one of mere disobedience of an outward God, I think the first sin was a denial of the Queer or God within. That first person denied the Queer within and thought there was something better at the tree. Unfortunately, our lives are a struggle because we have all fallen victim to the lie that you can find God somewhere else besides that image of God that is within you. When you start looking elsewhere for God and stop looking within, you start getting confused. When you start grabbing hold of normative identity to give value to who you are, you make the mistake of thinking that you could possibly bind the God that is within you.

From a queer perspective, I am going to take us deep into much of the Gospel of John today. Hang on...things will only grow queerer from here.

John 1:1, "In the beginning was the word, the word was with God and the word was God." When we flip the script a bit, things begin to grow queerer. "In the beginning was the Queer, the Queer was with God and the Queer was God." I believe that God has never fit our normativities and when Jesus lives into his queerness...Jesus is the Queer that was and is and is to come. The Queer in John 1:1 sits in juxtaposition with the thief in John 10:10, "The thief comes only to steal and kill and destroy. I came that they may have life, and have it abundantly." I believe that there are two forces at work in our world, one of queerness that calls you to be different so that you might have life and one of normativity that pulls you to be the same so that you might live dead. God is on the side of queerness. The queerest of them all is Jesus.

We are going to chase Jesus through John. There in John 2, we find Jesus at a wedding. I don't know if it was a gay wedding or a straight wedding...but I know that when Jesus showed up it quickly became a queer wedding. Love is exciting. Love is worthy of celebration. Our God turns the water into wine. But before we get ahead of ourselves, what prompted Jesus to turn the water into wine? The word at the party was that the wine had given out. I don't know how many parties you have been to, but when someone starts talking about the drink giving out...folks have had much to drink. The normative response of our churches is to regulate and restrict. Our God set the party off. If we are going to be the queers that God calls us to be, then we too will be the ones who set things off. Do we have the courage to set things off? As everyone danced and lived life in abundance, I can just imagine Jesus sitting there at the wedding and thinking that this is what he came for. Jesus came so that we might have life. Do we have the courage to embrace life? Do we have the courage to not leave anything on the dance floor?

In John 4, we meet an incredible woman from Samaria. We live in a difficult time for women. All you have to do is look at the news to see that violence against women is out of control. From domestic violence to false detentions to glass ceilings to all sorts of evil, the question of our age is: Will you stand on the side of the liberation of women? Are you going to be on the side of the thieves who constantly cause women to live in fear or are you on the side of the God who comes to liberate us all? We cannot talk about abundance for our self while people are being abused and mistreated. Are we willing to join the struggle so that all might experience abundance? Jesus meets this Samaritan woman and asks her for a drink of water. There are racial and gender dynamics at play. These two folks are not supposed to be talking to each other. White folks and black folks are not even supposed to be talking to each other...yet here is this black man talking to this white woman. These stories didn't just happen two thousand years ago...these stories are taking place right now. Jesus asks for a drink of water. The woman can't figure out why this man is speaking to her. Jesus tells her that he has some water that will make her live forever. Can you imagine someone coming up to you and offering you some living water at the gas station? Far too often we are too worried about why someone is talking to us and not paying attention to the living water that they bring. This woman has been married and partnered over and over again. Jesus offers to break the cycle of abuse in her life with a true love and justice. What are we offering? We can offer the water of life only when we are willing to change the way we think. We must stop thinking that men are more important than women. If we are to truly be queer, then we must change the way that we think. We must empower all with living water. If we don't, it is like we have tasted Jesus' living water and spit it out. The woman of Samaria has much to teach us about our time.

Next to the Pool of Bethesda in John 5, there is a sick man who has been lying there for some time. The normative thing to do in our society is to inquire whether or not he has health insurance...that is the first question on our tongues. Jesus asks in John 5:6, "Do you want to be made well?" If we are going to be a queer people, this will be our first question as well. We have to ask the question of wellness. When the angel stirred the Pool of Bethesda up and the first person in got healed, this sick man never had anyone to help him. All this man was asking for was a hand up and not just a hand out. The people of God must stand on the side of healthcare for all people. We have to stop leaving people lying on the roadways. So many of us see someone struggling on the side of the road and just hit the gas. The queer thing to do is to hit the brake. Jesus calls us to stop. I don't see how people of faith can fail to support universal healthcare. We must hit the brake and care for the vulnerable. If we wait, we will have the blood of millions on our hands. There is nothing queer about waiting for justice.

In John 8, we meet a woman that is caught in adultery. Jesus doesn't wait. This woman is thrown at the feet of Jesus. She is called a tramp, hoe, hoar, slut and probably a few other things. The Pharisees feel like they have Jesus trapped. Whose side are we on? When we see women and men giving their bodies over to reckless lifestyles, how do we respond? Will we be the ones calling them hoe, tramp, slut and hoe or will we be the ones seeking to help them be made well? Jesus doesn't just speak. Jesus acts. When the woman is thrown at his feet, Jesus lays down with her. Jesus gets down in the dirt with her. I am thankful that we serve a dirty God that is willing to get down in the dirt with us. Jesus is willing to take on the names that are being called. Jesus is prepared to die with this woman. When was the last time that we bound our bodies this close to those our society would call slut and hoe? The Queer God calls us to get dirty. Jesus is a dirty dirty God. There is nothing queer about being clean. Jesus is in the dirt as all of this slut shaming is going on. Perhaps there were even some racist, classist, homophobic or transphobic comments bantered about. There is all of this othering going on. Regardless of the comments, Jesus starts writing in the dirt. We are left to wonder what he wrote...but I think he wrote something like: I'm with her. By being down in the dirt and taunting the Pharisees, Jesus is declaring that if you kill her then you are going to have to kill me. The crucifixion almost came early. Are we willing to get down in the dirt with the oppressed and give our lives for their liberation? Everyone says that they want to be with the oppressed until their lives are required of them. If we want to follow this queer way, then we are going to have to give our lives. Jesus stands up and the Pharisees start walking away. I wonder if Jesus made a tactical error here. I wonder what it would have been like if Jesus would have called the Pharisees back for a conversation. Often we fail to talk to our enemies. When we think we have won, we consistently let the oppressors walk away. If you let the oppressor walk away while you declare victory, you have actually lost because that oppressor will be there to oppress you again another day. Until we are willing to turn our enemies into friends, we are not making any progress. Jesus is not about winning. Jesus is about redeeming. When we have the courage to be different like Jesus then we will be able to make a difference. After the Pharisees departed, Jesus says, "I am the light of the world. Whoever follows me will never walk in darkness but will have the light of life" (John 8:12). I wish those Pharisees would have heard such words. Jesus is showing us the path to the Queer. Jesus is showing us what it looks like to be queer. If you are willing to be queer like Jesus, then you too can stand on the corner and say, "I am the light of the world. Whoever follows me will never walk in darkness but will have the light of life." When the scriptures say in 1 John 3:2 that we will be made like God in the end, I think it is important that we start that process a little early...we can start living like Jesus now. Are you queer enough to stand on the corner and be the light?

The blind man gets spit in his eyes in John 9. Have you ever had anyone spit on you? Have you ever had anyone spit in your face? Have you ever thought that that spit could your salvation? Have you ever thought that spit could be your healing? When Jesus tells us to love our neighbor as our self, I don't think Jesus was just talking about those neighbors that we like. I believe we are called to love our enemies as our self too. If you are able to love your enemy as your self, then you will become invincible. Sometimes the spit is our salvation. The spit is what opens up the blind man's eyes. If you are dating someone and they spit on you...that better open up your eyes and help you get on out the door to claim your salvation. We go from blindness to vision through spit. If we are willing to be spit upon and not spit back, then we will capture the queer nonviolent spirit of Jesus. People spend so much time spitting on each other. What comes of it? How many guns will have to be fired and bombs to go off before we realize that you can't teach people not to shoot by shooting, not to kill by killing and not to bomb by bombing? The spit will only heal us and others if we don't spit back.

In John 11, we arrive at the story of Lazurus. Jesus is standing outside the tomb. Then the words hit in John 11:43, "Lazarus come forth!" Jesus raises the dead. What does it look like for the dead to get up? Sometimes I am the walking dead. I don't respond or interact in the way that God would have me to. I've always wondered what would have happened if Jesus would have called Lazarus and Lazarus would have responded, "No thank you, I have had enough." How many of us have had enough? How many of us miss opportunities to heal others because we are dead? Lazarus comes out stinking and bandaged. If you are living in a moment right now and you would rather be dead, know that the Queer is within you waiting to be activated and engaged to enliven and fulfill you. So many of us live our lives trembling in the corners of closets. Jesus says in Revelation 3:20, "Behold I stand at the door and knock..." Jesus came and knocked on Lazarus' door and Lazarus came forth. Jesus is knocking on the door of your closet. What are you going to do? I know so many people who talk about coming out of the closet and they remain just as closeted as they ever were. So many come out to declare their identity and live as normative as everybody else. What difference does it make if you are gay or lesbian or transgender or whatever if you are not different? I've come out! To what? If you are not going to live in a newness of life and be queer, then who cares what identity you claim.

Jesus washes the disciples feet in John 13. If you are queer, then you know how to massage other queers. When you are queer and out of the closet, then you want to help others feel like they can be queer and out of the closet too. When Jesus humbly washes the disciples feet, Jesus is not preparing those feet to walk backwards...Jesus is preparing those feet to run. When we have the courage to be queer, we have the courage to run. Washing the feet of others helps us to know how to wash our own feet and prepare our own feet to run. When we embrace the Queer, we embrace our feet and the feet of others. We wash feet to help people take those steps out of the closet and embrace the Queer.

The crucifixion is quickly approaching in John 18 and 19. Jesus is praying and upset. Blood is pouring down. Jesus is in anguish because the world is so normal and normative. There is nothing more normal than treating people like shit. There is nothing more normal than perpetuating injustice. There is nothing more normal than embracing evil. Jesus is not being killed because Jesus is like everyone else. Many churches and speakers try to spend their time teaching their followers how to get. You don't get killed for getting. You get killed for giving. Queerness is about giving your true self to the world. God comes out when we get together and be who we were created by God to be in the first place. Let God come out! One of the things that the LGBT community has to teach the church is what it looks like to make a difference by being different. How many times have we been in the same place that Jesus was and declared, "If only there was another way..."? If only I could force myself into a category or identity that is not as oppressed. If only I could perform my gender in a different way. If only I could be attracted to the opposite sex. If you went down one of these paths, you would find where God is not. God is where the Queer is. Everybody wants to talk about safe spaces...there is nothing safe about being the queer that God calls you to be. Jesus got killed ya'll. We live in a society where living queerly can get you killed. We all know that. But don't be fooled by the dangers that lurk about...there is no safer place to be than resting queerly in the arms of God. Jesus knew this...and grew queerer and braver as the night went on. If we will embrace our queerness, we will grow braver as the night goes on. Jesus is about to be taken away and Peter slashes off the ear of Malchus...the servant of the high priest. How often do we act like Peter and think we are going to help Jesus or help God? I see a pattern in activism and advocacy these days...everyone has out their swords and wants to just slice people up. Hurt people hurt people or slice people. We must be different. We must be about reconciliation. Jesus says in Matthew 26:52, "Those who live by the sword will die by the sword." We have to educate people that slicing people will only get you sliced. If you want to help people...If you want to help God...leave your guns and swords at home. If we don't, then we are no different than anybody else.

The story both ends and begins with the crucifixion and resurrection of Jesus. Three days after his death and burial, the women discover Jesus is not in the tomb. I can tell you that there is nothing queerer than being alive when you are supposed to be dead. When we are willing to live...When we move past all that was supposed to have killed us...we live into the resurrection of Jesus. We bring the message of God. If you want to follow Jesus, be alive...be queer. Don't go home thinking those same old thoughts. Don't listen to those same old bullies and abusers. Don't let anybody push you into categories that you don't want to be. Be alive! Be queer! Be who God created you to be! Don't live into the fear! Take courage with you today! Jesus walks into that space with the disciples and they weren't expecting him. Jesus lives beyond their expectations and continues to live past ours. Quit expecting and be...because in the being is the expecting. In the being is God! Thomas asks to put his hands where the holes were. In the touch and belief of Thomas, I believe we see one of the early manifestations of Jesus' queering of the world through the constant giving of his queer body to us. The queering of the world continues and the world is slowly being returned to right. How does Jesus do that? Jesus gives his body and shows the wounds. As you leave this place, be healers by being queers that show your wounds. The message of Jesus is to let people in by being the queer that God created you to be in the first place. Connect honestly and queerly with the world so that the world can connect to God through you.

Amen.

236.

September 20, 2014

Would Jesus March at Dallas Pride?

The many closet doors will be closed tightly at Dallas Pride. Behind the smiles and drunken debauchery, there will be terror about what it would mean to leave the new normal that many have developed. Most of the participants will have told their parents and friends about their sexuality or gender, but few will have come out of the closet of homonormativity that has developed in a race for a false equality. We live in a world that bestows privileges on those who fit and shuns those who don't. If your skin is not the right color, your bank account lacks the right amount of funds, your performance is considered to be too much or you have shifted from what is considered normal in any number of other variables you will not be welcome. There on the margins will be the true queers amongst us. Those who have had the courage to come out of the closet and be exactly the person that God created them to be.

For those who seek to follow the way of Jesus, we must ask particular questions about Dallas Pride: What benefit will it be to the hungry? Will the truly thirsty be given living water? Will queer strangers be shunned? Will the naked be welcomed? How will we invite the sick to participate? Will those in prison benefit? Jesus stands with the truly queer amongst us and questions the homonormative on their behalf: Will you welcome me?

There will be many who think that the questions of Matthew 25 are too much to ask of Dallas Pride. I don't think so. From the beginning, the wider queer movement has championed the uplift and inclusion of all people. Queers stood with those on the margins and not against them. Because of the beautiful history of the queer movement, my family and I went to Dallas Pride when we first moved to the Metroplex a few years ago. We just knew that it would be inspiring for all of us. It wasn't. From the credit card vendors signing drunk people up for cards with exorbitant interest rates to the blatant celebration of companies that oppress people all over the world to the utter disregard for diversity to the insults of breeder that kept coming our way, I realized that this was a place for those who could fit into a new homonormativity and not for those who desired to stand with Jesus on the margins.

On behalf of our social justice ministry Hope for Peace & Justice, I presently work as Minister of Social Justice at the Cathedral of Hope United Church of Christ, the largest LGBT church in the world. For a long time, our church existed on the margins of society. Now, we find our space inhabiting a new normativity of influence. We have to ask our self in this moment if we will choose to be queer or not? I think the question for the Cathedral of Hope is not all that different from the question for Dallas Pride: Will we have the courage to leave the closet and be queer? After a long discussion, our family has decided to march in Dallas Pride with our church. We will be marching to break down all the closet doors that will be so tightly closed all around us and for the inclusion of all those who continue to be left out. I think Jesus will be too.

Amen.

237.

September 21, 2014

Prayers from Pride Sunday at Cathedral of Hope

Today is a day of celebration for liberation. We are the people of God. We are the people of liberation. On this Pride Sunday, let us not forget those whose liberation is not yet complete. We remember all who still face oppression and marginalization in our world. Let us pray.

This morning we draw near to you God to pray for those who face sickness and infirmities. We pray for those who sit in hospital rooms with no one to visit them. We pray for those who suffer from Ebola and other diseases that are ravaging parts of our world. We pray for those who are suffering from the sicknesses of racism, classism, sexism, homophobia and all other sorts of isms and phobias that pervert the mind and soul.

We pray for those who have lost people that they love...all of those who are in mourning. We also pray for the dead this morning. We pray for those whose hearts are cold and dead to the injustices and sufferings around them.

We pray for the hungry this morning. We pray for those who inhabit our streets with no homes...for those who are looking for that net meal.

We pray for the thirsty. We believe that you are the giver of living water. May we be the purveyors of such.

We pray for the strangers in our midst this morning. May we welcome them into our lives and hearts.

We pray for the naked this morning. May we be the ones who clothe them.

We pray for all who sit alone in prison this morning and have no one to visit them. We pray for their liberation.

Lastly God, we pray for all who are victims of marginalization and oppression. We pray for those suffering under the weight of injustice. We pray for those who are the victims of hate.

May all be liberated by your love oh God.

Let us conclude by praying the words that you would have us pray:

Our God who is in heaven,

hallowed by your name.
Your realm come,
your will be done,
on earth, as it is in heaven
Give us this day our daily bread,
and forgive us what we oppress,
as we forgive our oppressors.
And lead us not into temptation,
but deliver us from evil.

For you are everything always and forever amen.

Amen.

238.

September 22, 2014

A Gender Revelation: The Forming Hood Twins

Sonograms are interesting experiences for parents who dare to believe their children are gendered unique in the image of God. The dichotomy of boy and girl seem trite and misguided when staring at the formation of life. I refused to allow the technician's misguided question of "Do you want to know the gender of the twins?" to distract me from the beauty of the moment. While staring at the screen and listening to the garbled statements of the technician, I echoed and internalized the words of United Nations Goodwill Ambassador Emma Watson, "It is time that we viewed gender on a spectrum instead of two sets of opposing ideals." I believe her. I also believe the uniqueness of gender is the truth of God's image revealed in each individual. The two sexual organs that our society calls opposite may mean different lives for my children, but it shouldn't.

For many years, I have functioned in many ways that are patriarchal and misogynistic. While much of the blame rests on the society that raised me, a good deal of the blame rests with my selfish choices. Over the last year, I have been intentional about seeking out a variety of uniquely gendered voices to teach me a better way. I thank all of my teachers. I will never be perfect. Among many other sins, I will always be a recovering sexist and genderist. Each morning, I will have to wake up and make a choice about how I will choose to treat people of various genders each day. I have started praying before I go to bed each night that I choose the path of equality and love that God has laid out from the beginning. Now that I have an awareness of the sexual organs of my developing twins, I will push my self harder and double down on working for a world where all on the spectrum of gender are free to be exactly who God has created them to be in spirit and in truth.

I pray that for the sake of my children and the children of others, you will join me.

Amen.

239.

September 24, 2014

following jesus

do not be afraid
yet i have fear
give without payment
yet i can't survive
shake the dust off
yet i'm still dirty
is this what we are supposed to do
travel around and die with you

240.

September 29, 2014

The Inaccessible Pulpit: Rev. Justin Hancock and the Struggle for the Rights of Disabled Persons

"I can't preach in your pulpit," United Methodist Rev. Justin Hancock informed the audience at the Cathedral of Hope United Church of Christ. Everyone looked around stunned, until someone finally gathered the nerve to ask, "What do you mean?" "Your pulpit is not accessible to persons in wheelchairs," Hancock poignantly replied. Ours is a congregation that takes pride in being a welcoming space for all people. Founded in 1970, the Cathedral of Hope UCC is the largest LGBT church in the world. Regardless of such platitudes, Rev. Hancock helped us to understand that his inability to preach in our pulpit has nothing to do with his ability or theology and everything to do with the fact that he has a form of cerebral palsy that leaves him confined to a wheelchair. To say that this was a convicting moment for the gathered is an understatement, but the worst was yet to come.

Through description of going on job interviews at numerous churches all over Texas, Rev. Hancock spoke of another tragedy. In congregation after congregation, hiring committees expressed tremendous confidence in Hancock. Time after time in place after place, the call would inevitably come: "Rev. Hancock you are a tremendously talented and were a inspiration to us in the interview, we just don't see how you would connect to the people of our church." People of faith constantly express an idealized belief that the call of God is what qualifies someone for ministry. The truth is that we don't live this out. Physical characteristics beyond someone's control disqualify people all the time. Under an exemption from the Americans with Disabilities Act and a recent US Supreme Court decision, religious communities have the right to discriminate against persons with disabilities.

Pushing further, Rev. Hancock challenged us to think about what it would mean for us to truly open our communities and hearts. "Each time I enter your space of worship and see row after row of pews, I know that you don't really want all of me in your congregation. You want me to sit in the space that you have carved out for me and stay in my place," Hancock asserted. I began to realize just how much we demand that people with disabilities stay in the spaces that we allow for them. Most churches are not ready to include anyone with disabilities that cannot be easily accommodated and controlled. Oppression is always about accommodation and control. Rev. Hancock also pushed us to expand our definition of disability. From mental illness to narcolepsy to HIV/AIDS, Hancock reminded us that people who are disabled are not always confined to wheelchairs and concluded with, "How can you truly be inclusive of all of God's children?"

Disability is a category that most of us fail to include in our calculations of inclusion. What causes us to hesitate? I believe that we are afraid of the expansion of our minds and hearts. If we expand, we will inevitably have to change. With change, comes the requirements of newly realized responsibility. In living out our responsibility to the oppressed, we will discover the loving God that created all of us in God's image. Now is the time to do right by our disabled friends. Now is the time for our repentance and transformation into true practitioners of God's inclusive love.

Amen.

241.

October 5, 2014

jesus is where?

jesus is here
not there
not somewhere
not beyond
not up
not around
not over there
not down
not close
not anywhere
jesus is here

www.ingramcontent.com/pod-product-compliance
Lightning Source LLC
Chambersburg PA
CBHW081756300426
44116CB00014B/2139